I Led 3 Lives

Herbert A. Philbrick, for years a counterspy for the FBI inside the Communist party, testifies before the House Un-American Activities Committee on Communist Affairs. (*Acme Photo.*)

I Led 3 Lives

CITIZEN · "COMMUNIST" · COUNTERSPY

by Herbert A. Philbrick

McGRAW-HILL BOOK COMPANY, INC.

New York   London   Toronto

Many names used herein are Communist party aliases. Should one of these prove to be the name of a person entirely unaffiliated with Communist activity, it is a matter of pure coincidence.

The names of business, philanthropical, political, and religious organizations are also to be found herein. In each case no criticism of these organizations is intended although it may have been necessary to point out how a Communist used the group's fine reputation as a front for his underground activities.

I LED 3 LIVES

Library of Congress Catalog Card Number: 52-5944

Published by the McGraw-Hill Book Company, Inc.

PRINTED IN THE UNITED STATES OF AMERICA

691

TO EVA, MY WIFE

Who proved that a woman can keep a secret

ACKNOWLEDGMENTS

I would like to acknowledge the invaluable assistance rendered by the many good friends who have helped along the way; to Fendall Yerxa, whose criticisms and editorial guidance brought order out of chaos; to Cornelius Dalton, for reading and checking the manuscript; to Ruth Chism, who threw away the clock to type and retype the manuscript and watch over a thousand and one details; and to Ogden R. Reid of the *New York Herald Tribune*, without whose encouragement and friendship this book would never have been completed.

ILLUSTRATIONS

CHAPTER 1

NINE LONG YEARS led me breathlessly down a tightrope to a small platform and a chair. It was a dozen paces through a doorway now to the end, almost within reach. The nearness made my prison seem smaller and more suffocating. I was held in the shadows of a darkened elevator. Outside the elevator door a special agent stood on guard. I must not be seen until the moment ripened.

It was 2:05 o'clock in the afternoon of April 6, 1949. Beyond the guard, whose back was turned, I could glimpse the crowded courtroom, hear a murmur of words and the rustle of the crowd. I shifted uneasily on my feet. There was nothing to sit on in the blacked-out elevator. I watched the bailiff on the side of the room that was open to my view, waiting for his signal.

Then I heard the District Attorney say, "Shall I proceed? Mr. Bailiff, will you call Mr. Herbert A. Philbrick." The moment had arrived. The bailiff nodded in signal. My guard motioned me to go. It was only a few quick paces through the doorway and onto the platform. The spectators in the crowded Foley Square courtroom moved restlessly, whispering and following me with their eyes.

The light in the vast room was diffuse. My racing thoughts, the hum of voices, and my vision of the room spun dizzily together in my brain. A circle of upturned faces whirled past me. I braced myself to recover my balance. A single figure rose out of the crowd, and I heard him speak.

1

"Do you solemnly swear. . . ." The mass of faces spun away, but one long row came distinctly into my view, separated itself from the crowd, and stood out. ". . . to tell the truth. . . ." Directly across from me at the end of the row was Jack Stachel, an unbelieving look on his face, as if a dangerous name had been called out of his past. Farther along I saw Bob Thompson, who also recognized me from earlier days. He sat morosely, chin pulled in against his big neck causing heavy pouches to bulge. ". . . and nothing but the truth. . . ." John Gates I remembered from Boston functions, also Henry Winston, his big shoulders hunched, powerful hands clasped in front of him, his face brooding and stony. Eugene Dennis reddened with anger beneath his brittle shock of graying hair. ". . . so help you God?"

"I do." My response startled me. I sat down stiffly, and glanced quickly around the room. For this moment I had been smuggled to New York. For this moment my presence, my very existence, had been meticulously guarded. My address was unknown even to my wife. For this moment I had somehow managed to live through nine years—for this moment and for this place, the United States District Court in the Southern District of New York.

High on the judge's bench, close by my right side, sat Judge Harold R. Medina, dignified in his robes and his spectacles. A long, polished table stretched across the center of the room almost at my feet. Behind it, in varying attitudes of defiance, sat eleven men in a row—The Eleven. I knew why they were there. "United States of America, plaintiff, *vs.* William Z. Foster *et al.,* defendants." They were accused of conspiracy to teach and advocate the overthrow of the government of the United States by force and violence. These were nominally the top leaders of the Communist party in the United States, exclusive of their chairman, Foster, who for reasons of illness was granted a severance of trial. They were there to answer to a little-known law, the Smith Act of 1940, making such teaching and advocacy illegal—a law never

2

before fully tested in the courts, and regarded with scorn by the defendants. I knew that The Eleven did not know why I was there—not yet. But the sands of nine years were fast running out in the courtroom at Foley Square.

Nine years of conspiracy, uncertainty, fear. Nine years in the shadows where glances must be furtive, where I looked in vain for the face of a friend I could talk to. Days of deception and guile, plotting every move, guarding my words, gestures, even my thoughts. Blind calls from telephone booths; the drop of a coin; a code number; hushed instructions hurriedly given. Sleepless nights and secret meetings on darkened street corners, where automobiles drove up, swallowed me, and whirled away. Nine years with my face smothered in a mask that could never be taken off; no face of my own to look a man in the eye and say, "I am Herbert Philbrick."

"Mr. Philbrick." I started inwardly at the voice, but training and habit checked me from giving any outward sign. "Where do you reside?" My eyes shifted slowly, inexpressively, to the speaker. It was Frank Gordon, special assistant to the United States Attorney General. The examination was starting. I slowly let out my breath.

"I live in Melrose, Massachusetts, which is a suburb of Boston." An average community, an ordinary neighborhood.

"What is your occupation?"

"For the past fifteen years I've been in advertising." Yes, I had led an ordinary life—Herb Philbrick, Citizen. The questions seemed to come from far off. The answers were automatic.

"Have you ever been a member of the Communist party of the United States?" I felt a stone slab drop down, and I seemed to hear my voice sealed in the silence of a nine years' secret. I had led two lives, the second life secret, unknown to my parents, my employers, my friends, my business associates.

"Yes, I have been a member of the Communist party since— well—for the past five years."

3

"Prior to the time that you joined the Communist party, were you a member of any other Communist organization?"

"Well, for the two years previous to the—" I shifted in my chair. It was a difficult story to begin. "—to my membership in the Communist party I belonged to the Young Communist League."

Under Mr. Gordon's patient questioning I told about my first encounter with Communists nine years before, in 1940. I heard other questions and my mechanical replies. "Yes, there were meetings—many, many meetings—yes, as chairman I—what's that?—I soon came to realize . . ." The Eleven were arrayed before me as if they were held in check, straining against some invisible leash. I saw the knuckles of a hand whiten against the polished table, and I felt the familiar clutch of fear.

In front of the eleven defendants, a lawyer jumped to his feet. "I object!" his voice cracked.

"And after you attended these meetings did you discuss anything about the group with any law-enforcement agency?"

"Objected to, Your Honor. We wish to plead surprise."

"I shouldn't wonder," Frank Gordon murmured.

"Overruled." Judge Medina's voice over my shoulder was firm and level. He turned to the witness chair. "Just say yes or no."

"Yes." I saw movement in the line of The Eleven. One or two started forward anxiously.

"And what was the agency?"

A stirring of feet, a rising figure. "Object to that!" Louder now, with desperation in the voice. "If the court pleases—"

"Overruled!" sounded in the courtroom like the closing of a door.

Mr. Gordon nodded at me by way of repeating the question. I felt something grasp hard at my right hand, nails digging into my palm. I loosened my fist and my hand was wet.

There was another secret to reveal to the court, a secret hidden from the world for years. I led three lives.

"The Federal Bureau of Investigation!"

4

The words slammed through the courtroom and echoed away in silence. I saw Carl Winter tighten his jaw. Ben Davis glared, his mustache cutting a straight line across his lip. I watched the mounting reactions of the others—John Williamson, Irving Potash, Gil Green, Gus Hall, all growing tense with rage. And I remembered them in different circumstances, their speeches, their written directives, their Leninist-Stalinist teachings.

The Federal Bureau of Investigation! I sagged back in the chair, suddenly relieved of a great, exhausting weight. Judge Medina's voice came out of the silence. "And when was it you did that?"

When was it? Nine years ago. Nine eternal years.

It was a day in late spring, 1940, in Boston. The east wind moved gently through the crooked streets of the old town, and there was leisure in the air. A young salesman starting his daily rounds shifted his heavy brief case of advertising samples from one hand to the other and quickened his pace toward Number 7 Water Street. He appraised his reflection in a store window as if to survey a new acquaintance. The young man in the store window was Herb Philbrick, in the twenty-sixth year of the life of an average Bostonian, an American wage earner pursuing his living.

My appearance, I think, was normal. I had no particular distinguishing marks to set me apart in a crowd; I was neither tall nor short and of medium build. This complete normality was to prove, in fact, one of my most valuable assets. Together with an extrovert's geniality, it turned out to be my best disguise.

The willing smile belied the serious view with which I regarded the world. It was true that in my twenty-five years no deep shadow had cut across my path. The ordinary problems and severities of life, yes; but these I passed with determination and the confidence of youth and inexperience. I intended that confidence to be discernible in my brisk step. After all, I was a salesman. The confident air was my stock in trade.

5

But beneath the salesman's exterior, I frequently paused to wonder about the world around me. It might be said that I had a New England conscience, for myself and for my fellow man. Although I had a good job and one I enjoyed, it had evolved more by chance than by planning and bore little relation to my initial quest in the world of professions. It was a long way indeed from civil engineer to solicitor for a direct-mail advertising house.

Despite the security of a steady job, no practicing Christian in the spring of 1940 could gloat over his good fortune and turn his back on those less fortunate. I found it difficult to ignore the fact that, out in Kansas, farmers burned the grain they could not sell to take the place of the coal they could not buy. At the same time, in Pennsylvania, coal miners—amid mountains of unmined coal—lined up at welfare soup kitchens to receive bread on dole. In a land of untold wealth of fuel and food, people were both cold and hungry. To a twenty-five-year-old, it didn't make sense that bread and coal could not be exchanged to the benefit of all concerned. I wanted to help in some way, to do something more public-spirited and constructive than what I was accomplishing at home and in my neighborhood Baptist church. I wanted to operate on a broader level. Yet when I searched for outlets, what did I find? Technocracy, perhaps? What was technocracy?

There was always hard work. That was something I had learned to believe in from the start. Hard work was cast in the rigid mold of a seacoast village, Rye Beach, New Hampshire, where I grew up as the son of a railroad trainman, descended from generations of farmers and fishermen, carriage makers, and sea captains. Studies were to begin at a spindly, scarred desk in a one-room, six-grade schoolhouse, but I received most of my education in Somerville, Massachusetts. Years later, however, when the one-room school at Rye was abandoned, I retrieved one of the ancient desks as a memento.

By high school, I had decided to be a civil engineer. Job experience began, selling newspapers and magazines, saving every

6

cent for college. But I was crossed by fate, even then. Two of the three banks in which my cash was placed closed their doors in the depression. College would have to be earned on a pay-as-you-go basis. I enrolled at Lincoln Technical Institute of Northeastern University in Boston, for evening sessions. Work in the daytime, study at night. Four years of five evenings a week, three of them for classes, two for home study.

To pay my way, I took any available job. Soap salesman was one of the first. From a Boston wholesale house, I purchased boxes of soap, each one marked prominently on the cover to show a retail value of $1.35 for seven assorted cakes, castile, shaving soap, aromatic pine. I developed a spiel. "As a special advertising offer to introduce our product in this area, madam, we are making this assortment available to you for only thirty-five cents—the ordinary price of but a single bar in this box."

The wholesale cost of the box was eleven cents. I pocketed the twenty-four-cent profit, and went from door to door, from job to job.

I worked as a plumber's assistant. As an aide to an interior decorator I painted walls, hung wallpaper, varnished floors. In heavy construction labor on a breakwater job, I swung a seventeen-pound sledge in the summer sun—the closest I ever came to civil engineering. I hired myself out as a chauffeur; saved the proceeds; purchased a four-door sedan; then hired out both car and driver in a package for a larger return.

On a day-and-night schedule there was little time for recreation. Occasionally I took a swim at the "Y" pool, or went bowling at the Huntington Alleys across the street from school. A favorite pastime for infrequent dates was the Boston Symphony Pops concert—twenty-five cents for a rush seat in the balcony.

The Baptist Church of Somerville was the focal point for most of my extracurricular activity. Of course, it had its curriculum, too, in the Philbrick family. Sunday began with church services at ten-thirty, Sunday school at noon. The young people's meeting was held at four o'clock, and then evening worship closed the day at seven. The young people's groups were both recreational and purposeful, and I was active in them. They had a church orchestra, a dramatic group, and a biweekly newspaper, *The Tattler,* where I discovered a liking for publicity work, promotion, and advertising.

Through development of this interest I obtained a toehold job in an advertising agency, in 1934. Finally, in 1938, graduated at last from the nightly grind of study and trained as an engineer, I hit the pavements of Boston in search of a job in that field. There was none. One prospective employer showed me a roomful of engineering drafting tables, the stools in front of them all empty. In the far corner of the room, two engineers were at work. "Even they wouldn't be working but for a government project we landed," the man told me.

I turned to advertising again. This time I took it up in earnest, working harder than ever at my job, studying advertising and salesmanship at Harvard and the Advertising Club of Boston. My engineering slide rule was put to work computing the returns from direct-mail advertising campaigns. I saved all I could from what I earned.

In the Somerville Grace Baptist Church young people's society, there was a girl, Eva Luscombe. At first we shared an interest in the church dramatic club. The interest became a fast friendship. On September 3, 1939, a hazy, warm autumn day, we were married and afterward took a short wedding trip through New England. In Alton, New Hampshire, the very day after our wedding, a shadow crossed our path.

It was the day the war began in Europe.

The shadow lingered over us, but Eva and I pretended for the moment not to notice it. We started our life together in a four-room cold-water flat near Harvard Square in Cambridge. The winter passed, the winter and the early spring of the "Bore War." I studied the newspaper picture of the French *poilu* seated on a chair along the Maginot Line, rifle held idly in his lap. But it

8

did not reassure me. My deep, New England, Christian roots were grounded in ardent pacifism. There was a war, however latent, and warlike talk split the country. I stood solidly with most Americans in those confused times on the side of pacifist measures. Anything, I thought, anything was worth while to keep us—this country, Herb Philbrick and his bride—out of Europe's eternal squabbles.

On this late spring day in 1940, then, I was twenty-five years old, happily married, busy at my job of selling direct-mail advertising, aware of the world around me, and sensitive to its ills and inconsistencies. Brief case in hand, I strode along Water Street in Boston and turned into Number 7 for a routine call.

Down the corridors I examined the doors, looking at the names, sniffing out likely prospects with a salesman's sixth sense. On one door was written, "Massachusetts Youth Council." I turned, knocked, and the door opened into a small room with a single window, stacks of pamphlets and booklets on tables and on the floor along the walls. There was only one occupant in the room.

"I'm Herbert Philbrick, and I represent the Holmes Direct Mail Service, in Cambridge."

"Yes, may I help you?" She was young, in her mid-twenties. Her face, under dark eyes and heavy black brows, was pleasant, though she wore no make-up. Her hair was straight, unadorned, and arranged in the fashion of a neat, well-disciplined person, but one who had little use for fussy, feminine adornment. She wore cotton stockings, a politico-social badge of protest against Japan, which was then popular in some circles. Her dress was plain, and her shoes, I noticed, were comfortable and utilitarian, flat-heeled and purposeful.

I glanced around the room again. The place was crowded with desks and tables, all heaped with campaign literature. Posters on the wall gave an indication of the nature of the campaign, and amid cartons of stamped and unstamped envelopes, I could

9

read the titles of some of the pamphlets. "Don't Be an Unknown Soldier," said one, and another, "The Yanks Are Not Coming." "The Case for Non-Intervention," read a third. There was a picture of a young child, labeled, "To Be Killed in Action."

"My business," I began almost apologetically, "is selling direct-mail advertising, but it looks as though you don't have to be sold." I picked up a pamphlet and glanced at it. The girl gave a little laugh. "This interests me," I said, turning over the pamphlet. "I am interested in peace. Another war would be a frightful thing—and for what?" I said, only half expecting that she should reply.

I knew there were powerful organizations working for peace throughout the country. Ten million dollars a year, it was estimated, was being spent in peace campaigns. I had heard of The Women's International League for Peace and Freedom, the peace work of the Christian Endeavor Society, the Carnegie Endowment for International Peace, the Epworth League, World Peaceways with its graphic posters, all heavily engaged in the battle for men's minds to keep the nation out of war. I believed in them, and I was glad to know I was not alone. These organizations had built up a membership between seven and ten million strong. Public-opinion polls showed that 93 per cent of the population were opposed to a declaration of war with Germany and to sending troops to fight in Europe.

The ordinary channels of communication were flooded with peace propaganda from more than sixty organizations in the United States. They all appeared, fundamentally, to be driving toward the same objective, and there seemed little reason to question their precise motives. The confusion arising from arguments I heard was easily resolved in my mind by the single motive—pacifism. I was willing to play my part in achieving it.

"What does your organization do?" I asked.

My dark-haired companion—she introduced herself as Mrs.

Nathaniel Mills, a name which meant nothing to me—was eager to explain.

"We are the Massachusetts Youth Council. We function as a clearinghouse for all sorts of organizations. Peace is certainly one thing we are interested in, now especially," she said with a wry smile. "But it isn't the only thing. The groups we try to co-ordinate are progressive youth groups, and all progressive movements for youth have our support."

"Such as?"

"Oh, such as jobs for young people, training opportunities, government-job counseling. We organize discussions and activities to help out the young people." Her voice seemed suddenly to catch fire, and the flame that burned in it was urgent and zealous. "We believe that we young people should get together and discuss these things ourselves rather than wait for the older generation to try to solve them for us."

I agreed, without pausing to consider precisely what "these things" were. It wasn't necessary. I knew from my church experiences how valuable young people's organizations were in building character, confidence, and stability.

"Where do you live?" Mrs. Mills asked me, quite unexpectedly.

"We've moved to Cambridge, my wife and I."

"Oh, Cambridge," she said with a detached air, as if a thought had crossed her mind. I half sat against a table, and Mrs. Mills took a chair. "We have youth groups all over the state working on joint projects through this organization," she explained. "The YMCA, YWCA, church affiliates. . . ." She paused, waiting for me to say something.

"As a matter of fact," she gave a toss of her head, as though a fresh idea was to be tried, "we know of some people in Cambridge where you live, who have already expressed interest in the possibilities of a Youth Council there. I could put you in touch with them, provided, of course, you are interested."

11

I assured her I was. We talked for another half hour, during which the Cambridge Youth Council, springing from behind the alert dark eyes of Mrs. Mills, grew in my vision to a splendid accomplishment. She gave me ideas, names; told me to call on Toni Grose at Harvard, a very aggressive person and just the one to help me, she said. Mrs. Mills explained that her husband, Nat Mills, was the head of the Massachusetts Youth Council, and if I truly wanted to carry on he would call on me to give me any assistance he could. I was grateful. I left her my business telephone number.

When I walked out of Mrs. Mills's office that day, stacks of Youth Council literature mingled with the direct-mail samples in my brief case, I stepped for the first time onto that long, treacherous tightrope of the nine years, the three lives.

But I didn't know that then—I felt elated.

CHAPTER 2

MY ELATION CAME from my selection for an interesting and important mission. The responsibility of organizing and running the Cambridge Youth Council fell on my shoulders by accident. I was a stranger when I walked into Mrs. Mills's office. I had a new horizon and a broader goal when I walked out. Mrs. Mills, I thought, had paid me a high compliment, not by any shallow flattery, but by entrusting me with something in which she obviously had a deep interest. She had even assured me that her husband, as head of the state organization, would call on me to help. I realized that I needed help, but I was also determined to meet the trust.

The early days of 1940 gave urgency to my mission. The fall of France carried the nation closer to war, and intensified the necessity for a strong peace movement. Congress argued over and barely passed the first peacetime conscription act, certainly a vital factor in the lives of the nation's youth. On the policy level, the country was torn apart—America First on the one hand, Aid to the Allies on the other, interventionist contending against isolationist. Unemployment problems were gradually disappearing in the accelerating national defense program, but new employment problems, still important to young men and women, were growing up.

In common with other young people I met in church and business life, I felt I was being swept along on a tide that nothing could stop. Yet the horror that was envisioned in a new world war made it worth while to do everything possible to avert it. The chance of maintaining peace was slight, but while any chance remained, it had to be taken. As the war and antiwar slogans raged around me, I knew only that I stood on the side of peace. I felt the strongest revulsion against Hitler's aggressions and disgust with the Russo-German pact. I believed in helping Britain to the limit of our abilities. But I favored first of all a strong America which could and would defend its peace.

I thought I stood with the majority. But the conflict was sharpening. In early June, columnist Dorothy Thompson called for immediate intervention by the United States, and loosed a deluge of mail, three-fourths of it in opposition to her. In my own Cambridge, at the Harvard class-day exercises the class-day orator, David Sigourney, of the class of 1915, was vigorously booed when he said that "as parents we should be proud to see our sons get in there and do the job again." It was a pride which did not seem to be shared by his listeners. The Boston *Globe* reported: "In the stands, men who fought in the last war and have sons in college sucked in their breath in sharp surprise and some in anger. Some cried out, 'No!'" The college newspaper, the *Harvard Crimson,* roasted Mr. Sigourney on its editorial griddle.

Everyone in the country was caught up in the debate as the war came nearer. Some pretended to ignore it, but I was one of those inclined to seek an outlet for expression. Mrs. Mills showed me how I could do something about my views. She explained to me the complex and far-reaching network of Youth Councils, and their affiliation on a higher level with the American Youth Congress. She demonstrated how, even in my own community, a Cambridge Youth Council, functioning as a coordinating agency for dozens of existing organizations, could reach down through all classes of people, inspire them to work together, and consequently wield tremendous influence for the common welfare. We could make ourselves heard, and we would.

The organization of the Youth Council confronted me with problems I had never before faced. It was one thing to mobilize my close friends in Baptist Church groups for a particular task. But it was quite another to start from scratch on a community level in a large city among people I knew only slightly or not at all.

I would have been lost if it had not been that at each turn I found the way paved ahead. Mrs. Mills was good enough to facilitate the first part of the job by giving me the names of youth leaders in Cambridge who could help me the most. At each step along the path there appeared a helping hand to take me to the next step. One person gave me the name of another to see; that one in turn made other names available to me. It was uncanny how those to whom I was most solicitously referred turned out to be the key figures in the brief and ignoble history of the Cambridge Youth Council.

One of the first was Toni Grose. Within the first few days of my new undertaking I called on Miss Grose in her office at the Harvard Student Union. Toni was big, hearty, and attractive, fair but with a deep tan, her long blond hair worn free. She was the embodiment of splendid health and vigor, an extrovert and an outdoor girl, such as one would expect to encounter on a summer's excursion through the youth hostels that were then popular with college groups.

Toni received me most cordially. Whether it was my mention of Mrs. Mills as a reference that simplified the introduction, or whether Mrs. Mills had forewarned her, I did not know. But at any rate she was highly receptive to the Cambridge Youth Council idea. She said it was exactly what college and other community youth organizations needed to orient their thinking and action on the current problems of war, jobs, racial discrimination, military service, training for national defense work, and other pertinent issues. She promised me the full support of her organization, assuring me that when the Council was called into ses-

15

sion, delegates from the Student Union would attend. Her group, she said, represented not only Harvard students, but students from women's colleges in the Boston area as well, Radcliffe and Simmons among them.

Toni protested that she was too busy with her own tasks to take on an active role in the functioning of the Council. Nevertheless she was a tremendous help in its organization. I found her always willing, even anxious, I thought, to sit down and talk about our problems, to offer advice, to make recommendations— and good ones, too—on particular persons to handle particular assignments. She made her office at 1384 Massachusetts Avenue available as my mailing address, since I could not handle the organizational material at my own office and my four-room apartment was now crowded with nursery equipment. Toni congratulated me on my impending fatherhood. She suggested that she could also answer any telephone calls that might come to me, and generally keep her eye on the Council's development—not that she wanted to intrude in any way, but as an aid to me, of course.

I observed later that throughout our first committee meetings in her office, Toni sat close by on the sidelines, intensely interested in everything we did. She gave me the names of additional youth leaders in the Cambridge area, young men and women on whom she was certain I could rely. Some of them, I remember, came, stayed a short time, and then dropped out of my sight.

Others remained until the end. There was Alice Solomont, then—and even now—a splendid youth leader in the YWCA, and my strong right hand through the periods of greatest trial. There were the Solomon brothers, Arthur and Sidney, to whom I was to become especially grateful in a fashion they scarcely intended. These two, together with Stanley Beecher, bore the hand of irony in the shaping of my destiny.

By no means were all of the contacts established through Mrs. Mills and her colleagues. Among my friends I found many stanch supporters for my early efforts, and I alone was responsible

16

for bringing in many members. One of them was Gordon Case, a schoolmate and Methodist youth leader, whose deep loyalty, I discovered later, made it impossible for him to disown me completely. No matter how despicable I was to appear in his eyes, he couldn't bring himself to believe it. There were others, too. One, a very good friend, then a student for the ministry, now a professor in a leading university, was one of the finest men I knew, whose allegiance caused me agonizing soul searching.

I had not long to wait before Nat Mills called on me. We had no telephone at home. He rang me at the office and suggested a luncheon meeting at a restaurant in Harvard Square. I found him as likable as his young wife, although he had none of her ease of manner. Tall and thin, he dressed conservatively, almost to the point of severity. His approach had a self-conscious formality, but no self-consciousness hindered his speech. He talked easily in a soft drawl, disclosing a perceptive and well-educated mind. He had a nervous habit of pushing his straying, unruly hair off his forehead with his left hand.

By this time I fully recognized the difficulties of my program, and I was delighted to have someone with whom to discuss specific measures. Organizational procedure was Nat Mills's specialty. He knew what made the machinery work, and understood all of its intricacies and refinements.

"The first thing," he told me in his cultivated drawl, "is to organize a provisional forming committee. I should think a dozen members would be a good workable number, and a representative one, too. You must have sponsors, and I think I can suggest some names for the sponsoring committee."

"What is their job?" I asked.

"First of all they will lend their personal support and perhaps the support of organizations which they in turn represent. But they will also serve as a sort of—point of reference, I might call it—to others in the community who do not know you or the younger members of your forming committee. They give the

17

organization adult stability, which is essential, especially if you have to raise funds; and you probably will, to carry on your work. They can also give mature direction to your policies. We always try to get well-known sponsors at every level of our organizational work—local, state, or national."

He showed me a list of American Youth Congress sponsors. I recall the names of Mrs. Franklin D. Roosevelt and John L. Lewis. There were others. (Mrs. Roosevelt had disassociated herself from AYC by this time, although Nat Mills did not tell me this fact.)

Now I began to see the light. Together we went over the names of youth leaders in the community, to serve on the forming committee, and of others to be invited as sponsors. I suggested a few, and Nat readily accepted them. He also filled in his own suggestions. From that point, with frequent assistance from Mr. Mills, we moved rapidly toward the organization of the forming committee.

There followed a series of committee meetings at Toni Grose's office in which I was elected provisional chairman. Most of those who attended these sessions proved to be ineffectual. It is usually the case in an undertaking of this kind that out of any assembled group a hard nucleus ultimately develops. It did now. During this series of preliminary meetings there emerged the influence of Arthur and Sidney Solomon and Stanley Beecher. Sid Solomon was most distinctive in contrast with his brother. Arthur was small, quick, with ferretlike eyes that sparkled with ideas and shifted constantly to take cognizance of everything around him. He was suave—the diplomat. Sid, on the other hand, was big, rather slow-witted, but a hard worker who hewed to the line laid down by his brother. Between these two and Stan Beecher, a bruiser who was long on muscle and short on finesse, there was nothing I couldn't get done, and some things that I didn't think of doing. I came to regard them as the Three Musketeers, not for any sense of chivalry, but because of their underlying unanimity, and the manner in which their personalities played against each other toward their common objective. They motivated the show almost from the very beginning.

Our first meeting was held just before the colleges adjourned for the summer, which may have accounted for the failure of some participants ever to appear again. On the other hand they may have changed their minds—or became discouraged more easily than we did. The drive to get the Council set up by autumn carried us through the summer. I talked with as many people as I could wherever I encountered them, in church work and in business and social activities. Many of them were well known in Cambridge civic organizations. There was far more work than I could possibly do myself, and without the Solomons and Beecher I would have been lost.

These three seemed to have unlimited capacity for work, so much so that I began to feel a little uneasy. While I didn't object to competition, I didn't want my position as prime mover and chairman of the Council to be usurped, nor especially did I care to have my conception of its purpose distorted by others. It seemed odd to me that such a tremendous amount of work should be volunteered and carried out by three to whom the Council idea was apparently an afterthought. At least they came into it on invitation; they didn't start it.

My experience in church work had taught me that the leader of a group usually has to take on jobs which his subordinates should do. Perhaps these young people were different from the church variety. In any event, the Solomons and Beecher got things done. If a letter was to be turned out in mass quantities, one of them had the immediate solution. In a day or two they would come back with mimeographed copies, produced by "friends." It was helpful for the sake of our nearly empty treasury that there was usually no charge for the work they extracted. My uneasiness grew into an uncomfortable awareness that a chairman was scarcely necessary for the functioning of the Cambridge Youth Council.

In November, we sent to more than one hundred Cambridge organizations our first call for a meeting of the full Council. The long three-page letter which my three aides drew up for my signature contained a platform of issues which we considered within our province. The paramount issue, of course, was the war. We pointed out that the vote for President Roosevelt in the election just passed was a vote for his peace promises, and we raised the possibility that the President was leading the country down the road to war instead.

The letter discussed the military-conscription law, and recommended action on a community level to provide services to drafted men—send-off parties for conscripts, correspondence with men in camps to keep them in touch with affairs and attitudes at home, and support for legislation that would help them. There were one or two points in the circular with which I disagreed, and I voiced exceptions.

One, as I recall it, was an implied recommendation that conscripts be given more frequent furloughs. I believed that if men were going to war they needed, not furloughs, but all the training they could get. However, it was a minor point, the letter was already mimeographed, and it seemed best to let it go.

In a subsequent circular two weeks later we fixed the date for the first Council meeting as December 6, 1940. We had received a good response from our initial call. We had an impressive list of local sponsors, including Professor Kirtley Mather of Harvard; the Reverend F. Hastings Smyth of the Oratory of St. Mary and St. Michael, also at Harvard; Ernest Collins of the Dunbar Associates; Dr. Albert Dieffenbach, Roland Forbes, the Reverend Walter Jerge, Miss Odile Sweeney, and Dr. Howard Whitcomb, all of them well known in Boston civic circles.

The principal speaker of the evening was to be Nat Mills. The agenda, worked out with the assistance of the Solomons and Beecher, centered upon the issue of job training for industry, an issue selected for a reason that later was to become part of a

20

familiar pattern—because it could be expected to stir up interest, provoke a lively discussion, and yet develop no strong disagreement or rancor.

Representatives of more than thirty youth organizations attended the opening session; from the standpoint of numbers we considered it a marked success. Arthur Solomon gave a report on the progress of job-training programs in Cambridge and guided the discussion. Nat Mills was unable to appear to make the keynote address, but Mrs. Mills came in his place. When she was finished, we raised other issues for open discussion, such as conscription, racial discrimination in both military and community life, and other pertinent topics.

Thanks to the procedural machinery worked out in advance, the elections were quickly dispensed with. I don't recall whether it was one of the Solomons or Stan Beecher who proposed my name as chairman, but the nomination was accepted by the assemblage and I was named. Alice Solomont was made secretary-treasurer. The hard work of the Musketeers brought its reward too; all three of them were elected to serve with Alice and me on the board of directors, or cabinet. Meetings of the full Council were scheduled for the first Friday of each month, while the cabinet was to convene every other Sunday morning at my apartment.

We quickly jumped into all kinds of youth activities, and also into immediate trouble. The first sign of strain came on the same question of job training in which Art Solomon was particularly interested. From time to time during our organizational phase, letters and circulars on a wide variety of subjects had been drawn up over my name, given to me for approval, and sent out to individuals and groups. But now came one that by-passed me entirely.

The specific issue was the National Youth Administration's work-experience project, then just getting under way with the aid of Federal funds. It was felt that the Cambridge School Committee, despite the availability of public money to help young people obtain part-time work, was delinquent in not taking advantage of the program. I discovered one day that more than a thousand leaflets, or "flyers," sponsored by the Cambridge Youth Council—and bearing my name as chairman—had been distributed in the city. They urged that the mayor be petitioned, and that a public hearing be held to start the ball rolling on local aspects of the National Youth Administration's program.

I was shocked that the leaflets had been circulated over what was supposed to be my signature without my knowledge. It represented to me a lack of scruples on the part of those involved, and a brazen usurpation of the authority vested in me by the membership, to whom I was responsible for all of my actions. At the same time I recognized some of the merits of the program, and my own experience certainly justified support for part-time work for young people. I could not but appreciate the zeal and initiative of my cabinet members. Furthermore, the campaign brought results. The School Committee voted to establish a National Youth Administration Work Experience Center in Cambridge to coordinate the search for jobs. It was the Youth Council's first tangible victory, and in the end I was willing to overlook the tactics involved in winning it.

But the incident disturbed me. I determined to be more careful. Many of my good friends, sincere, respected citizens of Cambridge, had thrown their support behind me and the Youth Council. My first responsibility was to them. As chairman of the Council, I realized that I must see that control of its policies and actions remained where it belonged, in the hands of the membership.

But one meeting of the cabinet proved how difficult that was to be.

Alice Solomont was unable to attend. Those present were the two Solomons, Stan Beecher, and myself as chairman. The key point on our agenda was a report to the American Youth Congress regarding our Council's position on a major issue of the day, pertaining to military aid to the Allies. The precise problem has long since been swept away. But its effect on me and my relations with my three colleagues was to endure. I had no idea it would endure so long.

When the issue was brought before the four of us for action, the Solomon brothers and Beecher all made their positions plain. They were in agreement, and they were directly opposed to my view. They rejected all programs of any kind to give military aid to Britain. I was in the opposite camp. I believed aid to Britain and her allies was urgently necessary.

"Look," I said, thinking now of the job-training leaflet, "I appreciate how you feel, and you are entitled to your opinions. But there was a meeting of the Council ten days ago—remember?—and the opinion of the majority then was—"

"You're crazy!" Stan Beecher seemed ready to use his usual battering-ram technique, but I was in no mood to temporize. I got on my feet to face him down.

"As chairman of the Council I can see no choice but to—"

"Sit down!" Beecher leaned forward and punctuated the order with a light but firm push against my chest which caught me off balance, and I plopped back into my chair. "Look," he said, before I could recover myself, "the National Board of the American Youth Congress has already decided to go ahead. We got no choice but to send in our hundred-per-cent approval."

"You're confusing the issue," I retorted. "We're not formally affiliated with the Youth Congress."

"We send delegates to it, don't we?"

"Sure, we've voted to send delegates to it, but I don't see that that ties us to what they do. Besides, this isn't democratic. Our members vote one way, we vote another. How can we—"

"Naturally," Art Solomon interjected, "we believe in democratic action." His eyes darted rapidly from one to the other of us. He spoke nervously, but his intention was to conciliate.

23

I didn't want things to get out of hand. Perhaps Art could smooth over the argument.

"In most instances, of course, we would act in full accord with the vote of the members," he said. "I think we can now. A lot of the delegates were absent from the last meeting, you know. Furthermore, they didn't have time to give full study to the problem. I'm certain that if they had every opportunity to get all the facts and analyze them, they would have voted the same as we are now."

Smiling, as usual, Sid Solomon chimed in. "Of course," he echoed his brother, "we have to take action on this now. We can't wait. The Congress wants our report. We know the facts. At the Council meeting all of the facts weren't in, and the members weren't fully educated. Don't you see?" he smiled at me.

I didn't. I wasn't thinking about the issue at hand. No amount of quibbling could possibly change my opinion on that. Besides, I was too stunned at the full realization of how ridiculous my own position was to concern myself with the hairs these three tried to split. Their minds were made up as much as mine was, and we were on opposite sides of the fence. The problem would never be resolved in meeting with them. But the thing that shocked me most was their attitude toward orderly procedures within the council.

"After all," Sid continued, still smiling, "the national board is sitting right there in Washington. They've studied the situation at first hand, and they know what's going on better than we do. Who is in a better position to make a good decision than they are, right on the spot? Besides, here's another thing. The Massachusetts Youth Council, our own parent organization, has already approved this thing. How can we step out of line? You're just being left behind in the present trends, Herb, that's all."

His line of reasoning flashed on a light in a far corner of my brain. What was it called, this method of thinking? The Communists had a word for it—democratic centralism? The top policy makers establish the "line" on a particular issue and pass it down through channels to the mob. They agree with it, rubber-stamp it, and pass it back. The policy makers then call it "the will of the people." Democratic centralism, that was it. Communist democracy.

My mind was suddenly clear—bitterly clear. The answer to all my doubts and questions became apparent. I had walked into a cleverly laid trap. One of the founders and the first chairman of the Cambridge Youth Council—in fact the Council itself— was nothing but a front for the plans and programs of a few behind-the-scenes operators.

"We're just bein' democratic," Stan Beecher was saying. "We're the board. You're outvoted, three to one. What else you gonna do but be democratic?" There was an implication in his tone: "Or resign?"

I left the meeting in black despair. Even if Alice Solomont had been there, I would have been outvoted, three to two. The cards were stacked against us. There might have been an easy way out, but if there was I didn't see it at the time. I knew I had to do something. It was fortunate that I didn't act on impulse. I turned the problem over and over in my mind. I kept it to myself. In a way, I was too abashed to talk about it with anyone. I didn't even mention it to Eva. She was busy now with the new baby, and besides, she didn't care much for some of the people who came to our house these days. She didn't seem to be in favor of the Council idea.

I knew that many of my friends who had supported and come into the Council at my urging would be terribly shocked if they knew how effectively the chairman was being controlled. Should I go directly to them? To do so would certainly wreck the Youth Council and destroy all of my work thus far. Should I bring the whole thing out in the open on the basis of the issue at hand? I didn't relish a public scene. I could resign; Beecher had made that clear to me at the meeting. But to resign would solve nothing. Beecher and the Solomons would carry on the Council work any-

25

way, probably with the unknowing help of another front man, and I would simply be discredited.

I wrestled with the problem day and night, going back over every phase of the development of the Youth Council and my association with these three who now proved to be my antagonists. Sometimes, I recalled, things had been a little too pat, policies too tailor-made. How did the Solomons and Beecher manage to get so much done? Who did it for them, and why? Why were they so anxious to take on the heavy work? I covered every link in the chain that had led me to them in the first place—Nat Mills, Toni Grose, my first encounter with Mrs. Mills. I studied the literature that we had published, letters and circulars. I compared them with circulars from other sources, dumped in my lap by the Solomons, Toni, and the others. Communism was an alien word to me. I knew little about it. I had no proof that any of these people were Communists—a few booklets and leaflets, but no tangible proof. They had never spoken of communism or the Communist party to me. Marxism? Yes, perhaps a mention of it here and there, but many of our delegates studied Marxism as an academic pursuit. Besides, Marxism was no crime. Even the Communist party was a legal political group.

I thought of taking the problem to Nat Mills. As head of the state Youth Council, he was certainly concerned. But I thought of the links in the chain, and decided against it. I still had confidence in myself to work out the problem.

But the situation grew steadily worse. I saw that I was losing my grip. Full meetings of the Council were too far apart. I couldn't bring my weight to bear effectively against the opposition in the cabinet. The atmosphere changed from mere difference of opinion to outright fraud. Actions were taken in the name of the Council and in my name which did not represent the true sentiments of the membership. The initial platform of the "peace" organization was arbitrarily expanded far beyond its original concept. We became engaged in a "fight against discrimination

26

in the armed forces." This was enlarged into a campaign against poll taxes, for Negro housing, and in behalf of other racial issues which, regardless of their merits, had nothing to do with keeping the United States out of war. The Council became a propaganda sounding board to arouse resentment and ill feeling. While its "spokesmen" fought for nonintervention in Europe, they were curiously "interventionist" in what was then called "free" China. They made statements declaring that Latin American countries should be "free from American expansionist colonial policies." Apparently there was no end to the issues which could be dragged into the Council program without consulting either the members or the chairman. I knew that I was in a bad spot and that it was getting worse every day.

I was unable to sleep. It occurred to me that I might go to the Boston police, but I was afraid they might dismiss me as a crackpot. After all, no laws were being broken. Then I recalled that at the American Legion national convention in Boston during September, J. Edgar Hoover had attacked foreign "isms," and warned that agents of other powers were active in the United States. He had cautioned against hysteria, and had advised anyone having knowledge of anything detrimental to the national defense to report it to the FBI for investigation by trained agents.

I tossed and sweated it out on a bed of uncertainty and remorse. How had I ever gotten into this thing in the first place? Eva slept quietly beside me. I wanted to awaken her and blurt out the whole story, get it off my chest. I needed to talk to somebody. I was angry—angry at others as well as myself. I felt tricked and outwitted. Precisely how or when this thing had happened I could not determine. It was simply no longer possible for me to evade the truth of the situation. The Youth Council, basically a decent idea with great possibilities for good, had gone out of control. It was out of my hands and in the power of others, who were distorting it to their own views. The Council had been subverted. I had gone blissfully along and had been made a fool

27

of. Something immediate had to be done to win back my friends and my self-respect.

The room was hot, despite the cold winter night. I tossed off a blanket, turned over, and tried to sleep. Suddenly I sat upright. Although we had no telephone in the apartment, there was a directory which I used for business and for Council work.

I turned on a dim bedside lamp and picked up the telephone book. I looked under the initial F. Not there. Perhaps it was under Federal. I turned the pages. "Fedl . . . Federated." No. I switched to the back of the book. "U.S. Government" in heavy type. "Justice Dept. of." Now. "Fedl Bur of Invest 10 POSq . . . LIberty 1155."

Eva stirred. "Is anything wrong?" she asked, sleepily.

"No." I glanced again at the address, 10 Post Office Square, and closed the book. "There's nothing wrong." I turned out the light, and slept.

CHAPTER 3

I OVERSLEPT FROM sheer exhaustion, and when the day crept into my consciousness my head was heavy. Eva called from the kitchen, "You'll be late, Herb."

I got up, pushing aside the weight of last night's decision. The baby, six-month-old Constance Ann, was crying in the other room. I shaved hurriedly. In the midst of dressing I thought I might have a chance to talk to Eva, tell her what was happening, what I had decided to do.

"Eva!" I called.

"What is it, Herb? I can't come now, I'm busy." No, it would take too long to recite the whole story to her, anyway. I felt a tinge of regret that I had not let her in on all of this earlier. Now it was late, and Eva was preoccupied with the baby. I had only a few minutes to get off to work.

"I just wanted to say, don't bother about my breakfast. I'll get it."

"I'm afraid you'll have to. The coffee is perking." I gulped down a cup and ate a piece of toast. Then I donned my heavy overcoat, grabbed my brief case, and left the apartment.

When I came out of the subway at the Old State House in downtown Boston, the wind off the bay was raw. I headed straight for Post Office Square, moving fast through the cold, but inwardly my steps dragged. For a moment I felt that I was being silly, indulging in an unnecessary game of cops and robbers. However, the sight of 7 Water Street, as I passed, and the upper-story windows where the Massachusetts Youth Council had its headquarters brought my problem into bold relief again. I wanted to get to the bottom of it. Just how the Federal Bureau of Investigation could help me, even if they would, I did not know. But I needed advice, and I thought that at least the FBI could tell me if I was on the right track, or just being foolish.

The lobby of the big office building across the street from the Post Office was comfortably warm. On a big index board inside the door I found the Federal Bureau of Investigation, Room 1014. I asked the elevator operator for the tenth floor.

A receptionist sat behind a small switchboard. "May I help you?" she smiled. I suddenly realized that I didn't know what to say.

"I think I want to see one of your agents," I stammered. I didn't know whether the FBI actually had "agents" working out of an office this size, but the girl showed no surprise, and I was relieved.

"Anyone in particular?" I shook my head.

"What is your name, please?"

"Herbert A. Philbrick."

"Where do you live, Mr. Philbrick?"

"Cambridge."

"If you'll be seated I'll have someone see you in just a moment."

I thanked her and took a chair near the door. The waiting room was bare and cheerless. I thought over what I would say to the agent. I hoped it would not be necessary for me to talk in the waiting room. How would I begin? "What can I do for you, Mr. Philbrick?" the agent would ask, and then stand there in that hollow room waiting for me to tell him. Should I ask to talk to him privately? A moment of near-panic seized me when the girl returned from the inside office. I saw a man behind her. He smiled thinly and beckoned me to come in.

We walked through a series of turning corridors and past a long line of small offices. We stepped into one of them, and my

30

escort closed the door quietly. It was a tiny room with one window, a plain, bare table, and two chairs facing each other across it. My glance swept over the unadorned walls, half expecting to spot a hidden microphone or camera lens. The agent motioned me into one of the chairs. He didn't introduce himself.

"So you live in Cambridge?" he ventured, and I felt better.

"Yes, my wife and I moved there a little more than a year ago."

He studied me slowly, my brief case on the table, my business clothes.

"Work in Boston?" he asked.

"Yes, that is, Cambridge. I'm with the—I'm in the advertising business."

"Is there something we can do for you, Mr. Philbrick? Perhaps if you'll just tell me briefly what it is. Is it connected with your business?"

"It's a personal matter, I suppose. But I think it's a matter of public concern. I need some advice."

He returned his thin smile. "We don't exactly give advice. But you'd better start at the beginning. You say it is a public affair?"

"I'm the chairman of an organization of young people known as the Cambridge Youth Council," I began. He nodded. "It is a group of youth leaders in many activities who are interested in current affairs. A sort of discussion group, I imagine you would call it. I'm the chairman, but I don't know what's going on."

I outlined some of its policies, its membership, and named the other officers and the sponsors. I observed that his interest quickened, and he began making a few casual notes on a piece of paper that was screened with his other hand. He interrupted only to ask short, pertinent questions, to ask me to repeat a name or spell one out.

I launched into a detailed account of how I had become interested in the Council, described my work to start it, and the

31

efforts of the others. Under his prompting I left nothing out. I warmed up to my recitation as I went along, encouraged by his close attention to every facet of the story. At least he was taking me seriously. I recounted how I began to feel like a useless figurehead in the group, how public expressions were made in my name without my approval and contrary to my true beliefs and those of the membership. I ended by telling him of my near-break with Stan Beecher and Art and Sid Solomon.

"And what is there that we can do?" he asked after a long pause when I was finished. "Has there been any violation of Federal law that concerns the FBI?"

"No, not that I know of."

He frowned. "You suspect that your organization has been taken over by Communists, is that it? Have you any proof?"

"No, I have no documentary proof. I thought perhaps others may have been involved in similar circumstances. I wondered if I had better resign or drag the whole thing out in the open."

"Have you gone so far as to break completely with these people? Is the situation entirely—hostile?"

"No, no," I replied, groping for the precise meaning of his question. "I wouldn't say it was beyond repair."

"Offhand," he said, keeping full control of the conversation, "I'm afraid there isn't much we can go on, Mr. Philbrick. We appreciate it when citizens like you are aware of this kind of thing. But until there is something more positive, I'm afraid it is beyond our reach. Don't misunderstand me. We always have time to listen. You are always welcome here, and we want to help you. But we are an arm of the law only, and we can act only on the basis of the law."

"I understand." I took my hat and brief case. I had received no solution to my problem and no direct answer to my questions, but I had been given a fair hearing. "Thank you," I muttered, "perhaps I will come in again." The agent accompanied me as far as the reception room. I neglected to ask his name.

32

The interview left me in a worse quandary than before. I was so chagrined at the turn of events in the Cambridge Youth Council that I wanted to get out, to resign, and take my lesson with me. And yet I felt that by staying in and trying to hold control of the Council for the membership, if necessary to force a showdown at the January meeting, I might still salvage something from it. At least I might vindicate the trust of my good friends, for whom I felt more responsible. I resolved to talk it all over with Gordon Case. I also determined equally firmly that I would not discuss it with Nat Mills, who, as the salaried head of our parent organization, the Massachusetts Youth Council, would appear the logical man with whom to have it out. I could not forget that he and his wife were responsible for my organizing the Cambridge group in the first place.

The New Year's business occupied all of my attention for the next few days. I worked hard every day, calling on my old advertising accounts and soliciting new business to start the year off with a rush. I was too tired in the evenings to pay much attention to Council affairs. Art Solomon called several times at my home, but I let him handle the job. I had expected a blowup from the membership over the report to the American Youth Congress opposing the program of aid to the Allies. But it never came, and I was not prepared to precipitate one. The Solomons and Stan Beecher apparently slipped the report silently through their well-greased machinery, and the issue never came into the open.

I had no opportunity to talk to Gordon Case before I had an unexpected caller at my office. I went to the reception room to find a genial, good-looking man I had never seen before.

"My name is Harold Leary," he said. Covertly he flipped open a leather envelope to show me his FBI credentials with his name in block letters.

"Oh, yes," I said, anxiously.

"You came to see us about a matter. I'd like to talk to you."

33

I glanced around me, uselessly, and explained there was no place in the crowded office where we could meet in private. "There's no rush," he said. "Suppose I pick you up tomorrow morning near your house. We can talk then."

"Eight o'clock," I suggested. He nodded. "Memorial Drive and Magazine Street at eight." He made a note on a scratch pad and jammed it into his pocket. We shook hands. It would be advisable, Leary said, if I made no mention to anyone that the FBI had been to see me. I told him he could rely on my silence.

I was reassured. I knew now I was following the best course, one that might lead to a solution. The FBI was interested after all. This, I knew, was more than a routine dismissal of a case, more even than a routine follow-up.

The next morning I reached the appointed spot ten minutes early just on the chance that Leary would be ahead of time. I paced the corner to keep warm, groping frequently in my pocket to pull out my father's old railroad watch. With it I could keep time almost to the second. It was a quarter of a minute before eight when a car detached itself from the stream of traffic and pulled up to the curb. Prompt, I thought, FBI promptness. I ducked into the car, Leary switched off the motor.

"We can talk here for a few minutes. Then I'll drive you to your office. Cold morning." He plunged directly into the business at hand. "I saw a memorandum on your visit to the office. Done anything about it yet?"

"No, I've been too busy. Besides, I don't know just what to do."

"You're married, I understand." I nodded. "Does your wife know anything about all this?" He eyed me carefully, half turned toward me in his seat.

"I haven't talked to anyone about it except the agent at your office."

He started to say something, but checked himself, evidently changing his mind. I was watching his every gesture, alert to

34

every word, certain that Leary had come out here to tell me something. So far, he hadn't.

"My wife doesn't like the organization," I said, breaking the silence. "The organization or the people in it. We haven't discussed it recently at all."

"What is your wife's objection? To the people, that is."

"One of her friends told her I was running around with a bunch of Communists. Not only that. Some of them have been to my house, and she just doesn't like them."

"Umm."

"Of course, she's right."

"Do you know they are Communists?" Leary asked.

"No. I couldn't prove it, and they haven't said so."

"If you're interested in finding out," Leary suggested, "couldn't you stay with this crowd—what is it?"

"The Cambridge Youth Council."

"Yes. And get close enough to them to learn what they're up to?" I tried to figure Leary's angle, but restrained myself from asking him. He hadn't indicated the FBI's interest in the case, not directly. But if they had no interest, it was unlikely that Leary would have driven out here on a cold morning to talk to me.

"What time do you want to be at work?" Leary asked.

I dug my watch out of my vest pocket. "We'd better go along, if you don't mind." He started the motor.

On the other hand, I thought, if Leary had a definite interest, he wasn't trying to develop it, so far as I could see. The questions he asked were general. He didn't seem to care about specific points, or about individuals involved. Perhaps if I gave him a chance he might come to that.

"What do you think I should do?" I asked.

"Well, Mr. Philbrick, it seems to be a personal problem. We can't be directly concerned with it. I just wanted to be sure we didn't miss anything."

35

My spirits sank and I felt keen disappointment. Yet I was unable to believe that our meeting had been for nothing.

"My opinion," he went on, "my personal opinion, is that you should stay with your group. After all, a lot of your friends are involved. You don't want to let them down. But more than that, you don't want to sacrifice your own principles. If you resign you'll simply turn the group over to these people by default. The fact is, I have a hunch that's exactly what they'd like you to do. They'd like to see you resign."

"You can let me off at the next block. My office is just around the corner."

"I'll be in touch with you again," he said. So Leary wasn't going to let it drop, even now. "Meantime you have my number. If there's anything I can do, call me." He stopped the car and turned toward me. "I still don't think you should discuss your problem openly with anyone. That's up to you. But I must ask you not to mention that you've talked to us. It couldn't do any good, and might be harmful. I suggest you just keep your eyes open. Maybe you'll come up with something. Any pertinent information that you think we ought to have, send it along to us."

When I got out of the car, I glanced around involuntarily to see if anyone was watching me. Leary pulled abruptly away from the curb. The situation took on the aspect of a game, between the Cambridge Youth Council on the one hand, and the FBI on the other. I was the spectator. I became more and more curious over what trick plays each of them would call, and whether either of them would reveal his hand to me.

In the Youth Council, I gave Beecher and the Solomon boys freer rein in the days that followed, and they prodded the organization into a frenzy of behind-the-scenes activity. Occasionally I protested their policies, but I purposely avoided a showdown. I soon learned that the membership was held almost entirely in the dark, and they were bound to stay there, to be used as pawns, as long as I kept silent. While I professed a con-

36

tinuing interest in the group, I actually did nothing. I made no more contacts, no longer solicited the support of my friends for various undertakings, and always managed to plead that I was too busy. Interest in the Council gradually waned, and attendance at subsequent meetings was never as high as it was the first time.

I began to feel like one of the conspirators. There were anxious moments when my best friends, the ones I knew I could trust, Alice Solomont and Gordon Case, expressed opposition to some of the things we did in the name of the Council. I had to dodge their questions and try to mollify them without confiding in them directly. I kept my own counsel.

My primary motive was to establish all the proof I could as to which members of the Council were also Communists. In only one important respect, therefore, did I alter my position. I did not once openly assert myself as anti-Communist. The result was that Beecher and the two Solomons drew perceptibly closer to me. We disagreed on issues. I could not permit my disguise to change too suddenly. They took great pains to "educate" me, and passed quantities of literature, Communist and Communist-front pamphlets, into my hands. I studied them all carefully. Eva was angry and scornful when I brought the material into the house. She refused even to look at it.

It wasn't long before my "literary" stock was increased. The New Year had broken clear and cold, the streets covered with icy wisps of snow, the topsoil frozen solid. The mercury plunged to a record low; the easterly wind, raw and salty, invaded every nook and cranny in Cambridge and drove most folks stoveside. One such bitter cold Sunday, a girl I knew only as Joy, whom I had encountered at various youth functions in Cambridge and Boston, trudged through the ice-covered streets to my door. She looked so cold that I immediately ushered her into the apartment and threw a stick of wood on the little stove which was already glowing. She had a bundle of newspapers under her arm.

"What in the world are you doing out on a morning like this?"

37

I asked, as she put down the papers and warmed her hands at the stove.

"Just making my rounds. I was hoping you might take a subscription to *The Worker*. We have a drive on for new subscriptions." She handed me a sample copy of the Sunday *Worker* off the pile. I glanced through its pages, thinking that it must require a peculiar kind of dedication to tramp out in the biting cold on a day like this to peddle such rubbish. For the first time, I was impelled to ask myself, "Why?" What was it that instilled such devotion into these fellow-traveling Communists, to labor so hard for such a distorted cause. What was it that got into them? Was it sincere belief in the prattle of communism? Was it disillusionment and frustration that led them into these paths?

Joy was telling me about the paper, urging me to give her an order. With a show of reluctance—I really wanted to get on the list, but restrained myself from showing too much enthusiasm—I agreed. "All right, send it around," I said. "The Sunday issue."

"It won't come by mail," she declared.

"No?"

"Oh, no, this is not to be a mailed subscription. We send it by mail to a few people, but to others—government workers, business people like you—we think it is wiser to deliver it personally. I'll bring it to you every Sunday."

Thumbing through the paper after Joy left, I came across the masthead and read the names. Louis F. Budenz, president; Howard C. Boldt, treasurer; Benjamin J. Davis, etc. There was none that meant anything to me except Davis. I had seen some booklets by him on racial questions. It was with curiosity that I recalled that most of them were non-Communist publications, or purportedly so.

In the weeks that followed I studied *The Worker* scrupulously. Out of its welter of doubletalk I was able to trace the line of the Communist party on the paramount issues of the day—condem-

38

nation of "imperialist" war; agitation for extremist strikes in industry, particularly, I observed, in defense industries; opposition to credits of sale of arms to "belligerents" in Europe; aid to "free China"; repeal of the conscription law.

There was no deviation from this in any of the publications of the American Youth Congress or the Massachusetts Youth Council. Not all of the issues were seized so boldly. They were screened behind a solicitude for youth, and translated in terms of their effect on young people. Other issues, less controversial, surrounded the larger ones in the publications of the youth organizations. The Massachusetts Council, for example, placed its emphasis on education and job training, a cause which many non-Communists would gladly espouse. But buried away in its platform was a demand for a resolution to limit the service of conscripts to one year, and to hold the draft army permanently within the continental limits of the United States, regardless of the course of the war. There was no question of aid to the Allies. After all, Hitler and Stalin were comrades, for the time being. The Harvard Student Union, Toni Grose's group, issued pamphlets on "the case for nonintervention," professing abhorrence of naziism, but assailing any measures, however remote, to aid in the fight against the Nazis.

Occasionally during the early spring I passed bits of information along to Harold Leary at the Federal Bureau of Investigation. I sent them as letters, keeping him informed generally of my activities and those of the Cambridge Youth Council. Harold and I had a few meetings under circumstances similar to those of our initial conversations. They were all held at his request. He said nothing about reports I gave him. Only once, by indirection, did he give me a clew to what he was thinking. It was also in the nature of a warning.

"Philbrick," he said, "I believe there are—certain people— who recognize you for your abilities as a leader. You have a head on your shoulders, and they know it. They may think they

39

can use you. If so, they will probably make overtures to you, certain suggestions."

"What kind of suggestions?"

"Oh, nothing particular." He shrugged his shoulders in deprecation, and I thought he knew more than he was telling me. "They may ask you to help them out from time to time, join with them in some of their plans, do some work for them."

"The Communists, do you mean?"

"Well, I wouldn't say that, exactly. But you may be approached. My point is that if you are, no matter what your reaction may be, don't turn them down. At the same time, play hard to get. Don't jump at it. Tell them you need a chance to think it over. Do you follow me?"

I nodded doubtfully.

"Now," he continued, "and this is important. If anything like that happens, get in touch with me immediately. The first thing. We'll talk it over."

I was too surprised to say more than, "All right, Hal." It was the first time he had ever given me explicit instructions, beyond his admonition not to talk. I didn't have to ask him if he wanted me to continue my occasional reports. I was learning that these FBI men couldn't be pushed. You had to take it easy with them, let them carry the ball. I still didn't know just what Leary was after. But I remembered the words of the agent the first time I visited the FBI. "We are an arm of the law and we have to act on the basis of the law," he had told me. Meanwhile, it was implied, we can watch them and wait.

During that winter and spring, the Youth Council concentrated its efforts on peace movements in the Boston area, sponsoring and helping to organize meetings to protest against the war. We circulated thousands of petitions which sought to place as many persons as possible on record against American involvement. In other words, to tap the normal and humanitarian abhorrence of war.

I followed the propaganda line carefully through the Sunday *Worker,* and also augmented my subscription to that journal by picking up the *Daily Worker* at a downtown newsstand. I was convinced now that the Communist party, with my indulgence, was dictating the policies of the Cambridge Youth Council. I strung along with them, sabotaging their efforts by neglect wherever I could, but at the same time staying close to them in search of proof of their Communist links. Evidence was not long in coming.

On Sunday, June 22, 1941, the Sunday *Worker* appeared as usual, borne to us by Joy. Its strident columns followed the usual pattern. There was one editorial which condemned rumors of strife between Russia and Germany as "warmongering," but I paid no particular attention to it. The rest of the paper was anti-war, anti-Roosevelt, anti-defense program, anti-aid-to-Britain, prostrike.

On that same evening, however, radio broadcasts carried the shocking news that Hitler had turned his Panzer legions loose in a blitzkrieg strike against his erstwhile ally, Josef Stalin. I heard nothing that night (nor for several days), from my colleagues on the Cambridge Youth Council. The next day I was unable to purchase my *Daily Worker* at the newsstand. "They haven't come in," the news dealer told me. "Haven't got the dope yet, I guess." It was not until Wednesday—the 25th—that I could obtain a copy of the *Daily Worker* for Tuesday, June 24.

Support the USSR in Its Fight against Nazi War. That was the paper's battle-cry headline, the new slogan of the "antiwar" party. It was still a fight against war. The lead article dodged and weaved like a back-pedaling prize fighter. "The armed assault by German Fascism and its satellites," it said, "is an unprovoked criminal attack upon the greatest champion of peace, freedom and national independence—the land of socialism."

The gauntlet was now on the other mailed fist.

"The military aggression by the Fascist rulers of Germany

41

is also an attack upon the people of Germany. It is an attack likewise upon the people of the United States and of the entire world."

England and the United States still were "imperialists," but the switch was on. The American people—"the workers, toiling farmers, the Negro masses, the middle classes"—were now taking the cause of the Soviet Union as their own, according to the *Daily Worker*. ". . . Full support and cooperation with the Soviet Union in the struggle against Hitlerism," the leading editorial proposed, "against all those reactionaries of every stripe who seek in any manner to aid Hitler's attack against the Soviet Union. For a people's peace based upon the liberation and independence of all nations."

I was sickened. At the same time there was an element of humor to it, which became more evident on closer examination of the pages of *The Worker*. The big switch was too sudden even for the comrades. A special series of articles condemning the Hollywood motion-picture industry as a tool of the "warmakers" had started in the paper on the fatal Sunday. But in the first issue after the party cartwheel, the second article of the series appeared in obviously abbreviated form and was captioned as "the concluding installment." At that, it was not cropped quite enough to cover the Communists' embarrassment.

"The motion picture producers," I read, "much as they like Mr. Roosevelt and anxious as they are to carry out his war program in the pictures they make, face that little problem of the public. . . . Thus, not only do they make war-inciting pictures which people do not want, but they agitate for war by putting propaganda leaflets in the pay envelopes of their employees."

In its "Stop, Look and Listen" column, devoted to railroad labor, the newspaper—in the midst of its confusion—had its signals crossed. It condemned the government's demand for no-strike pledges, and said, "Neither side in the present war has the purpose of bringing freedom or prosperity to the working people

42

of the world. . . . It is only a question of who shall rule the world and who shall profit from their labors. Rail labor, by preparing to strike for higher wages, can give pause to the warmakers."

By the following week the signals were straightened out. "President Roosevelt," the column said, "and Sumner Welles, following the lead of Winston Churchill, have said that the Soviet Union will receive cooperation from Britain and the United States. . . . We call upon the Railroad workers to see that these promises are kept." Obviously, the threatened "strike" was off.

On that fateful Sunday, June 22, Louis Budenz, then president of the *Daily Worker,* had castigated President Roosevelt's message to Congress: "The freezing of Axis funds, the closing of the consulates, the institution of 'patrols,' the demand for reparations in the Robin Moor case are all spun out of Mr. Roosevelt's determination to get the United States into a shooting war. . . . The people want none of this war."

Apparently "the people" changed their minds with the attack on Russia. For on June 30, Mr. Budenz printed a statement of the National Committee of the Communist party, which proclaimed, "This is labor's great responsibility . . . The liberty-loving masses of the American people are ready now more than ever to make all necessary sacrifices to defeat Fascism."

Until this very week, every effort of the party had been to keep the United States out of the war—to prevent America from contributing to or preparing for war—so long as Russia was not involved. When the field was suddenly reversed, the Communists tried to maintain their delicate balance by keeping one foot on the ground. They still did not call for aid to the Allies, only for aid to Soviet Russia. It was the closest I ever saw them come to revealing their true colors. It was, of course, a very serious error, because it revealed the unvarnished, unobscured objective with no frills, and it stated the primary interest of the party quite clearly. But it was not long until they shifted the line a little farther, and fed the public with a complete interventionist pro-

43

gram, calling for full aid to England and Western Europe, and for a united front of all factions fighting the fascists.

Joy, the party courier who brought my *Worker* the following Sunday, was almost in tears. "Isn't it terrible," she said. "We actually cried when we heard the news, my whole family."

"It is terrible—sickening," I answered, taking the papers from her and hurling them into a chair. I felt just as glum, but for an entirely different set of reasons. The big flip-flop of the Communist party in this country probably meant many things to many people. To me it was most significant as a penetration of the party's humanitarian disguise. Certainly it was bad news that the war was continuing to spread and grow like a prairie fire. But to most clear-thinking Americans the war had been bad news all along, right from September 3, 1939. This was not the first time to be saddened—except for the Communist party.

Here stand my "antiwar" friends, I thought. They had done everything they could to prevent the United States from giving any help at all to France, Britain, Belgium, Norway, Yugoslavia— to any of the people who, with pitifully small numbers and even smaller resources, had been standing alone against Hitler's vicious and deadly war machine.

In all of this, for twenty horrible months, the comrades had stood by, not because of a deep-rooted desire for peace, or for pacifism, but as a matter of political strategy. This was but a war between rival imperialist powers. Let them destroy one another. Thus, not only did the Communists refuse aid or sympathy themselves; the party members sought to sabotage the possibility of aid or help from anyone else.

And now Germany—a mad dog, to be sure—had turned upon an adversary with three times Germany's population and forty-five times her area. This was the country that Hewlett Johnson (the "Red Dean of Canterbury"), in his book *Soviet Power,* called "the socialist sixth of the world," a colossus compared with the previous victims of fascism. And my Communist friend stood before me with tears in her eyes. I turned away from her in loathing. Evidently she misinterpreted my temper.

"I guess they knew they could never trust Hitler," Joy said. "Stalin only signed the pact with him to gain time for the attack. He knew it had to come."

So, I thought, another new line! "Self-defense! We knew it all the time!" I couldn't look at Joy. At that moment I had little desire to continue "fellow traveling," for whatever purpose. I was sure that if I opened my mouth at all, I would say something most indiscreet, so I remained silent. Joy left the apartment to finish her rounds for the party.

I heard Eva snort in the other room. She came in and confronted me.

"Why do you fool with these people, Herb? Why do you listen to them? I slammed the door in that girl's face once. That rubbish!" She waved a deprecating hand in the direction of *The Worker,* lying with its garish headlines on the chair.

"Eva." I faced her squarely and took her by the shoulders. "Believe me, I know what I'm doing. I'm doing the right thing."

She turned out of my grasp. "What are you doing? Are you mixed up with these—these Communists? Bill says they are all Communists. We aren't Communists, Herb. We're decent people."

"I can't deny I'm mixed up with them, Eva, no," I replied. "But please keep one thing straight. Believe me, I'm not with them. I'd be very happy to be rid of them, and I know you would, too. But I—I must do this. In spite of their prattle for the 'masses,' you can see that these people have no Christian compassion, no true regard for the individual, no real respect for his integrity. Somehow I have to fight for these things. Right now I can do it best by mixing with them, to learn more about what they are doing."

"But how? What can you possibly do?"

"I—I don't know." I recalled Leary's admonition and avoided her gaze. "I can't tell you for sure, Eva. Perhaps—maybe I can

45

do something about it when the time comes. You've never doubted me, have you, Eva?"

"Never."

"Then please trust me now."

She gave me a perfunctory smile. "I've always trusted you, Herb, you know that. And I know that if you think something is right, nothing I or anyone else can say will change your mind." She paused. "But I certainly hope you know what you're doing."

So did I.

CHAPTER 4

HITLER'S SUDDEN TURN against Russia was the catalyst that revealed the Communists among whom I worked. When the attack came, the Communist party in the United States was left dangling like a yo-yo with its string run out, hanging on the end of the Kremlin's war policies. Time was required to wind up the string again, and the yo-yo was a badge of identification for the Communists. It made it possible for me to tell almost at a glance who among my acquaintances was subservient to the Communist party line. Many of my friends in youth organizations retained their independence throughout the violent flip-flop. The isolationists did not change their position overnight, and those who were interventionist before the attack on Russia remained interventionist.

But between June, 1941, and the Japanese raid on Pearl Harbor, it was only necessary to listen and compare. It was a revelation to me to discover the number of my associates who had been violently antiwar before Hitler's march to the east, and who jumped over the fence to ardent support of the war immediately after the attack on Russia. It was shocking to realize that their primary concern was not the welfare of the United States, but the USSR, and the beliefs dictated to them by the *Daily Worker* and other organs of the party.

"The people," blared *The Worker*, "demand aid to Europe now!" It was not entirely true. The average American did not display the party's legerdemain at switching lines. A strong isolationist and pacifist faction continued to exert tremendous influ-

47

ence right up until Pearl Harbor. Especially was this true in the youth movement, where the Communists had worked hard to build up a powerful antiwar front. Organizations like the Cambridge Youth Council, rallied around an antiwar program, collapsed almost overnight, as their Communist supporters and *agents provocateurs* dropped out. In Washington, a peace picket line around the White House, led by Frederick Vanderbilt Field, folded up its placards and vanished.

I could not mourn the passing of the Cambridge Youth Council, because its Communist members had so twisted and subverted its original purpose. As in so many instances, the Communists in the Cambridge group used as a front an issue which they and non-Communists alike could rally about, the issue of peace. As soon as the antiwar plank was taken out of the Communist platform, the Cambridge Youth Council was no longer of any use to the comrades, and they fled like rats leaving a sinking ship. The fact that the ship actually did sink was further indication of how completely they controlled its direction. They had supplied the manpower, overpowered the leadership, forced their own ideas on the membership, and made themselves the captain and crew of the Council. Then they vanished, scuttling the entire organization to die. In years to come, I was to see this pattern repeated over and over again.

By early autumn it became urgently necessary for the Communists to re-form their lines, and to reestablish their connections through front organizations with the "masses." But it had to be done now under a new banner—"Support the war, aid the Allies, more guns and less butter, help the USSR." Youth organizations, always a keystone of Communist power and influence, were given high priority in the realignment campaign.

In October, 1941, therefore, a call went out to youth leaders of the Boston area for a mass meeting at the Hotel Touraine in Boston. Every potential supporter listed in the Massachusetts Youth Council and its affiliated organizations was invited to at-

48

tend. Letters of invitation were, in most cases, followed up by personal appeals.

Arthur Solomon, one of those who had most readily accomplished the big reverse, called on me and pressed me to attend the meeting as a delegate from the Cambridge Youth Council. I played along with him and agreed to attend. I sent a quick report through the mail to Harold Leary, telling him that the big youth rally would be held, and that I would be on hand to give him a full report of its conduct.

I persuaded Eva to accompany me, which she did with great reluctance. The rally, attended by more than a hundred leaders of youth organizations throughout the state, was held in one of the public meeting halls of the Touraine. Eva and I sat with Art Solomon near the front of the room. I looked around for other representatives from Cambridge, but I recognized only one—my old school friend Gordon Case, who nodded coolly from across the room.

The rally was started off by Sam Abelow, a stocky young man with crewcut hair whom I knew only slightly from previous youth activities. Flanked by the presiding officers at the front of the hall, he stood behind a bare table and outlined the purpose of the meeting—to rally Boston youth behind the nation's defense program, and to crystallize the opinions of young people in support of the war against Nazi aggression.

Slowly he warmed up to his speech, offering a resolution which would place the group on record, and then marshaling arguments to support its passage. Sam wasn't at all sure of the sentiments of the group. After all, there were non-Communists as well as Communists in the room, pacifists as well as militarists, isolationists as well as interventionists.

But Abelow was an accomplished rabble rouser. His voice rose to a keener pitch and his tempo gradually stepped up, as he urged immediate aid to the Allies and to Russia, increased defense production, a larger army, adoption of the Atlantic Charter, and,

49

especially, repeal of the Neutrality Act to permit further support of the nations arrayed against Hitler.

There was little or nothing in his speech with which I disagreed. I was still a pacifist at heart, but I had long since come to the view that the best way to avoid war, if indeed it could be avoided for America, was to support England and her allies to the hilt and to prepare to engage the Nazi enemy directly if necessary. But as Sam rattled on and on, sounding like a recorded version of the *Daily Worker*, I could see the stamp of "stooge" written all over him, and it angered me. For only a few short months before, Sam was talking out of the opposite side of his mouth, assailing the war and all that it stood for with the same vehemence he now mustered to support it. It was more than I could stomach.

I knew the *Daily Worker*, too, by heart—knew what policies it reflected before the June attack, and after. Sam's tirade ran across my grain. I felt an irresistible impulse to needle the Communist "comrades" in the hall, to give them a powerful injection of the same narcotic to which they had once been addicted, and which they were trying desperately now to forget.

I clutched Eva's hand. She turned from listening abjectly to Sam Abelow, and responded by tightening her grasp. "Hang onto your hat," I whispered. "I'm going to try something out."

Sam wound up his appeal for the warlike resolution and sat down. There was a round of enthusiastic applause. I leaped to my feet and signaled the chairman with a wild waving of my arm.

"Will each speaker please give his name and the organization he represents. The chair recognizes this gentleman." His finger pointed to me.

"Herbert Philbrick, Cambridge Youth Council."

Then I blew off steam. For three long minutes, I raked up all the old discarded arguments of Sam Abelow, Art Solomon, and the *Daily Worker*. I blasted the "Wall Street monopolists who are dragging this country into war." I raged against cooperation of any kind with the "imperialist" British, French, and Dutch. I sounded off against the munitions makers and the industrialists who "have everything to gain and nothing to lose by embroiling the world in a bloody war." I used every approach to passion that I could muster.

An eerie silence, like the lull before a tornado, fell on the room, and my voice echoed through it. I felt Eva tug at my coat, but I didn't stop.

"Don't forget," I said, "that an appeal for 'defense' can be used as a screen for aggressive war. The Roosevelt program, with its emphasis on offensive weapons, is a clear indication that the President is leading the country down the path to war. The real danger of Nazi aggression concerns but a small portion of our people the economic royalists, big business, whose properties, markets, and investments are the real stake." I almost gagged on my own words. But I warmed up to the task, and watched with satisfaction the growing concern reflected in huddled conversations at the chairman's table.

"If this country goes to war it will be to defend these interests and not to secure the defense of America's people and way of life. Since the American people have nothing at stake in this war, does not history and common sense dictate no aid to belligerents if we are to stay out of it? War would destroy our much-needed social reforms, as it did in France—break the unions, undermine minimum-wage laws, increase the hours of slave labor, wreck social security, and abrogate freedom of speech and the press. The expansion of the United States Army is the framework of dictatorship. Naturally, we abhor Naziism. But we must not permit our abhorrence to be used as a propaganda lever to pry us loose from our democratic foundations, and drop us over the abyss into a senseless war."

When I sat down abruptly, the storm broke. Art Solomon looked at me aghast, and I returned a vacant smile. Speakers rose in all parts of the room and shouted for recognition. The chairman appealed for order. Eva directed exploratory glances toward the nearest exit. Some of the less genteel in the mob were making it plain that they were in favor of tossing me out of the hotel. But my next move was already plotted. I would demonstrate to these outraged people that I could subordinate my personal views to the will of the majority, but I would take my sweet time about it, and wait until the moment was ripe.

The meeting turned into a near-riot, directed primarily at me. Speaker after speaker ripped my arguments to shreds. A few endeavored to speak in support of me, tempering my views a little, but still appealing for peace. They were shouted down. The controlling element, most of them Communists in my book, rallied shoulder to shoulder, and got the meeting back on the track. For nearly an hour the speeches reverberated around the room.

At last, someone proposed that the resolution offered by Sam Abelow be adopted, and further debate curtailed. This was the moment.

I leaped to my feet again and demanded the floor. Arthur turned pale and tugged at my sleeve. Others half rose from their chairs in a threatening manner. I shouted at the top of my lungs, "Mr. Chairman! Mr. Chairman!" He could not avoid me. "The chair recognizes Mr. Philbrick." There was a groan in the room, and a few shouted insults, but quiet was restored.

"Mr. Chairman," I said in dulcet tones, "I wish to second the motion of the delegate from Dorchester." In the stunned silence that followed, I sat down, leaving them to make the best of my switch, and hoping I had not overplayed my hand. Then the sun burst forth. Arthur Solomon jumped up and shook my hand. Faces that were turned in my direction broke into smiles. Someone reached over and clapped me on the back. "We knew you'd see it right," he said. The whole thing dissolved in a wave of good humor.

Not so with everyone. I glanced around at Gordon Case. He

52

was leaning forward in his chair, staring at me with a sickened expression. My glance fell to the floor. The vote was taken on the resolution. I raised my hand in the affirmative. Nobody voted against it, although a large number, I observed, declined to vote at all. The chairman announced unanimous approval and the meeting broke up.

As the rally disbanded, I shouldered through the crowd to find Gordon, but I saw him walk rapidly through the door. His head was bowed, and he did not look back. I felt that I had turned a corner into darkness.

Eva, Art, and I took a subway to the Park Street Station and changed for the rapid transit to Cambridge. Eva was shocked into a puzzled silence. I was engrossed in my reactions to the meeting, wondering what the upshot would be, and at the same time mentally scribbling my report on the affair to the Federal Bureau of Investigation. Art was so jubilant and voluble that he failed to observe our attitudes. He chatted merrily during the ride, acclaiming the success of the rally, and expressing his glee at my support of the resolution. It was as if he had rediscovered a lost friend. He was still curious about my "deviation" at the beginning of the meeting, but he was so overjoyed at the outcome that he didn't press the point, and obviously didn't see the joke.

All the way home he turned the issues over and over, explaining how right I had been to do as I did, and how wrong I might have been. Eva and I watched the lights of the tunnel flash by the car windows, lost in our own thoughts. Art wanted to go somewhere for a snack and a talk, but I had had all I could take, and begged off.

"This is Eva's first time out since Sandra, the new baby," I said. "I think we'd better get along home. We have two of them to look out for now, you know."

"We'll get together later," Art said. "I'll be over." He gave me a final hearty handshake.

At Central Square in Cambridge we left the subway. It was a

53

pleasant autumn evening, and we decided to walk the rest of the way home rather than use our streetcar transfers. We strolled in silence down Magazine Street, hand in hand. Finally Eva looked at me in search of something to say.

"Well?" was all she could manage.

"I had my chance, didn't I?"

"You certainly did."

"What do you think?"

"Herb, if you know what you're doing—heaven knows I don't— and you know it is right, then you will go ahead and do it. So it doesn't make much difference what I think, does it?"

"Don't credit me with too much good sense. If I had a brain in my head we would have left that madhouse and gone for a ride in the swan boats."

"Silly. The swan boats aren't running. Besides, I'm proud of you."

My willingness to embrace the party line at the Hotel Touraine youth meeting was apparently the stripe which the Communists were waiting for me to show. It brought a resurgence of interest in me and my activities, all of which I reported to Harold Leary. "Good, good," was all Leary would say. "You're on the right track."

I had more and more strange callers at my house in the evenings. They showered me with pamphlets on every conceivable subject, many of them plainly marked, "Communist Party, U.S.A." I noticed that many of my visitors came in pairs. I was introduced to countless new young people, always by their "party" names—Margot, John, Nancy, Ray—and I wondered if they were real names or convenient aliases. Many of them did not attempt to conceal the fact that they were members and active workers for the Young Communist League, the youth section of the Communist party.

They engineered little soirees at my apartment, never with more than four or five outsiders. Eva usually stayed out of them,

54

frequently going out to the movies or visiting friends. Several times my callers asked about her, but I made plausible excuses.

The usual pattern was for someone to come bearing stacks of pamphlets or circulars, all of which involved social, economic, or political issues and problems. They even brought around occasional children's nursery books which closely adhered to the party line. Sometimes there would be a little sales talk along with the material, and I would be asked to buy it for the price printed on the cover. On other occasions, the literature was simply left without comment.

At the outset, I was questioned a few times on my "Trotskyite" deviation at the Hotel Touraine meeting, but the issue was never pressed, and they were apparently satisfied with the outcome. I would indulge frequently in little policy debates, just to demonstrate that I had an independent mind. I was asked to take part in innumerable campaigns, usually executed by means of the mass petition, one of the Communists' favorite devices. Most of them did not carry the party label. They always sought some combination of terms, tailor-made for the particular purpose, the Boston Committee——, the Citizens League for——, the National Congress of——.

I purposely turned down some of their invitations. It was not my intention to become so deeply involved that I could not devote myself to my job and my rapidly growing family. But one of the projects proposed to be by Arthur Solomon always the most frequent caller at my house—caught my fancy. He asked me to serve on the forming committee of a new youth group to be set up in Boston.

"What will it be?" I inquired with extreme caution, recalling the experience of the now-defunct Cambridge Youth Council.

"Herb, this will be right up your alley. First of all, it will function as a win-the-war group. The youth of Boston must be persuaded to give unstinting support to speedy victory in the war. There is no lack of youth organizations in the city, as you know.

There are hundreds of them in Boston. But what we need is a coordinating committee to point up the greatest needs of the country and to work most efficiently to fill those needs.

"The organizations with which we can work are already well known to you through your connections with the Boston Council of Social Agencies. How long were you with them, five years, wasn't it?"

I was surprised that Arthur even knew or remembered this long-buried detail of my career. I wondered how much more he had been finding out about me.

"Yes," I said, "that's right. I know a lot of them well."

"That's what I mean. You can be of tremendous help on this thing."

"What will be the principal objectives of the committee?" I inquired.

"Oh, things like salvage drives, blood-donation campaigns, defense-bond sales, recreation for service men. You know."

"I'll do what I can, Art," I agreed, "but I can't try to tackle too much."

Thus I was brought into the Boston Youth for Victory Council, a group whose origins were obscure. I did not know from Arthur's prospectus whether the program started in the Young Communist League or whether it began as a legitimate, non-Communist organization with the Communists moving in on it at the outset. Nevertheless, I went along for two reasons. I wanted to see what happened, and I felt the FBI would be interested to know, also. Furthermore, if Youth for Victory was to be dedicated to the winning of the war, and was to function as a legitimate group with America's interests at heart, then I wanted to support it and simultaneously work from within to help combat Communist influence and control. It appeared an ideal opportunity for me to try a little subversion in reverse.

Circumstances combined to make my job easy. The members of the Young Communist League who worked so avidly to worm their way into control of the Youth for Victory program were smothered under an avalanche of response from young, idealistic non-Communists, led by astute and experienced figures in the youth field. I recall Miss Emilie Everett, chairman of the Adult Advisory Committee for Youth Work at the Boston Council of Social Agencies; Harry Burroughs, of the Burroughs Newsboys Foundation; Carl Wetherell, head of the Boston Young Men's Christian Union (Carl was now supported and cultivated, in vain, by the Communists, who had previously cordially hated him for his espousal of aid to Britain before the June turnabout); and another, Reverend Augustine C. Dalton of the Catholic Youth Organization.

More than 250 youth organizations piled on the win the war band wagon, and under the controlling influence of good people the Communist infiltration enjoyed only limited success. Another factor which militated against them, of course, was the direct entrance of the United States in the war at Pearl Harbor, which eliminated the isolationists once and for all, and brought almost everyone in the country into the same camp. The Communists had no more ammunition for the time being, and they were never able to secure control of the Youth for Victory program.

But there were other reasons for their failure. The social workers of the city insisted that any activity of importance to the war should be coordinated with and receive the approval of the civil-defense authorities. Matters which were of keen propaganda interest to the Communists were effectively screened out. The significant lesson of the Youth for Victory organization was that Communist influence in legitimate activities can be held in check, and infiltration can be thwarted if the membership is sufficiently interested in the organization and its activities. This is true even in a case like Youth for Victory, where the Young Communist League obviously made the strongest possible bid to capture the group, and was deeply frustrated and angered by its failure to do so. I did nothing to aid them except appear to be helpful and act disappointed along with them.

Another group which I was invited to help organize during this period, and from which I learned something about communism, was the Cambridge Committee for Equal Opportunities, an organization purportedly devoted to the welfare of the Negro people of the community. It was a perfect example of the exploitation of legitimate complaints among Negroes for Communist ends. These people lived in squalid conditions and suffered heavily from discrimination and unfair treatment in their jobs and in their everyday pursuits. I visited their homes and talked to them, and saw them as a fertile field for Communist recruitment and development. I met frequently with their leaders, such as Miss Odile Sweeney, of the Cambridge Community Center, a veteran Negro leader and a non-Communist. Possibly she suspected the Communist influence in the Committee for Equal Opportunities, but if she did, she never spoke of it to me.

My Communist associates in the Committee worked over the community time after time. They staged rallies, and I saw how they kept rubbing salt in the wounds of the Negro people to stir up dissension and trouble. They organized picket lines, made promises, fought against discrimination, circulated petitions, and used every means at their disposal to gain support among the Negroes. Even though they campaigned vigorously and quite openly, I knew of only one Negro in the Cambridge community who was persuaded to become a member of the Young Communist League.

In whatever ways I could, I tried earnestly to lend my assistance where it might be of real benefit to the Negroes of Cambridge. But subversively, I would combat the Communist influence whenever the party began to assert its line, to enlist members, or, most of all, to grind money for the party coffers out of the pathetic incomes of the Negro working people.

The tactics used by the Communist comrades to twist Negro

58

thinking repelled me. I remember that we circulated petitions for a mixed battalion of Negroes and whites in the Army to put an end to racial segregation under arms. I remarked at one of our evening soirees that I thought it would be a wonderful thing to set up such a battalion as a demonstration that segregation was neither necessary nor desirable.

One of my visitors retorted with a sneer. "Don't kid yourself," he said. "These petitions won't bring any tangible results, and we don't expect them to. But at least they give us a wedge. They gain us a hearing among these people, so that we can accomplish our educational work among them."

"Educational work." The Communist jargon for "propaganda."

Such things undermined my determination to stay with the Communists and almost impelled me to break off my relations with them and with the FBI and to get out altogether. In March, 1942, I was afforded an opportunity. It became apparent at that time that my family was growing more rapidly than my business career, especially when Eva broke the news that we might have our third child in the fall. (This one, we expected confidently, would be a boy.)

I immediately started inquiries leading toward a better paying job. Through my connections in the Advertising Club of Boston I learned that there was an opening in the Paramount Theaters Division of New England, the M. & P. Theaters Company of Boston. One interview reaped rich rewards. I was hired as assistant advertising director of the group, and scheduled to start work in April.

Eva was delighted. My office would be in Scollay Square, just seven minutes' walk from North Station. We determined that, with the increase in our income, we could look for larger and better living quarters, somewhere outside of the crowded city but within reasonable commuting distance, in a place where the three children would have ample room to play, indoors and out.

Arthur Solomon showed up as usual, and we invited him to join us in a cup of coffee. We told him the news. I particularly enjoyed telling him about it, because I thought it would terminate my relations with him and his Communist colleagues. I was not only moving my office out of Cambridge, but I planned to move my home as well. The Young Communist League in Cambridge would no longer have any use for me, and I was glad of it.

Arthur was surprised, but he displayed no disappointment. "What kind of a job is it?" he asked.

"I'll be the assistant to Harry Browning. He's the dean of the entertainment press agents in New England. He has charge of advertising and publicity for more than one hundred theaters in this part of the country."

"Wow!" exclaimed Arthur. "That's great!" I hadn't expected his enthusiasm to equal my own. He began firing questions faster than I could answer them. Where will your office be? When do you start? When did you get the job? When will you move? His curiosity, I thought, was unlimited.

"How did you ever get such a good job?"

"Well," I replied, "mostly through my friends in the Advertising Club."

"The Ad Club of Boston!" Arthur almost leaped from his chair. "Do you mean to tell me you are a member there?"

"Why, sure, I've been a member for the last two years."

"God Almighty!" he exclaimed. "Why didn't you tell me before?"

"I didn't think you'd be interested."

"No? Why, that's terrific. The Advertising Club, and you're a member of it."

He asked questions far into the night. Eva yawned and bade us good night. I finally steered Arthur toward the door.

"Well," I said, "I'll be glad to get out of these Cambridge activities. I'm going to take it easy, put more time on my job, get to know my family a little better. Community projects are good, but they can take up too much of your time. I'll be glad to get away from them for a while."

Arthur's ferretlike eyes scrutinized me closely. "You'll never get away from it entirely, Herb," he said. "You enjoy working for people. You have it in your blood—organizing, managing, inspiring people. You'll never get away from it." I laughed at him and eased him out the door.

I found that Eva had gone to bed. I slowly untied my tie and slipped off my shirt, puzzled over Arthur Solomon's reaction to my new job, and especially to my membership in the Advertising Club. It was much more than polite enthusiasm.

"What do you make of that, Eva?"

"I don't know. He seemed pleased, didn't he? And the Ad Club, too. Don't your friends consider those people to be—'reactionary,' 'Fascists,' or something like that?"

"That's right, Eva. Do you suppose they would be so audacious as to try to bore into an organization like that? Or into a business like Harry Browning's?"

"Oh, no, Herb, they couldn't."

"I didn't think so, either. But now—I don't know. Boring from within. You know, I expected this move to spread the gap between me and these Communists. It's a move in the direction of what they call 'big business.' It seems to be outside of their world. I thought sure that Arthur would be displeased with the news. But I wonder. I have a feeling that the gap is narrowing."

The next evening a knock came at the apartment door. I found Arthur standing there, shifting nervously from one foot to the other. He looked worried. I invited him in.

"Can we be alone, or go some place?" he said.

"Eva's out for the evening," I replied. "What's on your mind?"

He paced the floor, his eyes darting about the room. "I can only stay a minute," he said. "Herb, by now you must realize that I'm a Communist. You must know something about the Young Communist League."

61

Now it was coming. I felt a shot of adrenaline jab into my heart, and I remembered Hal Leary's forewarning that an invitation might be made. I smiled.

"I'm not surprised, Art. I figured it wasn't any of my business to ask, but I wondered when you would tell me, and I'm glad you did."

"We want you to work with us," he said. "It doesn't make any difference, your moving out of Cambridge. The League is well organized here, and you know almost everyone in it. You could live wherever you want. Fact is, it might be better. If you go into a new community, they need never know, and you could carry on in the League here and do a good job. We need you, Herb. You can fill a big place."

My reluctance this time was not an act. "You know how I feel. I explained last night. I want to live my own life, at least for a while."

"Herb, you know we have to make sacrifices in times like these. We're at war. It's important that young people take control of things. We can't permit life to slip through our fingers."

Indeed, I thought, it is necessary to make sacrifices. Art turned on his most persuasive manner. He pressed me from all sides, appealed to everything he knew about me. I refrained from giving him a direct reply. I certainly didn't want to give my assent. If the choice had been mine, I would have told him no on the spot. But Hal Leary's admonition was ringing in my ears, and the long patience of the FBI now became clear to me.

"You'll have to give me time to think it over, Art. I don't know. There are a lot of things to consider." I was firm about it, even though he urged me to give him his answer then. I promised I would get in touch with him.

The following morning on my way to work I dropped into a telephone booth and got Harold Leary on the line.

"I have news for you. It's come."

"Is that so! And you told them . . . ?"

62

"I'd have to think it over."

"Meet me at Harvard Street and Massachusetts Avenue at seven o'clock tonight."

Hal made the rendezvous at the exact instant, driving up in his undistinguished automobile.

"What happened?" he asked, before I had closed the car door. He did not move the car, but waited for me to answer.

"They asked me to join the Young Communist League." Hal did not change expression. It was as if he had expected it.

"And what was your answer?"

"I carried out your request. You asked me to stall them. That was last night. I have to call."

"Do you know what your answer will be?"

"I know what I would like it to be."

"Before you tell me," Hal interjected, "let me explain that I can't help you reach a decision. That must be your own. If you say no, that's that. But if you decide to go along there are things you should know, and I can tell you what it would mean.

"The Bureau would like to have you stay. We know your work. We think that you have what it takes. The Young Communist League is simply the preparatory academy for the Communist party. You will go from one to the other, in all likelihood. We have good reason to believe that information—accurate, inside information—concerning the activities of these organizations is very important to the American people, and to the future of America. You know something of what they are doing. You are in a position to learn more."

It was not an easy decision to make, although I already suspected, deep down, what the answer had to be. "Hal, I haven't any doubt what you say is true. I have already seen enough to convince me. It's just that I don't like the idea of being a—a spy, even for the FBI. I'm not the type."

Hal brushed aside my objection. "I can appreciate your feeling," he said. "But the role must be played by someone, because it is

63

the only way through which the whole story can be learned, and learned in time. Normal methods of detection, where crime is involved, are important, but the detective gets the facts after the crime is committed. The counterspy gets them before the crime takes place. It has to be done, like it or not, where we have reason to suspect that crimes against society and the state are in the making."

I could see what Hal meant. It was true. Sometimes, for some unexplainable reason, in fighting to preserve what is worth while, you are forced to do things which are not in accordance with the very principles to which you are dedicated. A soldier doesn't like to pull the trigger, either, when he is confronted with a human being in the sights of his rifle. My thoughts came out aloud.

"If I said no, I'd be running away," I said.

Hal quickly interrupted. "Before you give an answer, let me finish.

"You would perform an important service, yes. But you would have to make tremendous sacrifices to do it, and your return may be nothing, or worse than nothing. We would want you to go as deep into the party as you could, give up much of your home life and many of your friends.

"I'm laying it on the line to you, Philbrick, because we don't want it otherwise. There would be an element of danger in it, physical danger. If you are identified as an FBI connection, you might suffer for it. If you are exposed publicly as a Communist party member you may lose your job, and you cannot claim the FBI to justify your position. It may never be learned that you worked with us. Certainly it can never come from you. If you are arrested in your Communist activities, you must expect no assistance from us whatever. We never heard of you. You are on your own.

"If you join, not even your wife must know what you are doing. Nobody will know. Not even most of the agents in the Bureau will know. You will be a code number. You must never appear in or near our office, nor be observed in conversation with us. Your operations must be thoroughly secret. You will send us regular reports, facts about the party, its members and their activities. Facts only. We will pay any necessary expenses that this entails. You will, of course, keep on with your regular job."

He stopped and waited, and I stared ahead through the windshield.

"I know you can't make up your mind on the spur of the moment. I don't expect you to. But you must give me a decision as soon as possible. Tomorrow, if you can. You mustn't keep the League waiting."

Leary started the car and drove the few blocks to my apartment in silence. He didn't let me out at the door, but turned the corner.

"I'll call you," I said. "Good night."

I knew when I stepped away from the car what my decision would be. The next morning I stopped at a cigar store and ducked into the telephone booth. I dialed the Bureau and asked for Leary.

"The answer is yes," I said. There was a slight pause, and then Leary, businesslike: "Good. Tell them. Then take it easy. You will hear from us. I wouldn't recommend that you close any more sales." I recognized the blind, and hung up.

I paused at the counter to buy a cigar. My hand trembled involuntarily as I picked up my change. You're a bungling fool, I told myself, and made a desperate effort to control my shaking hand.

To my surprise, I found that I could.

Counterspy.

CHAPTER 5

A TEN-CENT INITIATION fee made me a member of the Young
Communist League, a bargain rate to buy my way in as a Communist—and a government counterspy. A bargain, but it wasn't
paid for in money alone.

It was paid out in the racking of a conscience that rebelled
against the word "spy" under any terms; paid, too, in hard work
"grubbing" for the comrades; in suffering a thorough indoctrination in Communist policies and beliefs which, whenever they
were not completely detestable, were downright dull; in disruption of home life, infringements on business, uneasy moments,
and a long summer of preparation.

To change a free mind into that of an underground counterspy is a severe strain. I did not enter my relationship with the
Federal Bureau of Investigation by any long considered, well-
laid plan. My relationship grew from a foundation of anger and
frustration into a mutually agreeable working arrangement by
slow and natural stages. I had always been a non-Communist, but
when I initially approached the Bureau I was not a rabid anti-
Communist. The fact is that I knew so little about communism
and its hidden aims and methods that, like the average person
of those times, and many even today, I regarded the movement
more as a nuisance than as an acute menace. I was natively so
unreceptive to their doctrines that it was only by swallowing my
gorge that I was able to convince them they should take me in

the first place, and it is remarkable to me that I was able to disguise my attitudes well enough to stay in after they did.

In my early work with them, though I learned little about communism as a political science or social philosophy, I saw enough of their subversive practices to give me the will to dedicate as much of my life as necessary to combatting them. The deliberate fraud and distortion with which they victimized sincere persons and corrupted honest humanitarianism outraged my sense of ethics. I compromised my revulsion against spying by convincing myself that I was acting as a reporter to throw what light I could upon Communist activities in my community, and to fight where I could against the Communist infiltration of labor unions, professional groups, business, commerce, and government.

I was impelled to discover, if I could, why a mere political party, claiming to foster social improvement and public welfare, claiming that its aim was to impose its will upon the people within the framework of a strong constitutional government, should find it necessary to cloak its movements in secrecy and deception. What did communism have to hide and why the conspiratorial air? Why was it necessary to concentrate so much effort on an elaborate network of "fronts" behind which to exercise its influence covertly? If the keystone of communism was the will of the people, why then could it not, like other political parties, go to its source openly for support? Or did the Communists seek to usurp the will of the people, and if so, by what right, by what means?

When a man moves behind a disguise he may appear merely ridiculous. But if he takes his disguise seriously and persists in clinging to it, he is certainly suspect and he may be dangerous.

Arthur Solomon summed up the source of my curiosity when he called at my apartment to receive my reply to his invitation. I did not have to seek him out. He came before I had a chance.

"Naturally, your membership will not be known publicly,"

was one of the first things he said. "You needn't be afraid of that."

I had other things to fear, but Arthur wasn't aware of them. I was glad, for my purposes, that my communism would be under wraps, but at the same time I was unable to comprehend his attitude. Is our political activity based on fear? I was brought up in the tradition of the New England town meeting where each man spoke his own piece in public and feared no other.

"There will be nothing on the record to show your alliance," Art said, "no file with your name at the League headquarters. There are no membership cards. Your neighbors and business associates must not know that you are a Communist. Your life should be carried on in a normal way."

Live a lie, I thought and with a sardonic inward smile, a double life.

"Of course," Art was saying (looking at him—small, nervous, scheming, brilliant—I reflected that he seemed a comic character out of a cloak-and-dagger thriller), "of course, as a member of the League you are not a member of the Communist party. You understand that. The League is an entirely independent youth organization. But it is more than just a study club or social group. It is a training ground for leadership in the proletarian movement.

"It is not under the control of the Communist party," he lied, and he knew that I knew it. "The League you will find is the only interdenominational, interracial youth group on a national basis fighting for a better way of life, not only for the people of America but for the masses of the whole world.

"You will work at the start with a small cell of eight or nine members. It will be necessary to study hard. The members you meet will be a representative group—workers, students, business people, intellectuals. It will be interracial—Jews, gentiles, Negroes. You will probably be surprised when you discover who some of them are."

I pounded out a full report of the conversation, together with

68

some of my impressions, to Harold Leary, and sat back to await the next step. A few days later I received a telephone call at my office, where I was winding up my affairs preparatory to my new theater job.

"Hello, Mr. Philbrick. This is Miss Grose. Toni."

"Yes. Hello. How are you?" I had not seen or heard from her since the ill-fated days of the Cambridge Youth Council.

"You're a stranger," she said.

"I—haven't been very active. I'm afraid we didn't do very well. The council, I mean. Maybe I wasn't quite the man for the job."

"Oh, don't worry about that. But it just happens that I have some—unfinished business—I would like to talk over. Could we have lunch?"

"Sure. Glad to."

We met at the Waldorf Restaurant in Cambridge, just across the square from Harvard College and in the same block as Toni's Student Union office. We greeted each other warmly. She was still tan, still hearty and charming, a suitable cover-girl picture to be captioned "Typical American College Youth." We filled our metal trays at the cafeteria counter and carried them to a table, chatting amiably. She unfolded a paper napkin and placed it in her lap. I expected some preliminaries, to what I didn't precisely know.

"I'm glad to hear that you have joined the League," she said in her husky voice.

I glanced at her quickly. She was looking at me hard, but with a smile. I took off my glasses in a gesture which I suddenly realized was a habitual one whenever I wanted to hide an expression that might be revealing. Because I had observed Toni's close association with the Cambridge Youth Council and those who subverted it, I had long suspected that she might be a Communist. But I had no proof, and now the subject was like static in the air. Was this then the "unfinished" business? I replaced my glasses

69

with a realization that my life as a spy forced me to guard against such gestures, which might defeat their own purpose. I toyed with my food, suddenly no longer hungry. Possibly in answer to my blank stare, she added, "Of course I understand your membership will not be public."

"I'm very proud to be invited," I said, finding my lost voice. "It's a fine thing."

"I know," she said.

"I didn't realize that you were. . . ." I ventured cautiously.

She flashed her charming smile. "The League is very strong. You would be surprised to know who some of the people are." The same thing Art said. There was a pause while a man walked by our table, and Toni watched him disinterestedly. "Have you thought what you expect to do, what you hope to get out of your membership?"

"Well, I believe in its aims and its principles," I muttered inadequately. She took me right up on it.

"You don't know much about them yet." Her manner was still warm and friendly but there was a bluntness to it now, and her eyes were level on me. "What subjects are you especially interested in? Have you any suggestions for the League's immediate program? You've done a good bit of youth work of various kinds, I know."

She fired questions at me, scarcely pausing for replies, in the manner of an inquisitor—questions about my political views and even my private life, some of which I hesitated to answer until I realized that she probably knew the answers to them anyway. I had an unpleasant sensation that she was trying deliberately to trip me up. It would be foolhardy to depart from the truth.

What did my parents do and where did they live? Oh, good working people. Unionist, your father? What about your wife, how does she feel about the League? How much Marxism have you studied and what aspects of it would you like to emphasize? I answered each one as directly as I could, making plausible

70

excuses—the children and household demands—for Eva's inactivity.

"You have been interested in pacifism. Do you believe there is such a thing as a just war?"

My lack of understanding of Marxist philosophy crossed me up. "Well," I replied, thinking myself on firm ground, "of course I believe in this war. Once a war has been brought to us there is only one course to follow and that is to win it as soon as possible. Pacifism is valid until war is declared, and in this case we were attacked. But generally I have always thought that war was outmoded and that a civilized world should certainly be able to discover peaceful methods to settle its disputes. I don't think anyone wins wars."

She did not enter into a discussion but simply said, "Umm," as though she was making a mental note. When I filed my report later to the Bureau, for the first time I felt uneasy about my FBI connection. Where there were spies I was vaguely aware that there might be others spying on the spies. Toni Grose's scrutiny was too close and exacting for comfort.

The first meeting of my League cell was held at my apartment, 213 Banks Street, in April, 1942. Art Solomon came, and Joy, the girl who delivered my Sunday *Worker*. "Party" names were used in introductions: "Bea . . . Dottie . . . Alma . . . Dave . . . Betty . . . this is Herb."

"Will Sid be here?" I asked Art. No, he said, his brother belonged to another group and this was mostly newcomers. I expected to see Toni, but she did not appear.

Quantities of Communist literature were carried in and displayed on top of the cedar chest in our living room. We were given a little pep talk and urged to buy as much as we could for prices ranging from one to twenty-five cents. Some of the pamphlets bore the name of the Communist party, others were under "independent" sponsorship.

Arthur took control of the meeting, swung it over from sociabil-

71

ity to serious purpose, and announced that the subject for the evening's discussion would be, "Just and Unjust Wars." I felt a warm flush under my collar. One of the girls was named to lead the discussion and she brought out a portfolio of instruction material.

I learned that I had betrayed to Toni Grose a serious Marxist defect when I said that wars were outmoded and that there should be peaceful means for resolving international disputes. In the Marxist view, wars are necessary. There are two kinds of wars, the discussion leader explained, "just" and "unjust" wars. Communism is opposed only to wars of conquest, imperialist wars, and even those the Communists must attempt to convert into civil wars. Communists, the young instructress told us, do not oppose just wars waged to liberate people or to defend them from foreign attack. Such wars should be encouraged, should be supported.

To illustrate and prove a point made during the discussion, the group received as a "textbook" a pamphlet entitled, "Know Your Enemy—Japan." I expected to find it labeled "Communist Party," but was surprised and mildly curious when I noted that the imprint on the pamphlet was the Institute of Pacific Relations, 129 E. 52d Street, New York. Why was this organization being used to educate young Communists? I wondered.

It was war as an instrument of society, without compromise as to types of war, that I vigorously opposed on Christian principles. It was difficult for me to accept the Leaguers' differentiation. But I was actually less concerned with the issue than with the fact that this should be the first topic of my Communist indoctrination, coming only a few days after Toni Grose had raised the question and received my reactions privately.

"But isn't the Communist party ever pacifist?" I asked, recalling their pacifism in the CYC.

"No," came the response from one of the group. "Marxism refutes pacifism. They are incompatible."

72

This was a subject that was elaborated and amplified many times during the next few weeks of my initiation. I applied myself diligently to my studies so that I could give the best possible appearance of learning and accepting communism while still showing an intentional spark of independence on occasion. I learned that the public position of the Communist party can be, when occasion demands it, entirely at variance with the real party line, which remains inflexible.

I also learned that my independence would not be tolerated and caught my first inkling of the rigidity of party discipline. Independent thinking was not condoned. There was a straight and narrow line to follow, and in our discussions we would reach an impasse and progress no further every time I injected an alien thought, until the comrades were certain that my deviation on each point had been erased and a "proper" Marxist viewpoint instilled in its place. I suspected that this was one of the functions of the classes, and in fact the discussions themselves bore me out. They were arranged to detect any measure of deviation and to root it out and destroy it. It gave me an idea as to the success of the party in winning persons of varying degrees of intelligence to its way of thinking. They had time and patience.

The Marxist reasoning followed by this hard-eyed group of purposeful youngsters was a revelation to me. A peculiar pattern of "free discussion" was to appear. In group discussions, the cell leaders would invariably state a premise as a rigid conclusion—a dogma—and then call upon the participants to bring forth evidence that would support it. "Truth" was not found by accumulating a lot of heterogeneous data and then groping for a solution. It was reverse reasoning, from Marxist-Leninist "truths" to manufactured testimony. As I watched and listened to the questions, answers, and comments by the YCLers, it appeared to be a contest among the students to determine who could say the same thing over again the most often, in different words but with the same meaning; an attempt to express it with greater clarity, more pre-

73

cision—a refining process. All evidence at variance with the conclusion was argued into the discard, usually by applying other Marxist rules to it. Everything in the world could be explained in this fashion in accordance with the unchanging laws of Marx, Lenin, Engels, and Stalin. It was simple once I got the hang of it and I quickly found I could do it myself.

As soon as my indoctrination had progressed far enough in the League's eyes I was given my first Communist assignment, "grubbing" for the party. One of my initial tasks was that old workhorse of Communist action, the petition, this one in behalf of the release of Earl Browder, the party's national chairman, from his jail term on passport fraud.

We blanketed Cambridge with the petitions. I canvassed business houses, rang doorbells, solicited signatures on street corners. We played upon the argument that Browder had been "railroaded" on a charge that had never been used before for prosecution of a case, and we met with an amazing response. Thirty thousand signatures were obtained in Cambridge alone, more than one-quarter of the total population. It helped to bring results. "In the interests of national unity" Browder was given his liberty by President Roosevelt on May 16, 1942.

Throughout this work I felt that I was never free from close scrutiny by my League associates. I was constantly on guard not to say the wrong thing at the wrong time. I learned to weigh every word before I spoke it. Every occasion, even the most innocent one, was a potential booby trap.

There was one meeting of a youth group in Cambridge—a non-Communist group, I understood—which brought me into contact with a girl I knew only as Margot, Joy's sister. Joy was not present, and I did not know whether Margot shared her sister's enthusiasm for communism. The connection put me on the alert, although I had no positive link between Margot and the Communist movement.

The discussion at the meeting was abstruse and trivial, but in

74

the midst of it, while I was holding the floor and attempting to direct the talk, an indirect reference was made to communism.

"Those damned Communists," Margot suddenly blurted so that everyone could hear her. Someone in the room snickered approvingly, but a danger signal went up in my mind. Could it be that she was anti-Communist, with a hatred of her sister's affiliations? Or, I thought, was it possible that Margot was also a Leaguer or even a party member who knew that I had joined? Was it possible that she suspected my true role and was trying to make me reveal it? If so, I reflected, it was a naïve effort. But this was a non-Communist organization, and some in the room were ardent anti-Communists. It occurred to me that I would be on dangerous ground no matter which way I moved.

"I'm sure," I said as genially as I could after the briefest possible pause, "that the issue of communism has nothing to do with what we're talking about. We had better stick to the issue."

The brush with Margot increased my caution. I was beginning to understand that there was a sense of urgency in Communist ranks to protect themselves from government spies—a position for which I had a keener respect than some of the other members. My new comrades, furthermore, had already impressed on me the theory that the Communist party must represent the "vanguard of the working class," a carefully chosen few. Weaklings, pinks, fellow travelers, opportunists, and deviationists, they told me, must be constantly weeded out or sidetracked into harmless pursuits. Having come this far, I didn't want to be purged now. I recognized that Margot's probe could be a part of the purging process.

Discreet inquiry revealed that Margot's name was Margot Clark, and that she had been for some time in charge of a Communist-sponsored bookshop in Harvard Square. Furthermore, she attended meetings of a Communist cell in Cambridge. When I confirmed my suspicions and realized that, in fact, a trap had been set for me, I began to distrust my imagination and saw Communists,

75

spying on me, everywhere I turned. I grew suspicious because I noticed the same loiterers from day to day on the same street corners near my home or office. I began taking devious zigzag routes to and from work, and I thought I encountered some of the same faces every day. I was convinced that it was not just coincidence that there were more spooners parked at night on the two streets by my apartment, even more than the normal spring weather might account for, and they seemed always to be parked facing my apartment instead of the more scenic river front.

I took it up with Hal Leary at our next rendezvous. He laughed. "Don't worry about it," he said, and then he became thoughtful. "Could be that some of it is your imagination, or it might be special treatment. But if situations come about, or if there are any activities along those lines, anything out of the ordinary, we want to know about them. It might indicate something that we are not aware of and it might be helpful."

I was a little annoyed. "I don't know why it is that I can never get a straight answer from you. In fact, I can't get *any* answer from you. You might warn me about some of these things and save me some trouble." A big grin spread across his pleasant face, and it occurred to me momentarily to ask him how many of those people I thought were shadowing me might be FBI agents. But I put it aside.

"All right," I griped. "I know. I'm on my own. No help from the Bureau and all that."

He banished the grin. "None. You see, even if it were our policy, which it is not, it would probably do more harm than good. If we couldn't be sure—and if you couldn't be sure—that you could get by your first tests without assistance from us, then we wouldn't be sure that you could pass the next ones. Right? The Bureau can't possibly anticipate everything that's going to happen. Neither can we always be around to hold you up. Sooner or later something will happen with no warning, and if you don't have the experience to act on, you will sink like a stone.

"Perhaps you should know a little more about the Bureau. Naturally we're interested in you, but we're even more interested in the facts. However, we don't pass judgment on them. You give them to us, we organize them and pass them on to the proper authorities. That is our job."

I returned to my "grubbing." For the first time, I was ordered to report to the Young Communist League's Cambridge headquarters at 75 Magazine Street, right around the corner from my apartment. The place was identified to me as the apartment of Larry and Toni Locke, names I had never encountered. When I reached the apartment to accept my assignment, who should open the door but my blond friend from Harvard, Toni Grose. She said hello, and I did my best to conceal my surprise at learning that Toni was Mrs. Locke, if indeed that was her real name. I did not know how long they had been married, and we did not discuss it. Toni was busy and dashed off.

I glanced around the apartment. In one room were two typewriter desks, a filing cabinet, and several busy Leaguers. I noticed large stacks of writing paper and envelopes on the desks, all bearing the letterheads of different organizations, some of which were well known to me as non-Communist groups. I examined the stacks as unobtrusively as I could to see if there might be an old copy of our Cambridge Youth Council letterhead in the place. Could this headquarters or another like it have been the mysterious factory for all the paper work turned out by the Solomons and Stan Beecher for the Cambridge Youth Council?

I was interrupted by a League worker who handed me a letter drawn on the stationery of the Boston branch of the Russian War Relief Committee. Down the left side, almost the entire length of the paper, were listed the names of the committee officers and sponsors. Most of them, as usual, were well-known persons, locally as well as nationally. I remember that the honorary chairman was the late Dr. Serge Koussevitsky. The local chairman was Dr.

77

Hugh Cabot. I knew from my own experience that the "chairman" probably was not, from the viewpoint of the Communist party, the most important figure. I glanced over the list in search of the important Communist link I knew should be there. But none of the names struck me.

"I plan to be working more in Boston in the future than in Cambridge. Perhaps there is something I can do for Russian War Relief there. Who is the best person to see?" I inquired.

I was told to call on Mrs. George Faxon, the executive secretary of the Boston committee, at 123 Newbury Street. I was given a letter of introduction. It was doubly strange to me that the letter-head of Russian War Relief carried the Newbury Street address as its headquarters, and yet there was enough stationery here in the Young Communist League office to take care of a large volume of work.

The letter itself was an authorization to me as the bearer to act as an official solicitor for Russian War Relief. Another front! Manufactured in the mill of the Young Communist League! To heighten these mysterious shenanigans still further, the letter was signed "Alice Mills," my old friend and tutor from the Massachusetts Youth Council.

I was given a container and sent out to join the Russian War Relief canvassers in Cambridge. We worked from building to building, visiting stores, taverns, restaurants, and homes. For every evening or week-end day I devoted to the work I brought five to ten dollars back to the Young Communist League headquarters. I never knew where the money went, and I never received a receipt or an accounting.

The Russian War Relief campaign shed some light on Art Solomon's unreasoning enthusiasm for my new job as assistant advertising director of the M. & P. Theaters. One of the League's officer's proposed to me that I negotiate with my employer for permission to place war-relief solicitors in the lobby of the Central Square Theater in Cambridge. I did it with no questions asked, and thus materially aided the fund drive. Everything has its use.

I handled my "grubbing" assignments as diligently as I could, all except the sale of the *Daily Worker*, which was a regular task for all neophyte Leaguers. I took the number given to me, dumped them into the most convenient trash can, and paid for them later out of my Bureau expense fund.

My diligence quickly began to pay off. I was instructed to attend the state meeting of the Young Communist League, held on a beautiful day at a youth hostel at Kendall Green, Weston, Massachusetts. It was a box-lunch affair with the morning devoted largely to sports and games, and the "political" sessions following in the afternoon. The convention undertook no significant issues—those days were the doldrums of Communist activity—but many of my old friends were on hand, and I encountered some new ones.

I saw Joy Clark, now at work in a war plant; Toni Grose, or Locke, Sid Solomon in uniform, and Nathaniel Mills, who offered a "win-the-war" skit which he had written. I met Alice Gordon, the state chairman of the Young Communist League, and an important "Comrade Bob" who was otherwise unidentified.

Sid told me that Arthur was in the Army and had tried for officer training but failed. Someone in the circle suggested that there probably had been some "dirty work," and Sid remarked, "Oh, they probably had his name on a list somewhere." I began to feel uneasy.

"Those damned sneaking Trotskyite stool pigeons," Sid muttered. "We ought to give 'em all what Trotsky got." The sharp reminder that party discipline could be harsh increased my discomfort.

As usual, I communicated a full report of the convention to the Bureau when I returned that night. The problem of communicating with the FBI was the one chink in the armor which guarded me from detection as a counterspy. My activities within the party were permitted to progress in a perfectly normal manner entirely

79

at the instigation of the Communist hierarchy. All orders and suggestions came from them, and never did the Bureau direct me to maneuver myself into any specific position. The FBI approved courses of action laid out by the Communists, but Leary did not want me to appear overanxious. This was protection in itself. But the communications problem worried me until I learned how it worked. The Bureau established an elaborate set of precautions against detection. Just how we worked must remain a secret. But the system was planned in exquisite detail, changed frequently enough to add to the deception, and was provided with elaborate checks and cross checks to test its vulnerability.

Reports submitted by me in my early days as an informant for the FBI were long, opinionated, inferential, and vague. Hal set me straight about them. "All we want are facts," he said, "not deductions. There are more pieces to this puzzle than one man can possibly fit together. We'll do the fitting. You simply supply the facts, and don't leave any out."

As a part of these reports, I necessarily kept voluminous records together with large masses of printed material that fell into my hands. One warm day I arrived at the apartment in late afternoon to find the living room intolerably hot and a faint odor of smoke in the air. I rushed through the apartment looking for a fire and calling Eva in vain. She was not home. Frantically I searched through the apartment, but I was unable to trace any fire.

Finally my glance fell on the little wood stove in the center of the living room. I felt its steel belly. It was still warm. I raised the lid with the lifter and peered inside at a pile of charred papers burned to layers of ashes. I examined my desk and found most of my records were gone.

When Eva came home, I confronted her with my discovery.

"I burned them," she said in a matter-of-fact tone.

"Why?" I fumed. "I need them."

"Herb, I will not have that junk in the house! If you must carry on this way, all right, but I don't see why you have to bring that trash home with you. Mother has seen them, and we've talked about it, and Mother is worried to death about you. What can I tell her? I don't even know what you're up to, or if I do it sounds pretty funny to me."

Indeed, what could Eva tell her mother or her friends? What could I tell Eva? I went to Hal about the problem. He chuckled at the paper-burning episode, but I impressed upon him that it was far more serious than that.

"We have to tell her something," I said. "She's getting suspicious and I shouldn't wonder if she's a little frightened. Furthermore, it's hurting me among the comrades. They want to know why Eva doesn't become active along with me. I don't think they like it."

Hal was thoughtful. "That puts a different light on it. I was hoping it wouldn't be necessary to say anything to her, but at least I wanted to let it ride as long as possible. What do you think her attitude will be?"

"Eva? Oh, she'll understand, perfectly. There will be no trouble about that."

"Then you'd better explain to her. You can tell her, just in general, of course, that you are working with the government and how and why. But don't bring your mother-in-law or anyone else in on it, and be sure to tell your wife that she must not breathe a word about it to anyone. For your sake."

I waited apprehensively until the time was right. Naturally, I wasn't sure what Eva's reaction would be to a far-reaching program, a side-line career which she had no idea existed. Eva's interests were confined more to the home than outside activities. I knew she had no realization that I had gone so far in my double, even triple, life. When the youngsters were asleep, the evening's work done, and we had a moment to ourselves, I raised the subject.

"You've been wondering what I've been doing, Eva, in all of these organizations, in the League. I told you I was working against communism and the Communists, to fight them the best way I could?"

Eva looked at me dejectedly. She didn't like to discuss the affair.

"I'm doing it because the government wants me to. I'm working for—for an agency of the government, keeping them posted, turning in reports. All that stuff you burned the other night—"

"An agency, Herb? The FBI?"

"Well, not exactly. I'm on my own hook. It's entirely voluntary, but it is the way I can serve best."

Eva fell into the nearest chair. "Well, that's different. That makes sense. Oh I'm so glad that's what it is. Why didn't you tell me earlier?"

"I couldn't do it, Eva. I promised I wouldn't."

"But is it so secret that even your family can't know?"

"The fewer there are who know, the less risk of discovery."

"Herb, is it very dangerous?"

"I wouldn't worry about the danger," I laughed. "I can take care of myself. But we must be very careful to keep it secret."

"How? Why?"

"It would be easy to give me away without meaning to. Among our good friends at home and in business we have to go on just as we always have. When some of my other friends come around the house—you know who they are—you must expect me to act and talk like a Communist. The only danger could come from a tipoff. I'm sorry, but you mustn't tell anyone about this, not a soul, not your mother or anyone else. Only you and I may know. If it comes out in time, all right, but we must let things fashion their own course."

"Will it be the same after we move to Wakefield? Do we have to keep on there?" Eva wanted me to say no. Our new home in Wakefield was to be the start of a new life, which we had planned and talked about every spare moment.

"I think so." I hated to say it. "I'm afraid so."

The move to Wakefield, a suburb of Boston, was on us, the move I had once hoped might take us out of the whole thing and give us a more normal life. But I underestimated the leaders of the Young Communist League.

At the time of the move I was called to a special meeting at the Locke apartment, the League headquarters on Magazine Street. Larry and Toni Locke, Alice Gordon, and a League worker named Dottie Fleischmann were present at the evening session, the purpose of which was to lay down a set of instructions for me.

"We have a job for you," Alice Gordon, the state League chairman, said. "Wakefield is an important community, but it needs some groundwork. We want you to establish yourself as well and as quickly as you can in the town. Get to know people, lead a normal life."

Alice was a squat, stocky, square-jawed functionary of the party, a paid professional of communism. She was a plain proletarian, and like most party women she gave an impression of drab grayness, almost the uniform of Communist femininity. She was bossy, and could tell men what to do as well as she could tell her own sex.

My target, I was told, was the reestablishment of the moribund Communist party cell in Wakefield. The nucleus of the regular party. I was charged in a few brief terms with the responsibility of re-forming the ranks of the party in my new suburban home. It shocked me. I was not yet even a member of the party, merely a newcomer in its youth section, the Young Communist League. But this sounded as if my "grubbing" days were over, and Hal Leary was right. The party had plans for me. How had he known? I carefully studied the four faces in the Locke living room, but they were all impassive.

I was given the names of two men who would call upon me to give me a hand in reorganizing the Wakefield cell—Comrades Frank Collier and Gus Johnson. I was ordered to call a meeting

83

of Wakefield Communists at the first opportunity, at my own home. So I had passed the first stringent tests, and now I was entrusted with new and larger responsibilities. I was to reorganize a party cell even before I had become a party member myself.

"What about political affiliation?" I asked.

My consultants said they had been thinking about that. My family had been Republican. Wakefield was a gerrymandered district, they said, controlled by the Republicans. There was no Democratic organization in the town.

"It will be best for you to register as a Republican. Whatever you say will carry much more weight if you are speaking as a Republican."

I inquired about my activity in the Baptist Church, somewhat apprehensive that they might direct me to stay out of it.

"By all means get yourself firmly established in the church," Alice Gordon said. "Never separate yourself from your normal contacts with the masses, wherever they are. A good Communist is a leader of the people. If you were a factory worker, then you would join the trade unions and other associations of workers. Your background has been one of close affiliation with large numbers of church people. As a Communist you must not cut yourself off from them. To the contrary, you should strengthen your ties."

"Anything else?"

"No. Keep in touch with us. Let us know how you make out. When you get a full meeting scheduled we will send someone from the district office as a special speaker."

So geography was no escape. I moved my family to Wakefield, still wearing a false face and carrying a heavy heart. But Hal Leary and the FBI were pleased.

"Gus Johnson!" Hal exclaimed when I told him. He whistled softly.

84

CHAPTER 6

OUR NEW HOME, the big Parker residence at 8 Park Street in Wakefield, was a *grande dame* crusted with fine but worn brocade, and with anything but a conspiratorial air. The square, boxlike structure of ten lofty rooms demanded some minor repair work, and its tobacco-brown paint, heavily laid on some years before, was reticulated with cracks. The house crowded close to the asphalt sidewalk behind a big white fence with heavy, turned balusters. A huge, shaggy elm fanned over the front doorway, its branches touching the upper windows.

Largely because the house needed it, but also in an effort to lend normalcy to our movements, I ordered thirty gallons of white paint and a forty-foot extension ladder, and went to work on the outside of the old mansion. There is no better way to get acquainted in a new community than by painting the house. Neighbors came over to chat, and I was as amiable as possible with them. I learned all about the old house, about Mr. Parker, the sea captain who built it, and about the town and the more important among its sixteen thousand inhabitants.

The Philbrick family oozed respectability. I caught a morning train like the busy commuter I was, and until I had firmly established myself I rushed home in the evening to be with my family. I was a good, solid citizen, a respectable businessman interested in civic enterprises, a pillar of the church.

We were invited to join, not one, but three churches in the town. The Union Services, combining all of the Protestant churches in Wakefield, were being conducted for the summer in the Baptist Church. The easiest way to get a fast start in a new church is to arrive early on your first Sunday. I stood at the rear of the pews, looking a trifle bewildered. A parishioner recognized me and took me in hand. After the service I met the preacher, congratulated him on his sermon, and stood making friends on the church steps in the warm August sunlight.

My churchgoing was a serious matter with me, quite apart from the impression I was ordered to make, and within three weeks I was an usher, passing the collection plate on Sunday mornings for the free-will offering. Within a short time I was appointed chairman of the newly organized publicity committee and became editor of the church's new publication, "The Tall Spire," occasionally an outlet for harmless Communist propaganda slipped in to keep my party friends happy. A club for married couples was formed, the Mr. and Mrs. Club, and Mr. and Mrs. Philbrick were the first presidents. I soon became a member of the Administrative Committee, the governing body of the church, and the party functionaries in Boston were delighted.

By early fall, Eva and I were entertaining Baptist young people in our home; the big house was filled with gaiety, good fellowship, and devotion. But the old elm shrouded midnight secrets. Strangers passed under its whispering leaves late at night and slipped up the steps into the old Parker house—the town's new headquarters for Communist conspiracy.

The revival of the Wakefield branch of the Communist party was a difficult and onerous assignment. My heart was not in it, except for the sake of the Bureau. The atmosphere of Republican Wakefield was not conducive to Communist activity, and in those quiet days on the Communist front, when Browderism was in the saddle to support the war, there were no electric issues to serve as rallying points. There wasn't much for a Communist cell to do, after it was organized.

86

Comrades Johnson and Collier called at the house not long after we were settled. They had instructions from the Boston district. I could see on short acquaintance why the party had picked the two of them to help me with the spadework. In personality and make-up they were direct opposites.

Gus Johnson—whose name had been the cause of Hal Leary's surprise—was a hulking, florid Swede with a thick accent which was usually made even less coherent by the cheap whisky he dumped into his iron belly. He was amiable enough some of the time, but stupid, and a confirmed Bolshevik of the roughhouse school. "This goddam town," he bellowed when we were getting acquainted, "you got to watch every step of the way here. It's loaded with dirty fascist police."

By occupation Gus was a common laborer and general handy-man. But whatever honest work he did was just an inconsequential chaser for the communism that intoxicated him to the point of frenzy. He would tackle any job, preferably in agitation, and he loved party activity that promised a good brawl with the police.

I knew little about his private life except that he and his wife were at loggerheads. "Look out for Gus Johnson's wife," I was told by Jack Green, who was then in charge of internal security for the Boston party district. "She's a rat and a stool pigeon."

Collier was bookish, thin, sullen, and unhealthy. He rarely drank, but chain-smoked cigarettes, and his gaunt face had the pallor of ash. Frank had a deep appreciation of literature and a large library including the most complete private Marxist collection I ever encountered. Had Frank devoted to writing but a small portion of the energy he squandered on communism, I am sure he could have been at least a moderately successful author. Instead, he was only a mediocre newspaper hack. His eyes were bright and suspicious, and frequently flashed with his ingrown hatred of capitalism. I never heard him laugh. When he

87

enjoyed a joke, as he frequently did, he chuckled inwardly with a wrinkled visage and a tightly closed mouth, and a "hm, hm" sound was swallowed up in his spare, hollow chest.

The two comrades were not optimistic about the chances of building a strong party movement in Wakefield, but they had determination. They were, I thought, unduly insistent upon the deepest secrecy.

I inquired through outside sources and found out why. Two years before, Wakefield had experienced a Red hunt, inspired— it fitted so perfectly that it was laughable—by Mrs. Johnson. The lady was as rabidly anti-Communist as Gus was Communist. In the course of their domestic bickerings, Mrs. Johnson was reported to have told her spouse to get out of the party or she would cause trouble. It is not difficult to surmise what Gus told her, but apparently he underestimated the woman.

She marched straight to the police and delivered an exposé. Mrs. Johnson named names of party stalwarts in Wakefield, two teachers in the public schools and two ministers among them. The American Legion seized on the disclosures with vigilante ardor. Torchlight parades were held around the houses of those named by Mrs. Johnson. Insults and threats were hurled. Some of the victims fled town. The party cell was shattered. A feeble attempt was made to combine its remnants with the Malden branch, but the two communities were too widely separated; party meetings and activity, as well as dues collections, came to a standstill in Wakefield.

It was against this ominous background that Collier, Johnson, and I set out to exhume and revive the party cell. We had a list of some fourteen persons in Wakefield who were still listed on the party rolls. Frank and Gus knew most of them, and undertook to make the contacts. I was directed to stay in the background to prevent arousing any neighborhood suspicions.

The first meeting, however, was called at my house. It was to be the usual organizational and inspirational meeting with a speech

88

by Gus Johnson, and a collection drive for back dues from the delinquent membership. Collier and Johnson took pains to surround the session with utmost secrecy. The meeting was called for eight o'clock.

A half hour before the scheduled meeting time there was a knock at the front door, and a figure silently melted into the shadows of the living room. A few minutes later another, then another. One or two came in by the side door. No more than a single member arrived at any one time. No automobiles congregated in front of my door; if any were used they were parked at a discreet distance. Gus came by bicycle, his regular mode of transportation. By eight o'clock a dozen persons were assembled around the living room. Scarcely a word was spoken. There were members of the same families present, each of whom had arrived alone and now sat together. They came from all over Wakefield, some from its deepest slums—there were slums even in Wakefield —some from its neat, expensive homes.

The session was desultory, primarily devoted to the speech (with Gus in remarkably good control of his accents and his party fervor), the collection of dues, and arrangements for future sessions, which nearly all of them promised to attend. Eva sat through it all in a big wing chair, nervously winding and unwinding a piece of string in her fingers. When the meeting broke up, the arrival process was put into action in reverse. One by one, at intervals of several minutes, they slipped out the door into the night, walking briskly away, keeping to the shadows.

"We have to be careful here in Wakefield," one of them said to me at the door. "There are police spies everywhere."

The precautions were thorough enough to prevent neighborhood detection of the cell headquarters. I also was taking precautions of my own. After the meeting I trudged up the stairs, climbed a narrow stairway to the unfinished attic, picked my way across the open beams to the end of the room where stood a huge cedar closet. I reached for a concealed latch, swung the entire closet outward on its heavy hinges, and passed through the false end wall of the loft into my FBI operative's unit. Here, in a tiny room with a window screened by the big elm, compactly equipped with typewriter, dictating machine, and photographic equipment, I filed my report to the Bureau.

The little square room was a household sanctuary to which I could escape. But the secret room was also a prison to which I was sentenced for long dark hours on many nights after Communist meetings.

There followed months of intense activity. Besides my organizational work in the Wakefield cell of the regular party I was under orders to maintain formal cell affiliation with the Young Communist League. I climbed rapidly on the organizational ladder of the League, reaching out beyond the Cambridge unit, first into the Boston area and then into the statewide network of the League.

I attended cell meetings of different types—educational, cultural, social—in many different localities. There were sessions at Nat Mills's apartment in Boston. The identity of more and more Communists was revealed to me. I branched out into communities like Brookline and Dorchester. One unusual series of gatherings was held in a sumptuous apartment near Harvard Yard. Their apparent purpose was to make available to selected Harvard men a place of entertainment, liquor, and the companionship of well-groomed, sophisticated young Communist girls. Eva and I went to several parties there, where the affluence was tastefully displayed and controlled, the liquor flowed freely, and political "liberalism" was leavened with sophistry, popular music for connoisseurs of jazz, and the comfort of deep sofas.

Billed always by the party as a Baptist youth leader—the reason for the comrades' interest in my church activities—I was kept busy in front organizations, especially in the effort to gain control over the Youth for Victory Council. My professional acquaintances, through my job with Harry Browning and the

90

M. & P. Theaters, were immensely useful to the party. For the most part they were motion-picture publicists, advertising men, newspaper writers and editors, and radio executives. Mr. Browning's office became the headquarters of the New England entertainment industry's War Activities Committee, with the primary task of promoting patriotic campaigns. Since the Communist party at this time was also dedicated to the winning of the war, I was in a most advantageous position, for the party and for the FBI.

I was able to secure free radio time for the Youth for Victory group; I wrote radio scripts, prepared news releases under party direction, secured the assistance of the Office of War Information in some of the Communist campaigns, and served on the editorial board of the *Youth for Victory News*. I organized and staged rallies and fund-raising dinners. So thoroughly respectable was my front that at one big Communist-sponsored rally—without the Communist label, of course—I was able to obtain the services of a snappy Catholic Youth Organization band.

Out of the cell meetings I attended, I gained a new sense of party discipline and militancy. My fellow members were no longer the beginners of the original Cambridge cell. Weaklings were expelled, dropped, or sidetracked to menial tasks or back to "grubbing," and what was left was the hard core of the young Communist cause.

Meetings were devoted largely to reports by individual members as to their activities for the previous two weeks, and the issuing of new assignments. In the discussion of projects, there was always room for self-criticism, during which each member castigated himself for his own errors and shortcomings, or else was severely upbraided by the leaders. I soon learned that it was better to confess party sins quickly than to suffer the invective of the leadership. Sometimes I ducked an assigned task because it was simply more than I could stomach, or too dangerous to risk jeopardizing my position. But whenever this happened, I always took pains to accomplish some other less onerous task as spectacularly as possible, so I could shrug off the one and point to the other as an excuse. The value of my community contacts spared me serious criticism inside the cell.

The inexorable and unremitting training at the party's hands was, I soon recognized, pounding me into a Marxist mold, despite my resistance. I had to submit myself to the constant hammerings of communism. The sheer power of the party leaders with whom I worked—they were capable, highly dedicated, domineering people and not blundering dreamers—rendered me susceptible to their infectious poison. Wouldn't it be a fine thing, I often thought, if the evil I was trying to fight consumed me instead?

What kept my head above water was my natural Yankee resistance to the unrelieved bitterness, hatred, distrust, and atmosphere of doom that pervaded the swamp of communism. In the church near home I sought and found light, warmth, kindness, charity, and friends with healthy minds and souls, and I strengthened every tie I had with them.

This was the beginning of what I ultimately recognized as a manufactured schizophrenia. I was sinking so deep that it was no longer possible for me to "play" the role of a spy. I could no longer simply make believe that I was a Marxist. Like an experienced actor, who must sublimate himself to his part and immerse himself in the playwright's creation, whenever I walked into the stage setting of a cell meeting, I had to *be* a young Communist. The costume alone was not enough. No disguise would have been adequate.

I was so busy during our first year in Wakefield that I rarely had time for home life, or to enjoy the company of our third daughter, Dale, born two months after we moved in. My job with the M. & P. Theaters grew rapidly, and my responsibilities grew with it. Harry Browning assigned a secretary to me to take some of the load off my shoulders, and my staff increased from one assistant to a permanent group of six. This was augmented by part-time assistance from as many as ten persons. Fortunately, for the sake of my career, many of the tasks assigned to me by the Communist party dovetailed with my advertising and public-relations job.

Even so, there was almost more than I could handle. I frequently worked late in Boston on party affairs, made the milk train to Wakefield, filed a report to the FBI, and caught a few hours sleep before I was roused out for another business day. The physical strain brought on a series of colds and minor ailments. Eva frequently put her foot down and made me stay home in bed. She began to complain that I was doing more than my share, damaging my health, and neglecting my home and my family. She urged me to give it up.

It was impossible for me to argue with her, because she was right. I was trying to do too much, but no more than I felt I had to do. Rather than argue with Eva, I talked it over with Hal Leary. He was sympathetic, as always. Although it was a dangerous thing for him to do, and in fact very nearly caused serious trouble, Hal paid a few personal visits to our Wakefield house to discuss the affair, first with Eva alone, and later with both of us.

On his initial call, he introduced himself to Eva, and told her he was an agent for the Federal Bureau of Investigation. He was the first one she had ever met, and the only person besides me with whom she ever discussed my undercover job.

Hal impressed upon her that what I was doing was of great importance to the Bureau and to the country, and might even prove to be vital. He assured her of his desire to lighten the burden on my household as much as possible. He gave her his number, and instructed her to call him directly any time the going was too rough. He also asked Eva to cooperate with me and with the Bureau as much as possible in getting the job done.

Hal won her over completely, and the interview resulted in

93

Eva's attendance, still against her will, at more of the meetings held at our home, and in a membership in the Young Communist League to which I subscribed for her.

Subsequently Leary paid an additional call at the house, just to find out how things were going on the domestic scene. It was early evening and we were seated, all three of us, in the living room, chatting about nothing in particular.

There came a knock at the front door. I glanced at Hal, and Eva leaped to her feet. I went to the door and opened it to find Comrades Collier and Johnson in the entry. Effusively, and in a loud voice, I greeted them, while standing in the door as long as I could to bar their way.

"Hello, Frank. Hello, Gus," I bellowed. "How are you? Come in. Come in." I babbled in the vestibule, talked about the weather, asked Gus if he had his bike, requested that they give me their hats and coats, demanded to know what was on their minds.

"Just thought we'd drop in for a minute," Collier said.

When I could no longer delay their entry, I sauntered ahead of them, my heart in my throat, into the living room.

It was empty. Hal's hat was gone from the chair next to where he had been sitting. Eva came in through the dining room, wiping her hands on an apron she had quickly put on. I glanced at her anxiously, and the look she returned told me that Hal had safely departed. She was more than usually warm in her greetings to Frank and Gus, who were both sullen and incurious. "Whew!" I said, dropping into a chair with a sigh of relief, "we just got all the kids to bed and the dishes done. What a job!"

We turned to a discussion of party affairs, and especially to the proposed dissolution of the Young Communist League which was then under active consideration.

As in every mob movement of ruthless totalitarianism, youth groups have always been the touchstone of communism. In the United States for twenty-one years, the Young Communist League had been the rallying ground and the preparatory school for

94

Communist leadership. Now, in the summer and fall of 1943, the party was preparing for an unusual stroke—the abolition of the Young Communist League, and the substitution for it of what the party called "a new united anti-fascist youth organization."

The war was the heart of the issue. The purpose of the Communist party during these years was to weave itself as much as possible into the democratic American fabric, and to win the war. This, at least, was its public avowal, though the party took pains behind the scenes not to lose its grip.

Dissolution of the Young Communist League was a form of appeasement. Its aim was to do away with the name "Communist" in the organization, so the movement could embrace a broader segment of American youth under a different banner. For public consumption, notably in an article written by Max Weiss, president of the League, in the magazine *The Communist* for September, 1943, it was stated that the League would dissolve, merge itself with non-Communist youth organizations in the cause of the world-wide fight against fascism, and help—"help" was the way Weiss stressed it—to form "a new united anti-fascist youth organization."

It sounded like a magnanimous sublimation to the cause of unity. "It is clear," Weiss said, "that an organization such as the one we are discussing in this article will be completely independent of the Communist party, both organizationally and politically. It will determine its attitude to the proposals and policies of the Communist party on the basis of the merits of those policies. It will determine its attitude to all other democratic political parties and forces in the same way. It will be nonpartisan and will have fraternal relations with all patriotic, anti-fascist groups and organizations."

The issue was widely discussed at League meetings everywhere. As in every important change in party organization, the membership was primed in advance so that, in general terms at least, they would know what course a good Communist should follow.

The appearance of democratic action thus was maintained. Once the direction was pointed out by an edict like the Weiss article, each member had perfect "freedom" to carry that policy forward to a successful conclusion.

There was no internal battle over the dissolution. As was expected, it met with approval everywhere. I expressed hearty agreement in our discussions. As an organizer and director of many League projects, I argued that it would be most advantageous to have a single, broad win-the-war youth organization. At that time, I said, we were spreading ourselves too thin and duplicating too much effort, first through the League, then through Youth for Victory and other outside mass movements.

In mid-October, 1943, I received a call from Alice Gordon, the Massachusetts state chairman of the Young Communist League. She asked me to meet with her on a very important matter. We arranged to have luncheon together at the Waldorf Restaurant in Scollay Square near my office. Alice was to head the Boston delegation to the national convention in New York, where two days hence the Young Communist League was to write itself out of existence. She had already discussed with me the possibility of my doing some promotional work in the new organization once it was established in Massachusetts.

But I was hardly prepared for what was coming.

"We want you to attend the New York convention," Alice told me at lunch. "We will have an important job for you when the new unit is set up here."

"What is that?"

"You are going to be the state treasurer." I did not conceal my surprise—and pleasure—that I was to be slated as one of the five top leaders of the new organization when it came to Massachusetts. But I did not reveal my shock at her disclosure that the leadership of the new state group, as yet unnamed, was already firmly in Communist control.

"Don Bollen," she told me, "will be the chairman in the state."

96

Bollen was a prominent Young Communist League member and United Electrical Workers organizer. So this was the way the Young Communist League would "help" to establish a new, and ostensibly democratic youth organization! Now I caught a glimpse, from the inside this time, of what had happened to the Cambridge Youth Council.

"You should attend the organizational meeting of the new group as a Baptist. It will give strength to your position." The YCL dissolution meeting, Alice told me, would be held at New York's Manhattan Center on Friday, and the organization of the new movement would get under way Saturday and Sunday at the Mecca Temple of the Shrine in New York. I was to make a speech before the new group, as a Baptist, and I was to discuss subsequent affairs with Alice and Don Bollen at the conventions. Could I make it?

I thought quickly, and assented. Yes, I had some vacation time coming, and already was planning to visit some friends in New York. I could stay with a cousin.

There was little time to make the arrangements. I called Doug Keys, my cousin, and told him that I had to be in New York over the week end on business, and couldn't we get together? Eva explained to my office, on Friday, that I was ill and could not be at work. The sickness plan almost trapped me.

While I was gone, Harry Browning, whose generosity was usually impulsive, assembled a large basket of fruit for my sick table, all done up in ribbons and scalloped paper, a very handsome gift. He gave it to my assistant, Eddie Alfano, and to his secretary, Vickie, and dispatched them to my house in his own car.

Eddie and Vickie caught Eva flat-footed. Naturally, they asked if they could see me. Eva, flushing in confusion, told them that I had been quite sick and, to get me out of the hubbub of the household, she had sent me away for a few days' rest.

I can't imagine how we got away with it, but we did.

97

I talked to the Bureau, and they said by all means get to New York and cover the whole thing. I jumped on a train Thursday night and arrived late in New York.

The Young Communist League was buried by five hundred delegates from all over the United States at a special convention session Friday in New York's Manhattan Center. There was a speech by Earl Browder, stressing the importance of the dissolution in terms of national unity. There were no regrets, because everyone, on top at least, recognized that it was just a maneuver to change the name. In order not to jeopardize my future status with the new group, I attended the Young Communist League meeting not as a delegate, but as an "observer."

On Saturday and Sunday, the same crowd presided at the birth of the new organization, American Youth for Democracy, in the basement auditorium of Mecca Temple of the Shrine. Communist domination of the organization meeting was open and brazen. There were, by count, 156 delegates from the Young Communist League, and only 176 from other youth organizations. It would have been heavily weighted in Communist favor in any event, but was even more so in view of the fact that some delegates, ostensibly representing non-Communist groups—I was there as a Baptist youth leader—were actually underground Communists.

The statement of principles of the new movement was lifted bodily out of Max Weiss's article in *The Communist,* with all references to the Young Communist League deleted. Weiss magnanimously declined nomination to the national council of one hundred. It helped to have the national president of the old Communist League step aside. There was no concern over party control of AYD.

Robert Thompson, Army hero, former national vice-president of the Young Communist League, and later a big wheel in the party, was "elected" national co-chairman of the AYD. (Later Thompson became a fugitive from justice, following his conviction as a Communist revolutionary in the trial of The Eleven.) Carl

Ross, former New York state chairman of the league, was named executive secretary. Others on the slate of officers were well known to me, including "Comrade Bob" whom I had first met at the Kendall Green state convention of the YCL. He turned out to be William Robert McCarthy, of Quincy, and he was elected secretary-treasurer of the new youth organization, representing a Boston shipbuilding union of which he was president.

The platform of American Youth for Democracy called for an immediate second front, trade unionism, friendship among Britain, the United States, and Soviet Russia, aid to service men, and an end to racial discrimination.

When the convention broke up I went back to Boston—with an introductory lesson in Communist control behind me, and an advanced course yet to come.

CHAPTER 7

WHEN I RETURNED to the office Monday morning, everyone gave me a severe ribbing about the basket of fruit, from Harry Browning all the way down the line to the office receptionist. But I made up a story about going to visit my family at Rye Beach to escape from the racket of the house full of children and get over a bad attack of sinus; they all accepted it. The three-day convention pallor that I brought back from New York must have given credence to my story. Only Eddie Alfano, one of my advertising staff members, eyed me with some suspicion, but he was as good-humored as the rest.

I had seen the Young Communist League bow out with a fanfare that did not deceive all of the newspapers, and the new American Youth for Democracy, a nation-wide, "nonpartisan" group formed in its stead, under the firm control of the erstwhile Young Communists. Now it was our turn at the grass-roots level in Boston to impose our will on the essential character of AYD. Alice Gordon called me into another luncheon session within a week after the national founding convention.

"I don't have to tell you," she said, "how important it is that we achieve complete success in the coming phase of our work." I nodded. "Of course you realize that your role in our state organization will be as a non-Communist Baptist Church leader.

"And incidentally," she said, "it would be a good plan for you to find an opportunity to state publicly that you are a non-Communist. Naturally, if anyone asks you, or accuses you of being a member of the Young Communist League, you are to swear under oath if necessary that you are not and never have been a Communist."

"Don't worry," I grinned sheepishly, because it was only too true, "if my boss or any of the chiefs in my department discovered my affiliation with the League, they would hang me from a lamppost in Scollay Square before sunset."

"Now here is the schedule in general," Alice continued. She told me that by the end of October a forming committee—the same old device—would be organized. The task of the organizing committee would be to set up AYD clubs and branches all over the state. We would make a drive to secure charter members, and by the first of the year, 1944, we would hold a state convention at which permanent officers would be elected.

After this preliminary meeting with Alice, there followed a series of luncheon and evening sessions to plan the operation. All of those who attended these meetings were well known to me, and none of them was a non-Communist despite the AYD emphasis on cooperation with non-Communist youth. Their turn would come later—if at all. It was plain in these sessions that decisions were being made at a higher level than the one on which I was working. And the only higher level was the office of District One, New England, of the Communist party.

Our first meeting was held in the former Young Communist League office, already being dismantled, in the Little Building at Tremont and Boylston Streets, Boston. Immediately thereafter, a suitable AYD headquarters was established in another room in the same building. The desks and office equipment of the defunct Young Communist League were transferred to the new establishment.

A mimeographed letter was drawn up, proclaiming in brief the objectives of the AYD and inviting youth leaders from the Boston area to take part in an organizational meeting, November 7, to set up the AYD in the Commonwealth of Massachusetts.

"Every intelligent young American," the letter said, "has felt the urgent need for an organization uniting youth of all races, creeds and political beliefs. Around the program of American Youth for Democracy, it becomes possible to establish such unity in helping to shape the future of our generation."

The letter quoted from the statement of principles approved in New York. "All of us who adopt this program are active in the service of our country. We dedicate ourselves to the principles of American democracy. We place ourselves on the side of all that is just and progressive, and join hands with all youth in opposing everything that is reactionary and oppressive.

"This war, which now engulfs the whole world, was not of our making, but it is our war. Only by smashing fascism can we assure America's future in a world of peace and progress."

We discussed at length whether to include among the names to appear at the end of the letter that of Alice Gordon, who had been running the show thus far, but who was known publicly as the former head of the Massachusetts Young Communist League. Some argued against her inclusion, but it was finally decided to list her— not as a former Leaguer, but as a member of the National Council of American Youth for Democracy.

The other names were Anne Thompson, of the Young Women's Christian Association; Ben Barker, of Hecht House; Donald Bollen, of the United Electrical and Radio Workers Union; Jean Adams, of Tufts Theological School; Barbara Bennett, of the National Council, AYD; Herbert Philbrick, of the Baptist Church; and Francis Bailin, of the International Union of Marine and Shipbuilders.

The letter was mailed to a large composite list of youth organization leaders. Nat Mills furnished us the list of the Massachusetts Youth Council. Beverly Franklin secured the entire mailing list of the Youth for Victory Council. Frances Damon provided a list from the Boston Council of Social Agencies. The Communist party headquarters provided additional names from foreign groups. We put in hectic hours addressing the envelopes and getting them into the mail by October 29.

Then came the final session to map out the proceedings for the November 7, Sunday, organizational meeting. The former League leaders took no chances of anything going astray. Those of us who were running things met and drew up the agenda. The first items were to be the singing of "The Star-Spangled Banner" and the salute to the flag. One of the girls was designated to lead off the conference.

Next we got down to details. "Philbrick," I was instructed, "you will get up and suggest that we have a temporary chairman for the meeting, and you will nominate Don Bollen. Bollen, when you are elected you are to pick—at random, of course—the other temporary officers—vice-chairman, secretary, ballot counter, and so forth."

Then Bollen was handed a slip of paper. "Here are the names of the people you will pick for these positions," he was told.

The "democratic procedures" of the forthcoming meeting began to assume a definite shape.

The principal speaker was to be Bob McCarthy, the "guest of honor." Following his speech, Bollen was to call for open discussion and suggestions from the floor—open, except that Alice Gordon gave Bollen a list of speakers to be recognized and the subjects they were to discuss. Every speaker was to represent himself as a member or officer of his non-Communist affiliate. Each one would say what he was told to say, and would appear as a student, a labor-union member, a Negro, a Jew, or a Catholic. My assignment was to speak in impromptu fashion as a representative of Protestant youth.

Alice discussed my address with me later. It would be a good idea, she suggested, if I would express some doubts about the nature of the new organization. I could say that I distrusted it at first, but that I examined the constitution, attended the national convention, and met many of the young delegates there, and that

I was firmly convinced that AYD was all that it claimed to be. I, as a Baptist, could first plant a seed of Communist suspicion, and then stamp it out.

"I get it," I said. "I will say that I read an attack in the papers on the AYD, claiming it was a Communist front, and that naturally as a Baptist I wanted to make sure that it was not Communist dominated. Then go on from there."

Alice nodded her agreement. The major topic of my speech was anti-Semitism in Boston, and I was given an anti-Semitic letter to read as ammunition for an attack on the evils of racism.

The rest of the meeting was similarly planned, step by step, item by item. The resolutions to be offered were drawn up. Decisions were made as to who would offer them, and at what part of the program. Critical questions were planted, and the loaded replies were outlined for those who would give them. Sufficient members of the all-important nominating committee to assure control were designated, and the machinery for getting them into office was worked out. These nominating-committee members in turn were furnished with a complete list of the future officers of the Massachusetts branch of American Youth for Democracy. As Alice Gordon had arranged it, I was to be the secretary-treasurer.

Finally we discussed the possibility that genuine antagonism might break out on the floor. Possible attacks on our leadership were anticipated; those who would answer the critics were appointed, just in case. With a concealed smile I recalled my own experience at the Hotel Touraine meeting, and the speakers who answered me so spontaneously but with such devastating effectiveness.

The big meeting came off as scheduled. The conference room of the Little Building was jammed beyond its capacity of a hundred. A dozen or so comrades were scattered about the room, and everything had an appearance of normal youthful exuberance. Several persons who had been known publicly as leaders in the

104

Young Communist League were present, but took no prominent part in the proceedings. They assumed a discreet and convincing shyness.

The meeting started off in an atmosphere of good-humored confusion, as if no one knew exactly what to do. Then Don Bollen, after he was duly named temporary chairman, took over the chair and "selected" his assistants. McCarthy, a fine orator, made a stirring speech. Next, Bollen called for suggestions or ideas from the floor, and to his call he appended a request that was completely disarming in its candor.

"I don't know who all of you are," he said with his vibrant smile—Bollen was the ideal chairman, "so for purposes of identification, anyone who wants to speak please write his name down and send it up to the chair." The first speaker he called was Herbert Philbrick, "of Wakefield, representing the Baptist young people of his community."

As I threaded through the crowd to the speaker's platform I recalled grimly the smooth workings of the Cambridge Youth Council and the Massachusetts Youth Council. I had two audiences and two speeches, one spoken silently to myself as I moved through the crowd, addressed to my Communist comrades scattered about the audience; the other, the prepared speech for the unsuspecting newcomers.

You're not dealing with a gullible novice any more, my silent thoughts said to the comrades. He's been learning things; he's a different Philbrick now—Comrade Herb. You have caused him sleepless nights and days of worry. You have worked the hide off him, torn him away from home and family. You have fed him endless hours of Marxist-Leninist pap. You're pretty proud of your party hack. You are convinced that you have been successful. You think he is a Communist through and through.

It is entirely fitting—I smiled with genuine satisfaction as I turned to face the trusting young people who looked up at me out of friendly faces—entirely fitting that your chairman should call,

105

as the first "impromptu" speaker of the day, confidential informant Herbert Philbrick of the Federal Bureau of Investigation.

My audible speech, delivered for the benefit of the non-Communist innocents in the assembly, could not provide me the same personal satisfaction. With manufactured enthusiasm I swung into the speech of a good Communist playing his part with all the subversive, double-dealing skill that the party trainers had been able to build into me.

"That was a wonderful and inspiring address we have just heard from Bob McCarthy," I said, turning my mind swiftly to my task. I praised Comrade Bob's sincerity and his views, and I added, "I must confess that when I read attacks in some of the papers, charging that the American Youth for Democracy was a Communist-inspired organization, I had some misgivings about joining it and bringing it the support of my Baptist Church, I am sure you will agree, however, after hearing Mr. McCarthy, that some elements of the press have badly confused win-the-war patriotism with something else. Certainly you will agree that there was no communism in anything that Mr. Carthy said, and he is, after all, a member of our national board. There is nothing Communist about our constitution or the statement of principles to which we subscribed.

"I hoped that all the representatives of the press would be here today. They were invited, but it is obvious that some of them are more interested in Red baiting than they are in learning the truth."

I told about my trip to New York to the founding convention of AYD and what I saw and learned, and those whom I met there. Then I said that profascist elements in the country would do everything they could to break up organizations of this kind—up to and including use of the brand "Communist"—because AYD was interested only in the successful prosecution of the war, and the fascists and reactionaries were not. Finally I swung into my discussion of anti-Semitism in the Boston community.

My speech was roundly applauded. Other speakers were hand-picked by Bollen, who read the names each time from the slips of paper he held in his hand. At length the chairman looked at his watch and announced, "The time is getting on, and the hall has been rented for only a brief period. We must vacate it at a definite hour. We have a great deal of important business before we adjourn. Thus we will have to dispense with any more remarks from the floor."

No speakers had been called other than those previously selected. The meeting proceeded smoothly on its way—resolutions, telegrams, motions, the election of the provisional committee. Finally, when it was plain that the meeting was over, I took it upon myself to make the motion to adjourn. I'm sure I must have crossed someone up—somebody else must have been assigned to make the adjournment motion.

The response in behalf of the Massachusetts section of AYD was remarkable. Youngsters on the "home front," between the ages of fourteen and twenty-five, energetic and enthusiastic to tackle any project for victory, were rounded up. It was easy to join. Any group of ten or more young people could establish an AYD club in their community for a one-dollar charter fee. Dues were a dollar a year, with a special fee of fifty cents for high-school students.

A national magazine, *Spotlight*, was published for the organization, the first issue appearing in December. It was never an openly Marxist publication, because victory in the war, not Marxism, was then the stated objective of the Communist party under Browder. The magazine never mentioned the class struggle in so many words, but its pages made it plain to a discerning youngster that the class struggle was a vital factor in his life.

One of our most important tasks was to line up adult sponsors for the Massachusetts AYD, and according to form it was important that most of them be non-Communists. We recognized that any alert, mature person could easily trace the link between American Youth for Democracy and the Young Communist League, and we foresaw more serious problems of control.

The task of enlisting and aligning the sponsors was assigned to Don Bollen, Anne Thompson (whose real name was Anne Reid), and me, since each of us was in a position to speak as a non-Communist through a respectable front. We arranged a luncheon meeting for prospective sponsors to be held at the Young Women's Christian Association. But first we held preliminary meetings, again to lay the groundwork.

We made up a neat and impressive "package" of information about AYD—its constitution, membership blanks, an outline of the program, a list of national and local officers, even a blank check so sponsors could make money contributions to the cause.

We sought to anticipate objections from the sponsors, such as the fact that some well-known former Young Communists were on the provisional committees, and we discussed the answers— "AYD is a nonpartisan group, and, as such, members of all political parties are welcome to join. The sole aim of AYD is the winning of the war, and we proceed in democratic fashion. No one political party will dominate the movement."

We were gravely beset by budgetary problems. We already had an office for which to pay rent, and other overhead expenses. The three of us knew the financial support came mainly out of Communist party coffers. But we couldn't say so, and we had to be prepared to answer questions on our monetary affairs. Therefore, I, as treasurer, drew up a "dummy list" of contributors giving a total of about a hundred dollars a month. Anne Reid was put down for a small contribution and I "pledged" on paper to give ten or fifteen dollars a month. Others were similarly listed. Don Bollen kept the list.

"If by chance no one asks us about our finances, I think we

ought to have someone primed to ask about them," I suggested. "It will certainly be in the minds of some of them even if they don't express it." I was learning the Marxist way, and my suggestion was adopted. We planted other similarly loaded questions.

Some of the adults, I was told, could be depended upon to back the organization and our views—Stephen Fritchman, James J. Green, William Harrison, Elizabeth Jones, Grace Lonergan, Professor F. O. Matthiessen, Professor Kirtley Mather, Robert Mills, John Mitchell, and Francis O'Connor. But there were others who had to be handled carefully.

The advance preparations paid off, and the meeting was acknowledged a success. We were prepared to handle all kinds of questions, though there were one or two tossed in which momentarily caught us off base. But we were able to scramble back, and most of the prospective sponsors, with the exception of a few who pleaded the "pressure of other business," agreed to serve on the advisory board.

The objectives of the Communists in AYD were to enlist the support of young people for the war effort in which Russian communism now had a vital stake; to carry out an educational program of "proletarianizing" our members at every opportunity and aligning their sympathies with the "working classes"; and to gain as many friends as possible for the Soviet Union in peace as well as in war.

During the next three months we rapidly ran up the membership of AYD to well over a thousand in the Boston area alone; we also established many activities, including propaganda drives, canteens, and other services among members of the armed forces. Most of the AYD members were sincerely motivated young people who would have been deeply shocked to know that I, as their state treasurer, and the other officers of the youth organization, continued as usual to attend secret Communist cell meetings in Cambridge and Boston, despite the abolition of the Young Communist League.

For while the League had been eliminated in name, it had long been plain to me and other members of my cell that we were part and parcel of the Communist party, even though we did not hold formal membership. I had been entrusted with regular party tasks in Wakefield. I took orders from party functionaries at District One headquarters in Boston relative to the work of AYD. I was frequently called to the district office in room 546 of the Little Building, conveniently located three floors beneath the AYD office. I was warned not to be too open in these visits, and to make telephone contacts with the headquarters through pay stations rather than through my business telephone.

I also warned myself to be careful not to use the same pay booth for consecutive calls to party headquarters and the Federal Bureau of Investigation.

So the cell meetings went on as usual, every two weeks, with no variation in pattern other than shifts in the time and place of meeting. They were secret meetings because they were revolutionary meetings, devoted almost exclusively to the study of the fundamental techniques of violent revolution against capitalism. Over and over again, it was drilled into us that the Communist party was "the leading detachment of the working class, its advanced fortress, its general staff." We studied revolution through the voluminous *History of the Communist Party of the Soviet Union (Bolsheviks)*, the "bible" of communism, edited and authorized by the Central Committee of the Russian Communist party.

I first encountered the *History of the Communist Party of the Soviet Union (Bolsheviks)* at a cell meeting at 45 Dana Street in Cambridge, the apartment of Dave Bennett, a propaganda and cultural-division expert in the party. College trained, slight, and frail, Dave had a confidence, self-possession, and dedication to communism that were contagious. His special task at that time was to raise the "level of understanding" of young Communists. At the same time he was conducting a graduate course to prepare the young Communists for the next step up the ladder, member-ship in the party itself.

The bulky, paper-covered Communist history was placed in my hands for the first time only a few weeks before it was shelved by the party in the complete, though temporary, ascendancy of Browderism. It was at a session with Dave Bennett's class devoted to "dialectical and historical materialism," the foundation of Bolshevik revolution. This was the course and this the textbook that seized upon the dialectics of Marx and Engels to teach that "obsolescent, decadent capitalism" was a natural step along the way to socialism and communism, and further, that the develop-ment, while inevitable, can only be brought to practical fruition by utilizing the "contradictions" of society as the anvil on which to hammer out violent revolution.

Here I learned the Communist adulation of force and violence, the subjugation of individual principles and universal morals to laws which are entirely divorced from calm reason and historical lesson but are held aloft as immutable; laws promulgated by men who are merely men but believe themselves demigods. Here they tried to tell me that the political mentality can know everything, from the beginning to the end, and act accordingly. I was told that "the transition from capitalism to socialism and the libera-tion of the working class from the yoke of capitalism cannot be effected by slow changes, by reforms, but only by the qualitative change of the capitalist system, by revolution."

I was asked to accept the inevitability of the victory of com-munism, and I caught an important clew as to why so many young people are lured into Marxist paths. Marxism teaches them to resign themselves to the collective future, to give up the shaping of their own personal destinies, and to accept the alleged inflexible laws of class welfare and ultimate victory for the pro-letariat. They can simply let themselves go and be carried along to a goal they think they cannot escape. For weaklings flounder-ing in a sea of trouble, Marxist-Leninist philosophy appears as a

111

solid rock on which they can gain a footing—oblivious to the fact that the tide ultimately will come in and sweep them away.

Many ineffectuals who are incapable of footing for themselves in their struggle with life, who feel themselves to be rootless, unwanted, and insignificant, seize the rock and hold on. They find it gives them solace; they feel that they are playing an important part in an irresistible movement of history, its pattern so thoroughly worked out that they don't have to think for themselves.

Flattery plays its part. They are told that they represent a special class, a chosen few, the carefully selected vanguard of the masses. They are members of a formation of closed ranks, and they have the illusion of prestige in leadership. The party makes use of a person's talents, and many of its victims are men and women who feel neglected in their personal or business associations.

But there is more to it than that, and there is no easy single step from the cradle of political education to the grave of communism. It is a gradual process. One does not simply become a Communist by registering when he achieves voting age, like a Republican or a Democrat. Most of them are lured into the parlor by the spiderweb of Communist "fronts" spun to catch them. The front is an effective dual-purpose device—it pushes Communist influence outward, and it draws membership in.

Each front group in the network is baited with idealism. It is usually based on a legitimate and sincere motive, one which is compatible with certain principles of Marxism. It may be racial discrimination, as in the Cambridge Committee for Equal Opportunities; the aims of organized labor; job opportunities and training; pacifism, as in the Cambridge Youth Council, or any other worth-while cause. It may be a mild form of socialism, some cultural activity, or a burning political issue of the moment; but always the net is tossed out in perfectly legal waters, and while many fish swim by, a few are snared.

Once snared, a young person may be drawn downward through

112

fronts that are more durable and lie closer to the core of the movement, such as the Young Communist League and American Youth for Democracy. New recruits are put to menial jobs to test their abilities and their intentions, then to more responsible tasks; eventually, with no discernible transition, they find themselves members of the Communist party, and by the same process, conspirators. A great many wriggle free before they have gone very deep. Some simply lose interest and drop out. A very few are sucked into the inner circle beyond the power of resistance.

It was two long years from the time I joined the League until I entered the party, and almost as long before I was introduced to the revolutionary conspiracy of the Communist movement. Even then, in Dave Bennett's special course, it was innocent enough—the study of elementary revolutionary theory and practice on a basis that was historic and presumably harmless.

But it was revolution, nonetheless. In one cell meeting, I recall, Dave Bennett put his keen analytical mind to work ramming the Communist view of capitalism down our throats. Dave was supremely confident and suave. "Capitalism," he said, "is getting worse all the time. But capitalism is moving forward. It happens to be moving forward toward its death. Now, socialism is moving forward, too, but socialism as a world society is moving forward toward its birth."

"You mean that communism will grow out of capitalism?" a beginner asked.

"Exactly," Dave replied. "Karl Marx shows quite clearly that capitalism has within it the seeds of its own destruction. Likewise it has within it the seeds of socialism. Socialist society is born of captalism."

"But," he was asked, "can't the capitalist class do something to prevent it?"

"No, ultimately they cannot prevent it. I do not say they will make no attempt to prevent it. But socialism will come in spite of the fact that the bourgeois clique owns and controls all the means of production, in spite of their control over the state, the armed forces, the police, the courts. In spite of their spies and jackals and wreckers, their depraved attacks upon the working class, socialism will ultimately triumph." Dave's eyes began to blaze as his voice rose in fervor. "The rich become richer and the poor become poorer, and finally something happens."

"And that something . . . ?"

"Is revolution. Of course. As you all know the moment of transition from a capitalist to a communist state requires a violent revolution. But that is another subject."

So we were asked to accept the thesis, in our early training, not exactly that we could bring about a revolution if we tried, but that such a revolution was inevitable, inherent in the contradictions of capitalist society—that it would come no matter what we or anyone else could do about it. Our mission was to be prepared to espouse the revolution and assist it when it did come. Thus the party led the young Communists, in slow stages, from public denial of revolutionary intent, to the new insight that there would indeed be a revolution—but not through any fault of the innocent Communists, of course. Violence by capitalists had to be answered by violence from the workers. Newcomers in the movement are not immediately taught the ultimate party position.

During our class sessions I made marginal notes of the topics discussed and emphasized in the pages of my *History of the C.P.S.U.(B.)* and turned the copy in to the FBI—little knowing that I would find it again more than five years later at the end of my long road.

My own transition from the YCL to the party itself was deceptively easy. Evidently my teachers and observers over the years were convinced that I was a good pupil, a potential member of the elite. In February, 1944, Alice Gordon first extended me an invitation to join the regular party. She requested that I keep my membership secret, and declared that the party would do the same.

114

I had to stall for time to consult the FBI. But I had to be careful not to express any doubts about the party or its program. I was in too deep for that, for I had obviously already shown full agreement with the party and all that it stood for. I decided on the spur of the moment to plead that this was an important step that should not be taken lightly.

"It would be a great honor and a privilege," I said, "and it will be important not only to me but to my wife as well. But before I take the formal step I would like to talk it over with Eva, and of course ask her to join us, too. It would be better, I should think, if we both became members at the same time."

"Splendid!" Alice replied. "You could be assigned to a branch cell, probably in your own neighborhood."

"Not in Wakefield," I pleaded. "I've already done a lot of work in that area, as you know, and it's just effort down the drain. The cell is so intimidated and overcautious that they are practically immobile." I didn't want to risk detection by operating in my own community. "Furthermore, I've been out of touch with them for a long time."

"How about Malden?" she asked.

"Fine. It's right on the way home from Boston to Wakefield, and only a half-hour bus ride from my house."

Harold Leary fully approved my joining. Eva was willing to go along. The next morning at my office I called my secretary, Gloria Gradone, to my desk. "Gloria," I said, "will you please get Ben Redfield on the phone for me?"

"Who's he?"

"He sells life insurance. Tell him I want to see him right away."

I bought all the insurance for my family I could afford, and joined the Communist party.

CHAPTER 8

At the time I took out my first party card and became a member, in 1944, the Communist party, under orders from the unfortunate Earl Browder, had cast itself adrift on a placid sea of cooperation with democratic capitalism in the United States. This improvement in the party's exterior appearance, which began so violently with the flip-flop after the 1941 attack by Hitler against Russia, had settled down into a quiet policy of collaboration, obscured from public attention by the war.

It was a time of abnormal Communist activity. The party cooperated willingly and enthusiastically with the constitutional authorities, eschewed all obstructionist tactics, and with singular purpose aided in the prosecution and winning of the war. This was the mission of Earl Browder, wartime national chairman of the Communist party in the United States. Browder went in up to the hilt. In *Victory and After*, a work which he frankly admitted was "unorthodox," Browder laid down the national party line, and held out hope of collaboration with capitalism, not only in war but in peace as well, at least to achieve "scientific socialism."

The Communist party swathed itself in patriotism and gave itself wholeheartedly to the winning of the war; at the same time, in secret classes in Cambridge, it was teaching me the necessity of violent revolution to hammer out a Communist victory. But even this teaching did not go on for long. Browderism became so firmly intrenched that the leadership finally moved for a sort of public renunciation of international revolution, and proposed the abolition

116

of the Communist party and the substitution of another name—
The Communist Political Association. The move was a direct par-
allel to the previous shift from the Young Communist League to
American Youth for Democracy. It also paralleled the gesture made
by international communism in changing the name, if not the
character, of the Comintern, and calling it the Cominform instead.

It was the most peaceful realignment of party policy I ever observed. The ground was well prepared, so that there was little
opposition or confusion in the ranks. The only outward sign I saw
was the sudden termination of Dave Bennett's classes on Marxist
revolution. At National Headquarters, William Z. Foster protested
privately but went along. Sam Darcy, a central-committee man,
protested publicly and was expelled.

It was too peaceful. I had a strong suspicion that Comrade Browder's milk and honey might be a new palliative for the same old
poison. Two years earlier I had bucked the party line on different
grounds at the Hotel Touraine meeting. Now I wondered what
would happen if, as a regular party member, I demonstrated a
reluctance to go along.

My chance to needle the comrades and find out came during
one of our cell meetings with Alice Gordon soon after I joined the
party. The subject for discussion was the National Committee's
proposal for abolition of the party and creation of the milder and
more cooperative Communist Political Association. The matter
was so cut-and-dried that our new green membership cards in the
CPA were already filled out, marked with our first names and a
number. A registration fee for transfer to the new association and
our regular term dues were to be collected at the meeting.

As the discussion proceeded, on an even keel, I listened and
chafed. Then I decided to rock the boat. Joining the conversation
for the first time, I put in, "I don't know about this. I'm afraid of
it. I don't think we are doing the right thing."

All eyes fixed on me in a sustained silence. Some looked quizzi-
cal, as if they thought they hadn't quite heard me correctly. Others

117

plainly understood and were stunned. The silence was so oppressive that I feared perhaps I had been too rash. All of my comrades had adjusted their thinking to the new situation, and my negation of it was a deep shock. In spite of my vantage point within the party, it was impossible for me to understand such complete submission. It angered me to realize that the human mind could be so easily dominated, no matter what the cause. But I had stepped out of line, raising a question of party discipline, and they were flabbergasted.

"Why, what do you mean, Comrade?" Alice Gordon finally stammered. I pounced on the bait she offered.

"There, you see! You call me 'comrade.' But in the new association it is supposed to be 'brother.' That's exactly the sort of thing I mean. I can't get it through my head that what Comrade Browder says automatically changes everything. Not that I question the motives of the party—I mean, the association. I'm sure that it is proper and we should do everything possible to retain the Big Three alliance and support an all-out war effort now. I agree that we ought to make some concessions to capitalism during this period, that we help the country to make war, boost production, eliminate strikes. But—"

Another comrade broke in heatedly. "If you agree with the policies of the party, what are you arguing about? What are you questioning? Or are you just trying to be an obstructionist?"

"Now wait a minute," Alice said with a conciliatory tone, indicating that she was stepping over toward my side. "We are supposed to have a complete discussion of the subject, and every member has a chance to express himself."

Communist democracy in action? I felt it more likely that Alice was afraid of losing Comrade Herb, a good party hack with a lot of energy and some valuable connections.

"If Brother Herb has some questions, we ought to clear them up," she said.

I knew that I would be on unassailable ground if I stuck to a

118

theme of revolution, to the doctrines that had been drilled into me with such diligence.

"What I do question," I continued, "is not the party. It is the capitalists. I can't see us getting too friendly with them. We talk about cooperating with progressive capitalists such as Wendell Willkie. Who ever heard of a progressive capitalist? Personally, I don't trust the capitalists any more now than I ever did, and Comrade Browder can't change that. We talk about proposing Anglo-American trade agreements to guarantee Britain a share of world markets. What is all this about international free competition?"

I had read between the lines of Earl Browder's treatise even if the others hadn't. "When this war is over," I added, "you can be sure there will be no concessions by the capitalists toward 'free competition.' The capitalists are in this fight only for themselves, and everyone knows it. They are in the fight for world markets and world control."

We wrangled on and on. I quoted all I could remember off the cuff of the intransigent portions of Marx, Lenin, and Engels, and I watched my "brothers" and "sisters" squirm in their chairs as they tried to reason against my arguments. They could no more do it now than a few weeks before they could convince me of the inevitable victory of world communism.

"Look," I persisted, borrowing a page from the uncompromising bolshevism of Gus Johnson, "for generations the suppressed working peoples all over the world have been dreaming of the overthrow of their oppressors and the establishment of the dictatorship of the proletariat. For years we have been their champions in the struggle. Now are we going to throw all that out the window— admit that we were wrong, or acknowledge that we are weak?"

The question spurred someone to answer with the suggestion that the revolution was not being canceled, merely postponed. That was what I was waiting for. Alice Gordon, hewing to the national party line, said that, because of the wartime unity of the

119

Big Three, and because of their decisions at Teheran, the entire world situation was changed. Now, she declared, it might be possible to achieve peacetime prosperity, and bring about the changes we sought toward socialism by working through a democratic government and economic free enterprise.

There was no sense in prolonging the discussion. They had acknowledged that no basic change was intended, but only that new methods might be tried. It was to be a period of opportunism. I gave ground by degrees, until finally I was able to relent altogether.

"All right," I said, "I'll go along. But Teheran! The international capitalists and monopolists! Agreements such as those at Teheran are but pieces of paper. They will tear them up at the first opportunity and double-cross us as soon as they have a chance. But I could be wrong. I'll stick with you until I'm proved right."

The meeting broke up in confusion. Our cards were handed around, and we were instructed to make a mental note of the number and tear them up. Most members of the CPA would keep their cards, but those of us who were under cover would not run any risk of detection. We examined the new cards. A wastebasket was furnished for us to drop them in.

In the confusion of disbanding, with many of the cell members keeping me busy by informal continuation of the dispute I had started, I took a risk. I surreptitiously avoided tearing up my card, and slipped it in my pocket for transmission to the FBI. I took the chance that the wastebasket scraps might be examined, but fortunately they were not.

I was a little uneasy about how the tangent I had taken to the turn in the party line might be regarded in high places; at least I knew that I would need some little time to purge myself of it. Even so, there were strong implications in Browder's thesis which told me that his deviation was not so much a matter of principle as it was opportunity. The National Chairman hoped to achieve a social revolution through peaceful methods in the war's uncertain aftermath. Thus, with victory in the war coming closer, there was a strong possibility that the entire episode might rebound in my favor. At least I was down in the book indelibly as a Bolshevik, and it seemed unlikely that I could be chastised too severely for adherence to the traditional and historical role of the Communist party, only a few weeks previously the subject of intensive study in my secret classes.

Nevertheless, there was a distinct chill in headquarters circles, and I worked hard to overcome it. I was assigned almost immediately to the propaganda division of the district office, where the sign on the door had been changed to "Communist Political Association." My acquaintance with advertising, publicity, and public-relations work was put to use, and I began grinding out bulletins and news releases by the score on the old, battered office mimeograph machine.

Here was a chance to ingratiate myself again by demonstrating that my deviation did not affect my devotion. The mimeograph was in bad shape, and I suggested that it should be thoroughly cleaned and overhauled. But the manufacturer's representative in Boston wouldn't handle the job. So I ordered a quantity of benzine, acquired a bundle of rags, and went to work on it. I tore down the machine, cleaned and oiled it, ordered new replacement parts, and put it together again. It worked like new, and everyone was pleased.

Next, I devoted time and effort to the cutting of stencils, introduced some attractive lettering and art work in simple layouts and designs, and stepped up the quality of the bulletins. There was method in my desire to please. Gradually it paid off, so that when any important material was to be mimeographed for distribution, general or secret, I was called in for consultation and to help with the job. Therefore, few decisions were reached in party affairs, major or minor, that I didn't know about. And the FBI shared my knowledge.

The district office in the Little Building was the focal point of Communist operations throughout all of New England, and so I

121

was in an extremely advantageous position as an intelligence agent for the Bureau. Still, I had not yet gone as far in the party's confidence as I hoped. Therefore, I had to move with redoubled caution to avoid any misstep that would tip my hand prematurely.

Headquarters officers unwittingly helped me by screening my movements from the public and the police. The party itself wanted me to remain underground if possible. I was given careful instructions concerning my visits to the Little Building offices. I was told to come at different times of the day, to ride on different elevators so I wouldn't become too well known to the operators, and to get off a floor above or below the office and make use of the fire stairs. They were sound precautions. It would have been just as unhealthy for me to be recognized by business associates as a visitor to Communist headquarters as it would to be unmasked within the party as an FBI confidant.

The office suite consisted of four rooms at the end of a corridor on the Tremont Street wing of the building, next door to the Majestic Theater and directly across the street from the Hotel Touraine. There was a small anteroom with a receptionist's desk, typewriter, the rejuvenated mimeograph, and a bank of card files. Off the anteroom on one side were a corner office and a conference room. The corner office on the other side contained two desks and a table, the latter piled high with party literature. Over the table was a bulletin board for important notices. This room led into the inner sanctum of Fanny Hartman, the district organizer, and the real district leader.

Fanny was a graduate of Simmons College and a vest-pocket edition of party stalwart Elizabeth Gurley Flynn, but what she lacked in size and power she more than made up for in skill and precision. As the strategic brain of the New England Communist party, she demanded and received unwavering loyalty from everyone under her jurisdiction. She exacted it because of a basic foundation of toughness over which she spread a thin veneer of charm, so that while she had a pleasant way of putting things, she left no room for doubt.

As one comrade expressed it to me: "When Fanny tells you something, you damned well better pay attention, follow orders, and produce results."

She was a woman of few words, who could listen to hopeless wrangling among the other district leaders, and then neatly cut through to a solution, throwing off the trivial and the irrelevant. She had the ability to accomplish as much work as three ordinary persons in a day, and still retain inexhaustible strength and stamina. She was a mannish woman, at home in a man's world, and yet she commanded genuine affection and deep friendship from other women. Fanny might have asked—and would have received—a salary in advance of most men in business, yet there she was, working for a party pittance in the drab district headquarters.

She was in time double-crossed and crushed by the very machine to which she had enslaved herself. In 1945 she was elbowed aside by the national hierarchy in favor of Emanuel Blum, who was a more powerful political strategist but a blundering fool by comparison with her. Under his direction the District One organization began falling apart. Where Fanny Hartman used a scalpel with consummate skill, Blum wielded a club. It was unfortunate for Fanny and the Communist cause that the party traditionally honored the latter method for reaching its objectives. Finesse has little place in the class struggle of Lenin, which is perhaps one reason why Karl Marx himself has been so largely abandoned in favor of the more direct revolutionary science of Lenin and Stalin.

Otis Hood was the front man for the party in New England, nominally the Massachusetts chairman, a public Communist who perpetually ran on the party ticket for offices ranging from governor of Massachusetts to Boston school committeeman.

Another in the public eye was Anne Burlak, known throughout New England as The Red Flame, a title she acquired not from the

color of her hair—which was blond—but because of her leadership in violent strike activity in Lawrence, Lowell, Providence,
and other cities in the area. She was not averse to physical combat
with the police, and had been known to tangle with as many as
three at a time. During the ascendancy of Browderism, Anne
served as president of the Communist Political Association in the
district, but otherwise she rarely held party office. For a short time
she was a member of the National Committee, and for a much
longer time she served as a courier for national party directives and
instructions. Because of this she was understood to be the most
powerful person in the district apparatus. Burlak's "domination"
of District One was a demonstration of the power and control
exerted by the National Committee.

William Harrison was another occupant of the district office.
The perennial vice-president of the district, Bill held a title which
had neither meaning nor power. He was the editor of the Boston
Chronicle, a Negro newspaper. A foil for Communist agitation
and propaganda, Bill was a cipher so far as influence in the party
was concerned, but he always did exactly as he was told.

It was from Fanny Hartman that I got my first inkling of the
innermost secret organization of a political conspiracy that is
based on concentric circles of secrecy. The cell to which I belonged was too sour over my deviation, even though it was an
anticapitalist deviation, to elect me a delegate to the District One
convention in the late spring of 1944.

At the last moment, however, I received a call from Fanny
Hartman. "I think it would be good if you would come to the
convention," she said.

"I don't know," I wavered. "Don't you think it might be dangerous—too public?"

Oh, no, was her reply. It would be a closed meeting, with no
one in attendance but the most trusted members. Nobody from
the press. I agreed to go.

There were three types of cards for admission to the convention—one color for delegates, one for alternates, and a third for important and approved visitors, of whom there were only a few, such as observers from other districts and national figures in the party.

When I reached the credentials table barring the entrance door to the conference room at Horticultural Hall, I found myself without the proper password in the form of one of these cards. I explained my plight to the girl in charge, and said that Fanny Hartman had asked me to be present. The girl called Fanny out of the conference hall to check my story.

Fanny greeted me warmly, and then went into a huddle with the credentials official. Finally they produced a visitor's card on which Fanny wrote my first name. She paused reflectively a moment, then scribbled another entry on the card and handed it to me. "Here," she said, "this will take you in and out for the various sessions."

I thanked her and the girl at the door and passed inside, glancing at the card before I tucked it into my pocket.

Across the face of the card was written "Herb," and then the cryptic designation: "Pro-4."

In all of my associations with Communists and their front organizations I had never before heard of such a tag. At headquarters and elsewhere I had run across countless names of party cells and groups, names like the Dorchester Debs or the John Reed Club. But this was new to me, and for a long time—a matter of years—I wondered about and searched for the answer to "Pro-4."

I sent the Pro-4 information along to Hal Leary as another minute fact that might fit somewhere into the puzzle. By this point in my career I was thoroughly accustomed to my role as confidential agent to the FBI, and had a fair idea of what they wanted. I made no effort to draw any inference from what I saw or heard in my peregrinations around the party. In my reports to the Bureau, I expressed no opinions. I sent in assorted facts, many of them probably useless, some, as it turned out, vital.

125

The physical job of relaying such a mass of information was so great that I could not take the time to appraise it. I picked up everything I could without actually rifling the headquarters files —copies of directives turned out by mimeograph, sheets of discarded carbon paper on which a letter was legible, hasty notes on snatches of conversation, telephone numbers, and addresses. If a party functionary scrawled a memorandum on a tablet, I made an excuse to get the underlying sheet of paper off the pad.

"Let me make a note," I would say, reaching for the tablet, scribbling a brief notation in one corner, and leaving the main part of the paper undisturbed. Although the pressure of the pencil or pen that made the previous memo was invisible to the naked eye, the disturbance of the fibers of the paper was indelible, and the message written by the functionary could easily be deciphered by the Bureau's scientific laboratories.

My spying was entirely objective and impersonal. While maintaining as best I could the rigid discipline of a party member, I served as a pipeline to the Bureau, a funnel through which flowed a vast amount of material for the Bureau experts to screen, appraise, and use as they saw fit. More often than not the FBI knew of a forthcoming meeting, including the date, place, those in attendance, speakers, even what the speaker would say, long before the information was in the hands of rank-and-file party members. These things were discussed in detail over Fanny Hartman's desk, and I frequently sat in on the outlining of speeches, policies, and plans for meetings of party units.

I learned to appreciate the basic tenet of intelligence work, that it is inadvisable for the operative to know too much about the activities on which he is spying. There is always a long chance that a slip of the tongue may reveal his awareness of something he is not supposed to know. If he doesn't become too familiar with all the details, the risk of such a slip is minimized. This rule of secret service is especially applicable when working inside a group like the Communist party, where every member, no matter how "trusted"

126

he may be, is constantly under suspicion and subject to examination and tests.

For even while my spying was most active, I felt that I was most persistently spied upon. One night after a meeting at the Bennett apartment in Cambridge, I walked toward a bus stop on Massachusetts Avenue for a bus to North Station. I suddenly became aware that I was being followed. I thought it possible that my imagination might be deceiving me, so I determined to give it a test. It was a warm night and a dark one, an ideal evening for a pleasant stroll. I walked in leisurely fashion, enjoying the evening air, halfway across Cambridge, following a circuitous route down dark gas-lit streets, stopping to look into store windows, wandering almost aimlessly. I headed in the general direction of the Central Square subway station where I could catch a train to North Station. All that distance, despite the twists and turns I made across the city, the shadow stayed a discreet distance behind me until I entered the subway.

I was not immune even at home. In the summer of 1944 I staged an American Youth for Democracy outing at my house in Wakefield. Most of the crowd, assembling for a day of swimming at the nearby beach and games and social activities in our big, barnlike garage, came toward midday by train. But quite unexpectedly, two carloads of young members arrived ahead of them by car.

In a gay, holiday mood, the six or eight early arrivals swarmed into the house. Before Eva or I realized what was happening, they had fanned out through the spacious rooms. The girls wanted to "see" the house. The boys wanted to know where they could change their clothes and put on their bathing togs. They were all over the place, and it had happened so quickly that Eva and I, scurrying around in an effort to herd them, couldn't keep track of them. I found one of the young men on the attic stairway, peering curiously into the darkened corners of the attic toward the gable end, where the big cedar closet stood against the false wall. Fortunately everything they were looking for was behind that wall.

While the young Communist AYD members were prying into my affairs, I was able to turn a small-scale coup on them. As a motion-picture hobbyist, I made a complete film record of the outing, which went into FBI files for identification purposes—identification, that is, of those who attended. Few, however, persistently turned their backs to the lens.

The AYD affair had its sardonic aftermath. Barbara Copland at M. & P. Theaters, fully aware of my activities in the organization, cautioned me that I had better get out of AYD because, she said, it was about to be investigated by the Federal Bureau of Investigation. I asked her to identify the investigators, but she declined.

I was watched even at my work in the M. & P. Theaters office. The party worked comrades into employment with M. & P. where they could keep an eye on me. One of them, a girl who made no effort to conceal her sympathies, aroused the deep resentment of Gloria Gradone, my secretary, and frequently indulged in Communist discussions among the three of us. She tried to induce Gloria to join the party. Gloria was disturbed that in these discussions I could not come out in the comrade's presence with a firm stand against the Communists. Her loyalty would not permit her to believe that I was one of them, but she became so concerned about the apparent drift of my attitudes that she even went to Harry Browning to ask him to give me a raise. She argued that economic necessity was threatening to convert me to communism. I was beginning to make a good show of it in spite of myself.

There was another counterspy in my office, of whose mission I was unaware. She was an elderly woman, a reticent person who did not indulge in any overt Communist activity. I paid little attention to her until one day I was working on some Theatrical Post American Legion mailing pieces for Harry Browning. Just as the woman passed my desk while I was reading over some work, I abstractedly muttered, "Dear Comrade," a salutation frequently used among Legionnaires. The words stopped her as though she had been struck. She stared at me open-mouthed and flushing, then turned and fled in confusion. She quit her job shortly thereafter.

On the other side of the fence I had to be equally careful. I couldn't afford to be known in my private or business life as a Communist. The FBI, I had been warned, would not stand behind me to acknowledge that I was a confidential informer, and my career in advertising would have been ruined.

By the middle of 1944 I expected that I would soon be called up in the draft. I had taken my physical examination and had been classified as available for limited service because of an eye injury suffered when I was a youth. Anticipating the call, we moved from the big house in Wakefield to a smaller one in nearby Melrose, a house which Eva would be better able to take care of alone. The draft call never came. We settled down in Melrose, where we discovered that our neighbor across the street was Gus Johnson's wife, the same Mrs. Johnson who Jack Green had warned me was the "stool pigeon" who had started the anti-Communist ruckus in Wakefield several years before.

I had been assigned the task once more of moving into the party setup in Wakefield, to convert it from the Communist party to a branch of the Communist Political Association. In the course of this work, several comrades, or brothers and sisters, came to my Melrose home from time to time, and one of my most frequent callers was Gus Johnson. Gus was separated from his wife but was also living in Melrose. He visited his wife occasionally. I didn't like the idea of his coming to see me under Mrs. Johnson's watchful eye, and I said so.

Gus was hard to persuade. He didn't care for undercover Communist activity anyway, and held to the brash theory that every good Communist should be willing to stand up in the public square and be counted. But I convinced him that I was under orders to remain covered. Gus went ahead on his own and provided a "solution."

Gus liked the ponies as well as his whisky, and he confided

to his wife that I was a bookie. Word flashed rapidly around the neighborhood; I was considerably puzzled when some of the neighbors eyed me coldly, until I learned what had happened.

I was warned several times by the Bureau that traps would be set for me by the party, and to be wary of them. On one occasion I was scheduled to mimeograph and mail out a large quantity of party material from the district headquarters office. Several days before I undertook the job, Chairman Otis Hood made a special point of telling me that, on that particular night, all of the headquarters personnel would be busy elsewhere and the office would be deserted. On the appointed afternoon I showed up just before closing time. Hood suggested that he give me his key so that I could return after a quick supper and continue my work. He showed me exactly where to put the key when I left for the night —in the top drawer of the receptionist's desk by the front window —and admonished me to be sure to lock the office door and close it tight.

I assured him I would and went out to supper. When I returned there was no one in the office. This was my first perfect opportunity. Now I could get my hands on any quantity of material in the office files, in Hood's desk, in Fanny Hartman's sanctorum. It was too perfect.

Instead, I stayed right on the job in the outer office. I did not go into any of the other rooms. I worked at the mimeograph machine, at the card files, and at the typewriter by the reception desk directly in front of the window, where I could be seen plainly from the building across the street.

When I left I stepped to the drawer of the desk by the big window and carefully placed the key where Hood had ordered me. Then I closed the drawer, turned out the light, checked the snap lock on the door, and closed it tight.

There had not been a single indiscreet move on my part. For across the street in the Hotel Touraine I knew there were party watchers, scrutinizing me carefully with binoculars through the big front windows of the district office. They could see where I went and they could plainly observe me replacing the office key in the designated place. How I knew all this, at such an early stage of the game, must still remain a secret.

Had I pocketed the key and taken it out with me even for a few minutes, it would have been fatal. Had I poked into any files or desk drawers where I had no right to be, I would have been promptly expelled from the party and my usefulness would have ended.

But turnabout is fair play. During that long evening at the district office, where the party counterspies could watch my actions but not my plans, I was able to devise a scheme the details of which must still remain a secret. It gave to the FBI information they wanted on directives and secret documents covering the party's plans and policies in New England. The district leaders do not know to this day how it was done.

CHAPTER 9

IN THE WINTER of 1945, Arthur Solomon, the alert and intense young party agent who unwittingly recruited me into the Young Communist League for the FBI, was killed in action in Germany. He died on February 24, four days after he penned me a friendly V-mail letter which he signed, "Fraternally yours." Despite the incompatibility of our views, I was saddened by Arthur's death. He gave his life, I knew, in complete devotion to the Communist cause, fighting on the side of democracy in obedience to the orders of his opportunist leaders.

His sacrifice was ironic. For even at that moment the top echelons of the party both here and abroad were carefully laying plans to turn their big guns against the very cause for which Art died. I am certain that Art would have given his life just as readily in the pursuit of any course laid out for him by the party. Had he lived, he could easily have shifted his ground from the battle against naziism to the renewal of the party's all-out war against "capitalist imperialism."

Shortly after word came of Solomon's death, a letter written in the name of the French Communist leader, Jacques Duclos, exploded in the faces of the party leadership in the United States and shook the ranks of the party almost as violently as the infamous 1941 somersault to support the war. The Duclos affair was a full-scale internal revolt, although it was carefully screened from the public gaze.

132

It squelched Earl Browder's deviation and ended his hope of "American exceptionalism."

It rudely purged any illusions of future collaboration with capitalism.

It swerved the Communist party sharply to the left and pushed the nation closer to the ensuing Communist crisis.

It affected almost every member of the party. In my case, it moved me in from the perimeter toward the epicenter of conspiracy where I was in a better position to keep track of events for the FBI.

The Communist atmosphere in the fall and winter of 1944–45 was charged with advance warnings of the Duclos storm. The tide of war, both in Europe and the Pacific, had turned. There were still plenty of home-front issues for the Communist party to support on its win-the-war platform, but it was clear that they would not last forever. On the long-term planning level, the Browder party was faced with the ultimate loss of its central rallying point— the winning of a war which was now almost won. Cooperation with capitalism, as envisaged by Browder, would never keep communism alive. The party and its front organizations were losing membership. Something had to be done.

Once again it was within the Communist youth organizations, with which I, as a party "floater," was most intimately connected, that the signal flags first went up. Orders from above directed a tightening of policies and discipline within the ranks of American Youth for Democracy, of which I was the Massachusetts state treasurer. After reaching a peak of more than 1,500 dues-paying members in the Boston area, AYD rapidly lost ground on its win-the-war program. With the break-through into Germany and the Nazi failure at the Battle of the Bulge, the membership and interest in AYD dropped off.

A special meeting was called at the apartment of Dave and Barbara Bennett to start a new membership drive for the youth group. The session was limited to AYD leaders who were members of the Communist party. Barbara Bennett told us that the AYD would continue to function as a victory coalition, embracing Communist as well as non-Communist youth. But at the same time, she said, we must be more selective in our recruiting, and take care not to enlist any Trotskyites or antilabor and antiprogressive elements. I suggested that the Young Communist League should be reestablished, but I was slapped down for meddling with national policies. The failure to rebuild the YCL was a grievous party error. The Communist youth movement in the United States has never been the same since.

While an ideological purge was thus started on a small scale, it was also time to screen the AYD membership for possible recruits for the regular Communist party. The word came down to open a "leadership training course" for hand-picked youngsters who might be good prospects. We selected about sixty-five young people, and induced them with promises of leadership in AYD activities to sign up for the course. The old familiar spider web was spun again. The new indoctrination program was given a high priority; a national party functionary, Marcella Sloane, was sent to Boston to direct the training personally.

The classes were held at the big AYD auditorium on Huntington Avenue. They followed the pattern of my own preinduction schooling in 1942. Marxism was cleverly and covertly woven into a sturdy fabric made up of the most acute postwar issues, many of which were to be found even in the Republican and Democratic platforms. Among them were fair-employment-practices legislation, Federal aid to education, support of the Dumbarton Oaks agreement, measures to ensure postwar jobs, and any issue which might appeal to a progressive-minded young person. Only those quite familiar with party teachings could detect the Marxist warp in the cloth. Communism was never mentioned, except that all anticommunism was firmly but discreetly branded as "Red baiting."

I attended a number of the classes as an observer, and I found

134

Philbrick demonstrates how he, playing the part of an underground Communist, delivered top-secret documents to party headquarters. He placed the documents in a public locker in the Boylston Street subway station and then mailed the key to Communist headquarters.

Late at night in this secret room behind the furnace in his Melrose home, Philbrick typed out reports and developed photographs for the FBI. In order to take this photograph, a partition had to be removed.

The Philbrick family today (left to right): Dale Lorraine (9), Sandra Ruth (10), Herbert, Mrs. Eva Philbrick, Leslie Sue (2), Brenda Mae (6), and Constance Anne (11).

that several other seasoned party members, some of them out of my own former cells, were also to be present. We were admonished not to fraternize too closely in the presence of others, and to pose as beginners along with the rest.

I thought at first that most of the party veterans were on hand merely to keep an eye on the new students and help the instructor weed out any who did not show promise as Communist material. But there was more to it. These party plants gradually emerged as floor leaders for class discussions—discussions which were designed to instill the first principles of Communist action into young minds which would not accept it in large, heavy doses. It had to be done with subtlety.

Marcella Sloane, for example, would toss out a question regarding the attitude of AYD members on a Federal fair-employment-practices act. A newcomer would suggest that "of course, such a law should be passed."

"Why?" Marcella would ask, and a bright young student would come up with the answer.

"Well, to put an end to discrimination."

"Do you think a law will stop discrimination?" would be the next question, and the students would kick that one around.

"Why does discrimination exist, and where do you find it?" was the next logical step. Most of the students, who had never gone that far into it before, were puzzled by this one. They contrived all manner of answers based on history and sociology, as much as they knew about it, and Marcella would tolerate the discussion until she felt it was necessary to put across the party viewpoint.

Then, with the students sufficiently prepared to accept it without too much argument, one of the party veterans would come up with the "right" answer. "Racial and religious discrimination is found primarily in industry. Industrialism and its leaders must foster discrimination in order to force wages down, to create a second- or third-class labor supply which can be exploited at starvation

135

wage levels. It is simply a matter of the economy under which we live."

There it would stop, short of the next logical step regarding the "necessity" to overturn the existing system. There was no indoctrination in revolution, only the instillation of ideas which would lead up to it, the first planting of the seeds of class strife, the theme that every social ill has its roots in capitalism.

The Communist veterans in the class frequently asked just the right questions which would afford Marcella an opportunity to supply the correct Marxist answer herself. Their loaded queries and Marcella's prepared responses made it all appear as a spontaneous development of ideas in an atmosphere of free intellectual exchange. It encouraged the youngsters even as it steered them. There was no hint of the contrivance behind it. Now I recognized that not all of my fellow students in my Banks Street classes in Cambridge several years before had been rank beginners. There, too, party plants had been used to blaze the discussion trail; that was why it all went off so smoothly.

Some of the sixty-five carefully selected AYD fledglings dropped out midway in Marcella Sloane's course, but most of them went on later to a postgraduate course in the Samuel Adams School for Social Studies, the educational center in Boston which was sponsored and supported by the Communists even while the party vigorously denied it. The four-week course was designed to teach them about the "shining future" and to give them the party's slant on the United Nations, problems of national unity, and employment.

Once again, the schooling consistently stopped short of revolution. But whereas in their first indoctrination classes the social evils of capitalist democracy were infused, now the dicussions led to the absolute necessity of making sharp changes in the social, economic, and governmental system.

Among the instructors for the Sam Adams course was the school's treasurer, Harry Winner, a Malden, Massachusetts, businessman

136

and executive with the Converse Rubber Company of many years' standing, a man whose talents as a teacher were widely appreciated by the party, even if they were overlooked by his business associates.

While the ranks of the youth organizations were being tightened, the party hierarchy showed other signs that they sensed the unpopularity of Browderism and the impending swing to the left. The party leaders feared that the move away from Browder would leave a large segment of the fringe membership hanging in the air, unless some provision could be made to give them a footing and maintain control of their political influence for the party's advantage. Accordingly, the district officers turned their attention to the problem of finding an aboveground political-action group, free of the Communist label, to serve that purpose.

I was assigned by district headquarters to the task of infiltrating a liberal group known as the Massachusetts Political Action Committee, to survey the organization and determine whether the PAC could be taken over and used as a political front by the party. I reported that I thought the committee, composed of true liberals, was ill-suited to Communist party purposes, and that it might be better to establish a similar group of our own. Many others agreed with me. Thus Earl Browder's flabby Communist Political Association, which had shunned divisive politics during the war years, laid the groundwork for the Progressive party and direct engagement once more in the political arena. It was a sign of coming events.

Still another was the falling-off of membership which resulted in a scramble for funds to support party and front activities. Early 1945 found us in desperate need of money. A concentrated effort was decreed to pull us out of the hole. Every conceivable fund-raising dodge was used, and nowhere is Communist cynicism more fully displayed.

One of my major assignments during this period was a treasury drive for American Youth for Democracy. It was no longer sufficient to tax dwindling membership, or to rely on door-to-door solicitation. We had to seize a "cause," and convert it into cash. Here was a prime example of iniquitous party work. We decided to appeal for money to "continue" the work of AYD. But we had our tongues in our cheeks, because we knew all the time that what we needed was money to pay off back debts preparatory to liquidation of the organization.

Working with Don Bollen, the AYD state chairman; Bob McCarthy, national board member of AYD; Barbara Bennett, who replaced Alice Gordon as district leader of Communist Youth Work; Beverly Franklin, who was especially adept at raising AYD funds among the society ladies of Boston; and others, I drew up a plan for a "Youth on Parade" dinner, ostensibly to pay homage to the youth of Boston for their sacrifices both at home and on the field of battle. In consultation with district party leaders, we drew up a list of carefully selected young people to be the guests of honor and to receive certificates of achievement—a returning service man, a war worker, a nurse's aide, a canteen worker, an artist, a musician, a youth leader. We corralled Dr. Hugh Cabot, a frequent sponsor of and contributor to our causes, and a man whose name was synonymous with Boston, to officiate at the ceremonies. Professor F. O. Matthiessen of Harvard was to be the chairman of the evening.

I made the final arrangements for the Youth on Parade dinner to be held on the evening of March 19 at the Hotel Vendome in Boston. I was assigned to write the letter soliciting the usual sponsors for the affair. After receiving the approval of Communist party headquarters, the letter was signed by Professor Matthiessen. In our press releases and public notices, we manufactured an aura of community pride in the accomplishments of youth, which was to pervade the whole affair. But all the time we had our eyes on the cash box.

Those invited to attend the dinner—and to contribute to AYD—were carefully screened. The name of each prospective donor was written down on a card, together with an analysis of the best and most opportune manner of approach. We studied the particular appeal to which each was most likely to respond, whether it was politics, philanthropy toward young people, interest in interfaith or interracial work, tolerance, or simply good citizenship. We had at least one such "weak spot" for everybody. We also asked each donor to give us the names of friends who might be expected to make contributions. Tables at the dinner were sold to civic organizations and trade unions for fifty to a hundred dollars.

It was an evening of good will, good food, music, sparkling conversation, and a spontaneity that belied the careful preparations. One of the guests of honor was Mrs. Harold A. Fletcher, Jr.—Martha, as she was known to hundreds of Boston young people for her youth work in the Unitarian Church. Martha was tall, with beautiful classic features and a long brunette mane. She had a bright mind, a warm personality, and a self-assurance that was reflected in her modulated, vibrant voice. Poised and charming, she made a sincere appeal for continued support of the "magnificent" work of the AYD.

She was the hit of the evening—and likewise the star of the motion picture made of the entire affair, for the picture files of the FBI.

The dinner raised approximately a thousand dollars for the treasury, one hundred of which went into the national office of AYD. The rest was used to pay off telephone bills, rent, printing costs, the salaries of Don Bollen and Bernice Rogers, who was state chairman of the Sweethearts of Servicemen program; and to shrink the AYD down from its spacious Huntington Avenue headquarters to a small office at 7 Water Street, the same building in which I started my Communist career.

While the Communist Political Association was thus girding itself, financially, physically, and spiritually, for the Duclos shock, I was momentarily diverted from business and party life by an incident that happily drove me back for a welcome sojourn with my much neglected famly. Our fourth daughter, Brenda Mae, was born on April 27, 1945, and for a week's vacation I stayed at home and ran the household.

It was also in April that the Duclos letter fell on soil that was prepared for it; it took root quickly, and blossomed into a full-fledged anti-Browder revolt. The letter by Jacques Duclos was published in *Cahiers du Communisme,* the theoretical organ of the Communist party of France. Long-winded and dull, replete with dialectical gymnastics, the letter was actually a directive from the international Communist movement, ordering the party in the United States to put its house in order. It was understood to have the backing of the Cominform and the Kremlin, and it was accepted as law.

Few people outside the party plowed through Duclos's article, but it was widely circulated in the party as required reading. The letter pounced on the hapless Browder for dissolving the party and creating the Communist Political Association. It chastised him for taking views which led him to say in a speech at Bridgeport, Connecticut, that he would "clasp the hand of J. P. Morgan" if Morgan would go along on the Anglo-Soviet-American alliance and the Teheran agreement. Duclos called for the rejection of collaboration, for the burial of the Communist Political Association, and for the restoration of a powerful and militantly Marxist Communist party in the United States. He listed the following major flaws in Browderism:

"1. The course applied under Browder's leadership ended in practice in liquidation of the independent political party of the working class in the U.S.

"2. Despite declarations regarding recognition of the principles of Marxism, one is witnessing a notorious revision of Marxism on the part of Browder and his supporters, a revision which is expressed in the concept of a long-term class peace in the United States, of the possibility of the suppression of the class struggle

140

in the postwar period and of establishment of harmony between labor and capital.

"3. By transforming the Tehran declaration of the Allied governments, which is a document of a diplomatic character, into a political platform of class peace in the United States in the postwar period, the American Communists are deforming in a radical way the meaning of the Tehran declaration and are sowing dangerous opportunist illusions which will exercise a negative influence on the American labor movement if they are not met with the necessary reply."

He decried Browder's hopes for peaceful measures toward a constitutional socialism and placed the party back on a forceful footing.

"Furthermore," he said, arguing this point, "one can observe a certain confusion in Browder's declarations regarding the problem of nationalization of monopolies and what he calls the transition from capitalism to socialism.

"Nationalization of monopolies actually in no sense constitutes a socialist achievement, contrary to what certain people would be inclined to believe. No, in nationalization it is simply a matter of reforms of a democratic character, achievement of socialism being impossible to imagine without preliminary conquest of power."

He raised the postwar cry of neo-fascism, and said, "The American Communists have an especially important role to play in the struggle taking place between the progressive forces of the earth and fascist barbarism. . . . And it is clear that if Comrade Earl Browder had seen, as a Marxist-Leninist, this important aspect of the problems facing the liberty-loving peoples in this moment in their history, he would have arrived at a conclusion quite other than the dissolution of the Communist Party of the United States."

This directive was a ringing challenge timed to coincide with victory in the war and to bring back the sharp class struggle in an atmosphere of anticipated demobilization and domestic turmoil. The gauntlet flung down by Duclos was quickly picked up by most

141

Communists in the United States, who saw the handwriting on the wall. Browder, of course, could not reverse his field and stay in with any grace. Whether or not it was by prior understanding with the Cominform, he would have to be sacrificed as the scapegoat of the conciliatory wartime Communist party in this country. Browder had served his purpose. As a faithful party member he would have to go; in all probability he would make a good show of lone opposition so that it would look like a domestic party affair, free from international pressure.

The reaction to the shot in the party's arm by Duclos was swift. The National Committee of the Communist Political Association obediently began groveling in self-criticism over the errors of its ways, and took steps to act in accordance with the Duclos letter. A draft resolution was prepared for submission to state and district conventions of the Association, calling for the prompt dissolution of the CPA and restoration of the party in its old form. It was to be strengthened, however, by a new constitution which demanded a more vigorous form of "democratic centralism" and tighter hierarchical control of the party's destinies.

I was in the district headquarters when some of the directives concerning the Duclos affair came in from national headquarters. I was not permitted to see them, but the discussion in the office told me which way the wind was blowing. Sitting on the corner of a desk, I heard the party functionaries—Otis Hood, Fanny Hartman, Jack Green, Anne Burlak, Alice Gordon—go through their verbal gyrations.

Green blasted Earl Browder straight down the line. "I never did like the bastard," he cried. "He's been bought out by the capitalists and turned the party over to them lock, stock, and barrel. It's about time we got rid of him."

"I don't know," I hazarded. "Let's look at this thing from a sales point of view. We've had a good many members come in on the basis of Browderism. Look at AYD, for example. We've just enrolled several new party members through them, haven't we?" I looked at Alice Gordon. She nodded, giving me the answer to a question of interest to me and the Bureau.

"O.K. Now we've gone to a lot of work to get these people. We've been telling them that Browder is a hero. We might lose them if we turn right around and make Browder out to be a heel."

Green turned on me fiercely. "Don't tell me you've fallen for that tripe, Comrade," he sneered, looking at me so that I was sharply reminded of Green's position as the chief security agent of the district, whose job it was to weed out deviationists in high places and low.

"Quite the contrary," I shot back, returning his gaze as firmly as I could. "I think my record will bear me out."

Alice Gordon backed me up. "That's right," she said. "In our cell it was Comrade Herb who held out the longest of all against Browder, and from the very beginning."

I didn't pause long enough to let it sink in, because I was afraid someone might ask me what had caused me to change my mind. "I'm looking at this thing purely from a practical angle. When you say that we've got to get rid of Browder and his whole gang, I agree. But I don't want to lose any more of the membership than I can help. I can see a drop of twenty per cent anyway, but I don't see why we should ask for a fifty-per-cent drop. I think we ought to take steps to hold onto what we have."

Otis Hood, who was much more congenial than Jack Green, and the district's best student of Marxism, agreed with me and offered an explanation.

"Your position is sincere, I know," Hood said, "although it constitutes a Menshevik error. You are right. Many intellectuals, professors, university and high-school students will remain outside the Communist party even though they may have joined such a group as the Communist Political Association. But the party

143

itself does not need members who shrink from party discipline and are afraid to join it. At the same time we will not lose their political influence, because we will have a place for them."

"And where is that?" I asked.

"The Political Action Committee."

"The PAC?"

"Sure. Many who will refuse to become dues-paying, card-holding party members will still enter into an alliance with us in such an organization. These people are the *khvostists*—the coat-tailers—and Comrade Green is right in saying that they are not to be trusted as party members. But that does not bar us from inviting them to join a political-action group with us, eh?"

My exchange with Green and the others served two purposes. First, it brought to the attention of the district leadership in this time of crisis that I had been a strong Marxist revolutionary even when Browderism was most rampant; second, it gave rise to a maneuver which was apparently unique in the District One organization. A special four-page flier was printed, with planted material defending Browder. The object of the scheme was to let the National Chairman down easy, so as not to disillusion too many of the new party members with a rude rejection. Someone had to take the pro-Browder role in the district, and by prearrangement the task fell on Otis Hood, who was, during the Browder interval, a minor official in the district. Anne Burlak, as titular head of District One, was to accept the brunt of party criticism for steering the party along the Browder line. Hood, also by prearrangement, was to be given an opportunity to switch his position later, and clear himself by confession. Thus the party contrived a deliberate show of "democracy" in the great Foster-Browder debate as a concession to new members who joined during the era of Browderism. The Browder position was put up like a tin can on the fence, so that we could shoot it full of holes with the big guns. Such are the ways of Communist manipulation.

But the switch back to a militant party was not to be denied,

144

and the party leaders took no chances of a mutiny, even while they made concessions. The soft days of Browder were dead long before the formal *coup de grâce*. Security was the watchword, discipline was the slogan of the day, and members were expected to go along or be kicked out. Discussions based on the Browder line were abruptly canceled out of cell schedules and indoctrination classes. Big Three unity was no longer importuned. Division was stressed, and Marxism was restored.

The government, through the FBI, watched the trend of the party with renewed interest. There was a flurry of exchanges between me and the Bureau, and the questions put to me by them were much more probing than those asked by the man in the street. It was obvious that the party was preparing a big shift to the left. The question that Harold Leary wanted answered was how *far* to the left it would go. I tried in vain to find out. The leaders and the party hacks in District One were full of words, but to a man they declined to make any flat predictions. Would this revival of Marxism include the imminent destruction of capitalism and a swift move toward violent revolution in the war's immediate aftermath?

One of my first tasks in connection with the castle revolt was to serve as courier and emissary between the district headquarters and the Malden branch of the party.

"Go down to the Progressive Bookshop at 8 Beach Street," I was ordered by Dave Bennett, the state secretary, "and pick up some material there. Tell them you are authorized to do so without payment. We'll see that it gets straightened out later. They will tell you where to take everything."

So I made my debut at the public propaganda headquarters of the Communist party in Boston. The Progressive Bookshop was a few doors down from Washington Street. I was surprised to find my old Wakefield cell comrade, Frank Collier, in charge. He was as morose as I had remembered him, and permitted himself no demonstration at seeing me again. The bookshop held shelves of

145

Marxist-Leninist classics, current and back copies of Communist magazines, racks of the *Daily Worker* and *The Worker*. Some books, such as the old reliable *History of the C.P.S.U.(B.)*, were sold to trusted customers.

Collier packed up a bundle of pamphlets and circulars. I asked him for directions. "These go to 34 Holyoke Street, Malden," Frank told me.

On the appointed evening a day or so later I made my hot, dusty way by streetcar and bus to a section of Malden that was unfamiliar to me. The address turned out to be a four-family, double-deck house in a working-class district. Under the second-floor apartment number given to me there was listed simply the name Mills—my old friend, Alice Mills, now the leader of the Malden branch.

Alice looked better than she had when I first met her more than five years before in the Massachusetts Youth Council. She told me that Nat was in military service, but she appeared to be weathering his stint well. She was in charge of the activities of some hundred party members in neighborhood cells in Malden, Somerville, Everett, Melrose, Wakefield, and Stoneham. The cells were composed of residents of these communities, mostly workers and housewives.

In the subsequent orientation meetings with the cells in Alice's bailiwick, we disseminated the new party line to the membership in preparation for the district convention of the party, scheduled for July. Following the outlines prepared for us by district headquarters, we castigated Browder and harped endlessly on the necessity for restoration of the party. We envisaged for the membership a sharpening of all the inner and outer "contradictions" of American capitalism, an intensification of the class conflict in the United States, a renewed struggle in behalf of the colonial peoples, and a sharper division between the two world systems of capitalism and socialism. All comrades in the branch were corralled into cell meetings and belabored with hours of indoctrination.

146

The Malden branch was instructed to elect three delegates and three alternates to the big July convention. The windup saw me elected as one of the alternates on the six-man delegation. This was fortunate for the FBI, because if they had asked me to crash the convention, I could not have done so. It was the most carefully guarded and secretive convention ever held in the district. First of all, the headquarters was zealous in its efforts to keep out spies, newspaper reporters, party wreckers and deviationists—anyone who might upset the carefully planned program. Furthermore, the party was anxious to show its own members that the careless era of Browder was ended, and that the new, tough "vanguard of the working class" would brook no nonsense.

Cards were issued for those who were to attend the three sessions spread out from Saturday evening to Sunday. It was not enough merely to be designated as a delegate by a party branch. Each representative's name was forwarded to headquarters for careful screening by Marc Alper's credentials committee. Only after approval by him were the cards issued—one color for delegates, one for alternates, and one for the very few visitors who were invited to be present. Each card listed the real or party name of the delegate, and it was stamped with a serial number for cross-checking against a master list.

But the best laid plans go slightly awry. In my case it was ironic that a counterspy for the FBI should receive not only an alternate delegate's visa but also a special invitation that entitled me to a visitor's card. Somewhere in party headquarters the wires were crossed up, and I received a special communication.

"Dear Friend," it said. "This is to extend to you a personal invitation to attend the special convention of the Communist Political Association of New England to be held in Boston on Saturday and Sunday, July 21 and 22. . . . Fraternally yours, David P. Bennett, Secretary."

I ducked into a telephone booth and called the special number that took me straight through to Harold Leary at the FBI. "Hal?"

"Speaking."

"You know that big convention next week end?"

"Yes, I do. What about it?"

"I'm going to it—twice."

"You're going? That's fine. What do you mean, twice?"

"They want to be absolutely sure that no stooges get past the door into the hall. So they gave me two tickets."

CHAPTER 10

IT WAS A THOROUGHLY casehardened "Communist" who set out through the hot, sticky night of July 21, 1945, as an alternate delegate to the crucial convention of District One, Communist Political Association, in downtown Boston. I crawled into my Marxist compartment, shut the door, and stayed there. This was a trick that four years of concentration had taught me. It would have been impossible for me to go so far in the party and still escape detection as a government agent if I had not been able to control my emotions and reactions, especially in an atmosphere such as that which pervaded the muggy, tense Saturday evening when the convention opened.

Nevertheless, there were some chinks in the compartment. The July convention, we were told in advance, was a major turning point in the history of the party. It promised to be a hurly-burly which would stretch my powers of self-control and credulity to the limit. If I was to be called on to play a role, I was not sure how I would play it. The question both the Bureau and I were seeking was as yet unanswered—how far to the left would the party swing? What would be its program on a practical level from here on? Every comrade felt that until the new Communist platform was fully set forth, it would be extremely dangerous for any individual to take a stand. I felt the same way and determined that, until at least a partial answer was provided, I would stay in the background, keep faith with my party orders to function as a semi-underground member, observe what I could, and remain as unobtrusive as possible.

Most of the party meetings I had attended during the previous year, since the 1944 district convention, had been small gatherings. But now the Charter Room and its foyers at the modern New England Mutual Life Insurance Building on Berkeley Street were crowded with several hundred of the party's faithful. Mixing in large Communist gatherings was a precarious occupation for me. I felt a cold fear that somehow, somewhere, there would be one member of the crowd who might put the finger on me. Even with two passes to the convention in my pocket, I was uneasy, and my very uneasiness made it worse, lest I give myself away by a display of nerves. The Bureau was anxious to have a full report of this convention, and I didn't want to be tripped up on the way in.

I mingled with the crowd and descended to the downstairs lobby. Across the room I saw Marc Alper's gimlet-eyed gate watchers at the door. I sought to avoid them until I felt perfectly composed. I strolled over to the literature table which was a perennial fixture at all party meetings and conventions. I engaged in light conversation with the literature attendants whom I knew, and bought several books and pamphlets. The old party "classics" were there, dusted off and brought down from the high shelves where they had been for over a year—the *History of the C.P.S.U.(B.)*; *Imperialism, the Highest Stage of Capitalism,* by Lenin; *Foundations of Leninism,* by Stalin; the *Communist Manifesto,* by Marx. Routine party propaganda journals were there, too—stacks of *The Worker,* the *Daily Worker,* and the magazine *Political Affairs.* I asked for a copy of *Socialism, Utopian and Scientific,* by Engels, but was told that it was sold out and I would have to wait until the Progressive Bookshop, the party propaganda center, received a new shipment.

There was a tipoff to the nature of the convention on the literature table. Every work from the prolific pen of Earl Browder—his *Victory and After, Teheran,* and all of the "great" books of the erstwhile hero of the Communist Political Association—was missing. Up to this point no vote of any kind had been made by the membership on the fate of Mr. Browder's leadership. Yet it was obvious that the decision already had been made. At all previous meetings, Browder's books and pamphlets had occupied the forefront of every literature table. Now they were gone. His doctrine was already *non grata* in the party.

I ran into several old friends in the hallway. Margot Clark, the girl who had put me to the test in my early days in Cambridge, was one of them. Whenever I saw Margot now I felt a little flutter in the pit of my stomach. To me, her presence echoed the dread sound—NKVD—the secret police. I had no definite proof that Margot was a member of the NKVD or its United States counterpart, but I had enough circumstantial evidence to make me apprehensive and very cautious. For one thing, Margot was not a member of the state board, nor did she hold any party office. And yet this slight, grave, and almost fragile young woman had an air of poise and competence that could not be missed by the party. She was given many important tasks, and on this occasion had the job of housing for the convention, which meant that she must know not only the names and addresses of a great many of the comrades, but also some of the details of their family life, how much extra room they had to spare to take in others, who should be billeted with whom. There are very few comrades even in the higher ranks who ever get around enough to know the intimate details about large numbers of the membership, and those who do are prime candidates for the dreaded Review Commission, the party's undercover counterspy ring. Margot seemed strangely involved in matters of party purging and discipline. I passed her by with a warm enough greeting, but I did not pause to get involved in conversation with her.

I also ran into Don Bollen, now, like me, a former officer of the AYD; Elba Chase Nelson, the grandmotherly New Hampshire Yankee whom I had met at the 1944 convention; Phyllis Helene, one of the new officers of the nearly bankrupt AYD; and Arthur Korb, pianist-composer who had played at our Youth on Parade dinner.

Finally I spotted Fanny Hartman near the entrance door. I felt that it was an opportune moment to make my entrance. Walking up to Marc Alper's barricade, I handed in my alternate delegate's card, greeted Fanny just inside at the same time, and unconcernedly engaged her in conversation while the clerks at the desk checked my card and its number against the long sheets of paper spread out in front of them.

The sheets contained every name approved to attend the convention, like a voting list, together with the delegate's card numbers and other information. As each card was handed in, the name was crossed off the list, to make sure that no one would get through the door on a forged or duplicate card.

"This is a beautiful place to hold the convention," I said to Fanny.

"Sure is," she returned. "Even the air conditioning works, thank heaven." In the midst of these banalities, my card was handed back to me and I passed through, fully accredited.

I found the Malden delegation about midway in the auditorium on the left side, seated at a large, bare table set up on sawhorse supports. Alice Mills was the principal delegate and the central figure of the group, which also included Frank Collier and a Malden girl whose party name was Grace Smith, known to many simply as Comrade Grace. I pulled up a chair next to the wall where I could face outward and obtain a good view of the entire gathering. I was immediately conscious of the distinctly different atmosphere of the meeting. There was a buzz of efficient activity, but unlike the usual political convention there was no turmoil. No buttonhole parleys were being held in corners; there was no lobbying around delegates' tables. Nor was there any loud or boisterous conduct. Everyone was there for a very definite purpose. It reminded me of a newspaper city room, where each person has a job to do and knows exactly what is expected of him.

The convention started with "The Star-Spangled Banner"—a last remnant of Browderism not yet obliterated. Anne Burlak, as president of the state Communist Political Association, gave the main report. Anne must have known that her number was up. Her address was a masterpiece of flagellation in the best tradition of Communist self-criticism. She had been wrong to embrace Browderism and realized it now, she said, and she was willing to assume full responsibility for leading the organization down the pathway of deviation.

Anne offered to the convention the National Committee's draft resolution, based on the Duclos letter, and urged its adoption in full. She said that Comrade Browder had been guilty of the most grievous errors in developing a reliance on monopoly capital which had sabotaged the vanguard role of the party. She said that she agreed in full with the Duclos letter, and she called for an immediate return of Marxist-Leninist policies and the reconstitution of the party.

"This is the most important turning point in our history," her voice shrilled over the public-address system. When her long, biting harangue was finished, it was Otis Hood's turn to carry out his previous orders, and pull back from the pro-Browder role he had been called on to assume in print. Now, in his speech, he merely quoted Browder without supporting him. But by this time Browderism was thoroughly whipped, and no one came forward to defend it. One planted speaker in the rear of the room read a watery letter from an "unidentified" comrade, which sought to defend only certain minor parts of Browder's program.

From there on, the convention got into full swing. It followed the familiar pattern of our first American Youth for Democracy meetings. Those who wished to speak sent their names to the chairman on cards furnished for the purpose. At the rostrum, the chairman—the post rotated for the various sessions—gravely sorted out the cards and with equal gravity "called upon" those who had been previously approved as speakers. As an experiment, knowing that I had been assigned no role as a speaker, I submitted my name, and of course I was never called on. Alice Mills also sent up her name. I knew in advance what she would say, and the FBI already had an outline of her blast against capitalism, coupled with her demand that the new party widen the gap and sharpen the conflict between the proletariat and the bourgeoisie, not to cover up the "contradictions" between them as Browder had done.

One after another, speakers rose to denounce the ways of Browder in terms which occasionally went even beyond the limits predetermined by hierarchical policy. So far to the left did the pendulum swing that the meeting began to get out of hand. Only the card system for calling on speakers saved the day. The leadership tried to apply the brakes, but they were greeted with hoots and howls. One major issue was the National Committee's program for continued adherence to the wartime no-strike pledge given by the Communist Political Association. The United States, after all, was still at war with Japan, and the atom-bomb end of the war was not yet in sight. But Russia was not involved in armed conflict with Japan, and there was a temper in the meeting for abrogation of the pledge, to begin now to stir up as much trouble and confusion as possible on the domestic economic front, and strike action was the favorite Communist weapon for dissension. The hate program outlined by the preliminary speakers worked too well. *Hate! Hate! Hate!* reverberated around the room from wall to wall, ceiling to floor. The extreme left wing of the district organization jumped on the band wagon. The roars of rage and hate were most vehement in one corner of the room, where I spotted the squat, flamboyant figure of Don Tormey, radical CIO United Electrical Workers organizer. (Tormey's Communist-controlled faction of the UEW has since been expelled from the CIO.) Tormey was a young, militant scrapper with twelve

154

years of rough-and-tumble labor experience behind him. Now he was red-faced, perspiring, his shirtsleeves rolled up, his tie askew at his open throat, clamoring for the floor. But he was not on the approved list of speakers, and could not get a hearing.

Nevertheless, from the storm center in his section of the auditorium, a full-scale revolt was in the making. Older comrades recalled the Jay Lovestone battle many years before, when the party was split asunder. The district functionaries were worried, and with excellent reason.

When the meeting finally broke up at a late hour in an atmosphere of turmoil and exhaustion, not everyone went home. Key leaders were called into a secret midnight meeting at the Little Building offices to thrash out the procedure for the following day. I was not invited, but reports of the strategy meeting came to me by the grapevine. I made a hasty telephone report to the Bureau on the party revolt that seemed to be shaping up. Then I went home to light the lamp in my own study, where I typed up a summary of the session for Hal Leary.

Sunday morning's conference opened with an announcement, obviously the result of the previous night's strategy meeting, that several features of the program would be changed, and a series of panel discussions would be called off. When the convention met again, it was apparent that the hate campaign had been set aside, and that anticapitalism would be soft-pedaled by the leadership. The revolt against Browderism, instigated by the party leaders, had almost gotten out of control, and blood pressures were still high. The morning session was a long wrangle which lasted well beyond the noon deadline. Dave Bennett, sitting as chairman, proved an able conciliator to rampant charges and countercharges of Browderism and every other shade of deviation from Marxist principles. But the compromises did not entirely satisfy the extreme left wing.

It was not until the final Sunday session that Don Tormey managed to break through the barriers opposing him and gain

155

the floor. Once he got it, nothing could stop him. He waved the red flag of disruption, confusion, and civil strife with the intimation that now was the time, following Marxist principles, to turn the imperialist war into a civil war and pave the way for revolution. Tormey urged rejection of the no-strike pledge in the proposed party platform, and drew sufficient support to forestall routine adoption of the National Committee's program. The convention committee had hoped to close the convention with a single vote, but Tormey forced them to take up the resolution point by point, section by section. His tirade included a blanket denunciation of the leaders and membership of the district for clinging to remnants of Browderism. The leadership was already beaten to an ideological pulp by the Tormey revolt. They needed a defense, and fortunately for me, it was Alice Gordon who rose to it.

"First of all," she cried, "many of the policies which we followed were entirely proper and correct, in keeping with Marxism-Leninism. They were win-the-war policies which would and should have been followed even if Browder was not the leader of the party.

"Not only that, but Comrade Tormey"—the membership was already back to the "comrade" salutation—"Comrade Tormey is incorrect in his blanket criticism of the entire membership. I know that some were not so easily diverted to Browder's views. It is well remembered that Comrade Herb of Malden, for example, held out to the very end, and then only accepted the Browder program for the sake of party unity."

I flushed and tried to crawl down into my coat collar. Fortunately Alice had not gestured in my direction to single me out and thus damage the anonymity I coveted. My fellow comrades at the Malden table looked upon me with new regard. My needling of the cell more than a year before on Beacon Hill came home to roost, and I knew now that the results would be advantageous to my party future, and to the FBI.

The draft resolution was offered to the convention section by

156

section, and gradually the leadership stemmed the tide of the left-wing revolt. But not without compromise. Some of the opposition was allayed temporarily by coupling with the no-strike pledge a demand that employer "provocations" of labor disputes must be stopped. Fanny Hartman proposed further "study" for issues that still remained in dispute. It was a narrow victory for the party leadership. So strong was the swing to the left that it was necessary to permit "abstentions" in the voting—an unusual procedure in the party, and one that I had never before witnessed. There were a large number of abstentions.

Exhaustion and the National Committee's program, at least its substance, finally won out. Late in the evening, V. J. Jerome, a member of the National Committee, stifled the audience with a speech that was so long and so vacillating that few listened to it and no one remembered it. It served its purpose. Delegates began drifting out; the convention broke up, subject to recall, August 11 and 12, after the national convention in New York.

My twenty-page typewritten report to the FBI required several late evenings of work. I sent in a list of names which, I was surprised to find, included nearly a hundred of the three hundred persons attending the convention. I also sent literature, pamphlets, and voting lists together with a summary of the full convention in an effort to analyze where the party was heading and how far it was going to go. I concluded, from the convention proceedings and from the debate I had heard, that if Russia came into the war against Japan, then the party would string along with the nation's war effort. But if Russia should disavow any military interest in the Far East, or should the war in the Pacific come to an early close, the party's attitude would be sharply changed, and a new war against "American imperialism" would begin with obstructionist fervor on the home front.

The advent of the atom bomb and Russia's hasty entry into the war against Japan just before the Armistice solved that problem for the comrades. Had the war against Japan dragged on, without

Russian participation, I was convinced that "American imperialism" would have replaced Japanese fascism as the party's prime target.

After the convention I attended a series of meetings at party headquarters to discuss the details of the August session. I asked Anne Burlak, "What will we take up?"

"For one thing," she flashed with a vehement glance, "you may be sure that we will discuss the matter of party discipline." I felt uncomfortable, wondering whether she was thinking of Don Tormey or of me. "Under the new program we will have to know where our members stand."

"Good," I said, trying to suppress the involuntary flush which I always felt stealing over me at times like this, and which I knew was my worst security flaw. "It's about time."

Before the August meeting came around, Don Tormey was severely reprimanded for his left-wing revolt. He was put on the black list, which merely meant that he was given no assignments. The Tormey incident emphasized the tightening of party discipline; no one, not even an archrevolutionary, was permitted to deviate from the policy laid down by the National Committee.

My own ranking with the district leadership rose a notch or two as a result of Alice Gordon's reminder that I had been from the beginning a reluctant Browderite. A few days prior to the August convention I was assigned to work with Alice to "set" the membership of the Malden branch in the new line and to pave the way once again for the convention deliberations. A series of special branch meetings was called, and I was designated as the lead-off speaker. Frank Collier mailed out the notices. He assured me that it would be perfectly safe for me to talk freely in addressing those present because the notices were going only to bona-fide and trusted members of the party.

Many of my old friends from the Wakefield cell turned up at the meetings, and I was a little surprised to find that so many of them had successfully weathered the violent tacks, from the party

158

to the association and back to the party again, from "comrade" to "brother" and "sister" and now once more back to "comrade." But there were also several new faces on hand. Following what had now become standard procedure, no introductions were made; if any identification was used at all, it was invariably by first names, real or assumed. A few could not conceal their identity. One of those I picked out of the crowd at the first of our meetings was Harry Winner, the widely known and influential Malden businessman, who as a teacher in the Sam Adams School for Social Studies had assisted in the Marxist indoctrination for prospective young Communists in the AYD. I was surprised at Winner's presence because of Collier's assurance that the meeting notices would go only to the membership.

Winner was an enigmatic figure. I could not bring myself to understand his position—a prosperous business executive, well liked and respected in his community and business life, yet apparently active as an underground member of the Communist party. He was one of many among the membership who remained aloof, unlike the avowed Communists who could approach each other freely and openly, at least at party conclaves. I understood that I must shun him, in and out of the party. It occurred to me also to wonder from time to time what his role was. If I were a member of the Review Commission, I thought that I would automatically suspect Harry Winner as a secret government agent. But perhaps I was overestimating the man. After all, I was one of a very limited number who had proof that the government had infiltrated the party. And then again, I reflected, Winner was, like Margot Clark, just the type who might without too much stretch of the imagination be a member of the Review Commission itself.

The new party, in its disciplinary ardor, was becoming nervous about security. Mutual suspicion cut through all ranks from the top down. In mid-August, the reconvened sessions of the District One convention were held at the same place with the same delegates and alternates. The checking and double-checking of credentials were more intensive than ever, and the guards on the door were more formidable. But I was a part of the convention now, and I came and went at ease. The convention itself was a dull, routine affair, which merely rubber-stamped the New York reconstitution of the party and listened to an artful inspirational address by Elizabeth Gurley Flynn, the big, jolly, powerful oratorical whip of the party. Miss Flynn's harangue was what the convention needed. Her magnificent sense of timing, her accurate measure of the temper and response of the audience, roused them to the only enthusiasm of the two-day meeting. Browder was dead. Long live Foster!

Comrade Flynn's colorful history in American radical movements dates back to her close association with the famous Socialist leader, Eugene V. Debs, and with labor leader "Big Bill" Haywood, in the early years of the twentieth century. (She was later indicted as a second-string Communist leader on charges similar to those against the original Twelve.

A new district board was elected. Under the new constitution it was given the responsibility of naming, in turn, the new officers. A budget of fifty thousand dollars was adopted, along with a fresh and intensive program for agitation, recruitment, training, and dues collection.

But the most important aspect of the August convention, from my point of view, was a report by Justine O'Connor, a vice-president of the state committee and a member of the state board. She proclaimed the edicts for the toughening exercises of the party on an educational level, and called for the setting up of a state educational commission to carry out an elaborate program of training in Marxism-Leninism. She proposed a speakers' bureau, a series of training classes for all cadres of the party, the preparation of study outlines and pamphlets delineating the new and more vigorous party policies, an active "cultural" group, and the training of new teachers to carry the message to the rank and file.

I was almost exhausted, mentally and physically, from the fever

160

of activity in the summer of 1945. Communist party affairs had been especially demanding, and of course I had to keep them secret from my business associates. The intensification of security measures within the party made me nervous. My long nights of filing reports to the Bureau robbed me of sleep. The Eighth War Loan Drive conducted by the New England War activities Committee of the entertainment industry through Harry Browning's office also took a great deal of my time.

Eva and I broke away for the first two-week vacation since our marriage six years before. We determined to get as far from the stress of our lives as possible. We attached saddlebags and carriers to our lightweight touring bikes, loaded them with rucksacks, cooking utensils, clothing, provisions, and blankets, and threw them aboard a Boston & Maine train headed for the "high" side of the White Mountains to the north, in New Hampshire. For two solid weeks we coasted south, avoiding civilization, sleeping out nights in a mountain tent, hiking, swimming, mountain climbing, and only occasionally pausing in a town or village to restock our provisions. For two weeks we read no newspapers, heard no radios.

When I returned after Labor Day, it was fortunate that I was well rested. Everybody was waiting for me. The Baptist Church in Wakefield was clamoring for copy for its monthly issue of "The Tall Spire," the church publication of which I was the editor. My office was still wrapped up in the War Loan drive, and, to make matters worse, was tangling with the problems of reconversion to normal peacetime activities. There was a stack of mail and work on my desk. On the pile of messages I found one which told me cryptically that I was to get in touch with the FBI quickly. And the Communist party had three meetings scheduled in which I was to participate.

The call to the Bureau came first, and I learned that it required one of our personal contacts, which by this time had become exceedingly rare, and then very devious. I was under strictest instructions never to be seen talking with anyone from the Bureau office, and in order to be doubly careful I purposely avoided curbstone conversations with any business or social acquaintance who might possibly look to prying eyes like an FBI agent.

The contact was set up. I left the office a few minutes before the appointed time, headed across Scollay Square toward the Suffolk Savings Bank at the far end. Along the side of the square a man fell into step with me.

"Hello." It was Comrade Roy, a newcomer, possibly a party underling or a recent district "floater" whom I had encountered at the state office, but whose mission I did not know. Whatever it was, I did not want him with me now and had to shake him quickly. I returned his greeting without slackening my pace as I glanced at my watch and noticed that my FBI contact was less than a minute away. I looked over my left shoulder and saw that the Bureau as usual was on time. Comrade Roy and I strode across Pemberton Street to the corner cigar stand, where I paused and decided to make the plunge.

"I'm being picked up by a friend," I said, stepping to the corner and raising my hand in signal to the car heading through the square toward Tremont Street. The automobile bore a single distinctive marking which no one would notice unless he was looking for it. "Sorry to duck off, Roy, but I have a business appointment uptown. You know how it is. Oh, could I give you a lift?" I added, with perfect confidence that I could if he wanted it.

"No, thanks," he replied. "Just going up the block a step."

"So long."

I climbed into the car and closed the door. The driver turned to face me with a barely perceptible smile which indicated that everything was all right. "Head down to Park and out Beacon Street," I said. Then I sat back until we had passed the Parker House and left Comrade Roy in our wake.

My contact in the driver's seat, a Bureau agent whose name I

162

was never told, spoke up. "There's an envelope down behind the seat," he said, turning up Park Street. "Take a look." I fished for the envelope and came up with it. Inside I found a passport-type photograph of a heavy-jowled, middle-aged woman.

"Ever see her before?" asked the agent. I examined the picture carefully.

"Nope, not in this area. What level is she?"

"High."

"Who is she?"

"Probably be known by the name of Helen," the agent answered. I searched both the picture and my recollection for a clew.

"I know two Comrade Helens, but this doesn't look like either one of them."

"O.K.," said the agent, with a trace of disappointment in his voice. "If you do run into her, let us know. Name is Elizabeth Bentley. What's doing?" he added in an offhand tone, as if to change the subject. I knew he would have no more to say about the Bentley woman.

"Plenty," I replied. "Right now we are lining up what the rank and file will be digesting this winter."

"Who's running it?"

"For the young members, the Bennetts. For the adults, Fanny Hartman. Tell Hal the party is getting suspicious of everybody. I can't be too careful."

The agent drove me across the Charles River to the Central Square Theater, where he stopped and let me out. "Sorry I couldn't help you," I said, standing beside him for a moment to go through the motions of saying good-by to a friend, just in case I had been followed.

Pondering over the woman in the photograph, and wondering why the Bureau was so anxious to have information about her, I returned to the office by a roundabout route after a routine call on the theater manager, and cleared away the work on my desk as rapidly as possible. Then I got in touch with party headquarters.

From the very first meeting of the reconstituted Communist party, the new spirit of grim militancy was in evidence. All of the leadership received explicit instructions: "There will be a tightening of the party cell and club network. Each leader will be responsible to the district executive and will take orders from him. Iron discipline will prevail throughout."

I learned at district headquarters that a highly secret training class for a dozen or so carefully selected candidates for party teaching posts was in the offing, and that I was on the list which was then being carefully screened through every agency of the party. The purpose of the class would be to train teachers, who in turn would go out to cells in the network, to break down the new party line into its component parts and define a course of action for the membership. I also learned that, despite my close affiliation with the headquarters and the district leaders, I was even then undergoing renewed scrutiny by the Review Commission. The Commission never considered a case to be closed, whether the party member was a lowly "grubber" or one of the top brass. Evidently the Commission was busy.

Browderite deviationists were being frozen out of the party in wholesale lots. They received no more notices of meetings, no assignments, no party communications. For comrades who were thoroughly imbued with communism, in spite of their deviation, it was harsh treatment. They felt a psychological amputation which was mentally painful to them, more so than an outright expulsion under direct charges. Under these conditions it was not unusual for the victims to become so distraught that their families and friends became fearful of suicide.

The new security drive gave the district party, from top to bottom, a severe case of the jitters. Naturally, I did not know all of the ramifications of the screening through which I was going.

But it was dropped into my ear that the Review Commission was on my trail, possibly in the expectation that if anything was wrong my nervousness might betray me. Alice Mills even paid what to all appearances was a routine social call on Eva, but she stayed a long time to chat, probing our household views on racial prejudices, economic problems, and corollary issues. She discussed with Eva the question of the upbringing of our four daughters and Eva's account of the afternoon visit provided interesting counterpoint to the party line for the adult members. The function of women and girls is changing, Alice reminded Eva. . . . A growing girl can look forward to motherhood, but should not be taught that this is her only function. . . . Boys who want to be modern have to include girls in their games when they play soldier. . . . If we prepare our children for their vanguard role we must not hem them in by the narrow restrictions of conventional middle-class sex patterns of behavior.

Since we had no boys, we did not have the regrettable problem that the Communists found in many bourgeois homes. In the culture of these families, according to Communist theory, male children are preferred and are considered better than their sisters. The effect on girls of this "male chauvinism" is deep and permanent. But girls as well as boys should learn the meaning of the picket line.

Such was the conversation between two Communist mothers. Eva was probably the most reluctant Communist on record. Since the Communist party aims to influence the "culture complex" of a nation, this most certainly includes the children; special attention is given children's literature in Communist homes. Thus, when the party Review Commission checks the homes and families of party members, it includes a check of the reading material for the children. The censorship of the party in this respect is severe; such bourgeois accretions as Mother Goose nursery rhymes and fables are considered especially evil. Any fable about a prince or princess is an obvious glorification of the idle rich. *Little Black*

Sambo is deemed an insult to the whole Negro race, and the comrades find that anti-Semitism and "white chauvinism" run rampant in children's classics.

I distinctly remember three children's books lauded and approved by the party although, as far as I know, their authors had no affiliations with the Communists. About the time of *Grapes of Wrath,* Doris Gates wrote *Blue Willow* for children from ten to twelve years old. The party expressed favorable opinion—sharecroppers driven off the land, "dirt-poor" family, etc. The party objected, however, to its "romantic ending which destroyed its reality." Later on, in 1948, the party applauded Lois Lenski for *Judy's Journey,* for "an appreciation of economic struggle not ordinarily found in children's books." Also approved was *Anchor Man,* by Jesse Jackson. A Negro is the hero of the story, the Negro school is "underprivileged," and the hero's brother is "sold down the river" by a white fight trainer.

Eva acquitted us well, and at the same time demonstrated to Alice that four small girls, ranging in age from five months to five and a half years, were so demanding that Eva could not possibly spare the time to engage in party activities with me.

I began to be wary of traps. At the twenty-sixth anniversary meeting of the Communist party in Boston, I thought I spotted one. It was a semipublic meeting, and Eva attended with me. As we walked down the aisle of the big New England Mutual Life Insurance Company auditorium that night, a slightly built, bespectacled lad followed on our heels. He stopped and took a seat beside me. He engaged me in conversation initiated by himself despite my rebuffs. He gave me his name, told me that he was of German descent and had been in the United States about two years. He tried diligently—and in vain—to draw me out. He mentioned the names of numerous members of the party hierarchy, on both the national and international levels. He set the conversation up as a perfect opportunity for a government agent to go after valuable information. It was a highly irregular performance

166

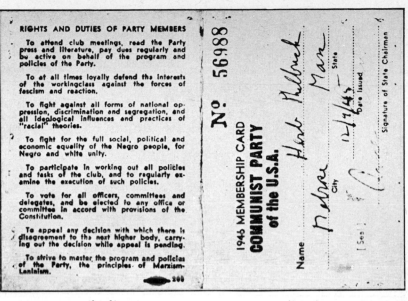

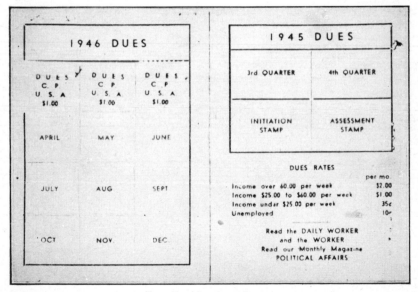

(back)   *(front)*

(inside spread)

Two views of Philbrick's 1946 Communist party card. When the party instructed him to destroy it at the time he was assigned an underground role, Philbrick sent it to the FBI for safekeeping. The signature of the state chairman, which is difficult to read, is that of Anne Burlak, "The Red Flame."

Judge Harold R. Medina, who presided over the trial of the eleven Communist leaders for nine grueling months. (*Acme*)

The eleven Communist leaders, convicted of conspiracy to overthrow the government of the United States. Philbrick knew many of them personally and the evidence he gave against them as the government's star witness at the trial was an important factor in their conviction. Left to right (seated): Robert G. Thompson, Henry Winston, Eugene Dennis, Gus Hall, John B. Williamson; (standing): Jacob Stachel, Irving Potash, Carl Winter, Benjamin F. Davis, Jr., John Gates, Gilbert Green. (*Acme*)

for a good Communist. I reflected that if he was a spy he was a very crude one, and refused to encourage any of his conversation.

Following a long series of speeches, tableaux and pageants, I nudged Eva. "Let's get out of here." She nodded. I turned to our friend. "I'm sorry," I said, "but we must leave." He shot me a glance full of disappointment and approbation. "The sitter problem, you know." He looked a little relieved and smiled that he understood. We slid past him in the darkness, but before we left I turned, leaned toward him and whispered, "By the way, my friend, it is not wise to talk so much."

The party's security consciousness was given its deepest shock when, on October 10, 1945, Louis Budenz abruptly announced his resignation as managing director of the *Daily Worker,* his renunciation of communism, and his return to the Catholic Church. The uneasiness of the membership turned into cold rage. This was treason in high places. The rank-and-file members had already been fed the "treason" of Earl Browder. This was perhaps the first time in party history when the ordinary members looked askance at their leaders. Suspicion was rampant. If a top member of the national organization could be a traitor, so could an officer of the district organization or a branch leader. The shock gave credence to Don Tormey's argument that the evil spirit of Browder still lingered in the hearts of some of the party functionaries.

Self-criticism was no answer to this problem. A hard and vicious counterattack was decreed. New efforts were ordered to quell once and for all any criticism of national or local leaders within the party. I attended one secret meeting for discussion of the Budenz affair. Our speaker was unknown to us. "Comrade Sam" was his only name. He was plainly in a belligerent mood.

"We have no reason to cover up the Budenz betrayal," he told us, as we huddled in the warmth of a small, dingy room under the glare of a single overhead lamp. "Who was Budenz? From the very beginning his background was sinful and treacherous. He was an underling who wormed his way into a position of leader-

167

ship for his own profit. Budenz," Comrade Sam said with an air of stern warning, "was incorrectly promoted without sufficient testing.

"The main lesson we have learned is that we are not only surrounded by the class enemy. The enemy's agents are at work within our ranks, too. We will find them out."

His emphatic pause fell on a moment of intense silence. Comrade Sam's face was cruelly etched by the slanting glare of the single electric lamp. The pause was punctuated by the measured breathing of twenty men and women in the room.

Everyone stared straight at the speaker or the wall behind him, not daring to steal a glance at his neighbor. While I felt an intense discomfort, as if the eyes of the person behind me were drilling through my head, I knew that I was not alone, that everyone in the room, whatever his position in the party or his motives in being there, was uneasy. The speaker let his glance roam about the room.

"The party must and will act ruthlessly," he went on slowly, pausing after almost every word. "From top to bottom the Review Commission will root out and destroy the agents of the enemy who smuggle themselves into our ranks. We will overlook nothing.

"There are many in the party who, like Budenz, are not innocent. That does not mean that all comrades will be disciplined for connections with the class enemy in the past, so long as the past has been repudiated and the comrades have proved themselves in the struggle. It does mean that all comrades must be doubly conscious of their past."

The speaker continued with the usual discourse about discipline, the elimination of weaklings, and the necessity of building a strong, tough party ready for any struggle. We were more relaxed by the time he had finished. But when the meeting broke up, no one had much to say to anyone else. From that time on, the name Budenz was seldom heard in the party.

168

CHAPTER 11

SECRET UNDERGROUND PRESSES are a vital adjunct to the Communist party in every non-Communist nation, including the United States. Propaganda and education are the keystones on which the movement to subvert a people and their government must be built. Communication and agitation by means of the printed word, through pamphlets, magazines, leaflets, and newspapers, are essential to the structure.

During the "legitimate" phase of Communist party activity, printing operations are carried on through legal, aboveground presses. But every party member is instructed that in any nation, as communism gains strength and becomes a serious threat, vigorous countermeasures will be taken by heavy-handed legal authorities to suppress it. And one of the first of these will be an effort to close down the presses which grind out reams of "agit-prop" (agitation-propaganda) material daily. If its presses could actually be shut down, the party would suffer a crippling blow. But the fact is that they cannot.

For as the party goes deeper and deeper underground its presses go with it, and operations continue more energetically than ever. Communists in the United States are well prepared for the ultimate outlawing of their press. As early as 1945, when I became a member of the six-man Educational Commission of the Massachusetts Communist party, I first became acutely aware of the existence and constant strengthening of a far-flung network of underground presses.

Some of the party's stand-by presses and equipment are kept in dead storage against the day when they may have to be used. There is also a considerable stockpile of scarce paper and printing ink held in reserve. But for the most part, the "underground" party press is already on an operational footing, not lying idle and concealed in secret cellars. They are working in the open behind legitimate and respectable business fronts, making and taking in money through every available source for their own support. In some cases they represent large and well-known printing and publishing houses. But they are run by trusted party comrades who will be ready to take them underground when the word is given. In the meantime, they frequently turn out covert material for the party, material which it is inadvisable to print on the organization's open and legal presses.

My job as assistant advertising manager of the M. & P. Theaters in Boston brought me into close contact with the printing and publishing trades, and also with the Communist underground press. First of all the party made use of me, sandwiching its publication orders for its front groups into my regular business orders, and I learned which printers were in the pocket of the party. I was instructed to take care to spread these jobs around to avoid giving too many of them to one house. I paid the bills in cash and was reimbursed by party headquarters.

As a member of the propaganda division of the party, I came to know many of its skilled personnel, including its printing-shop operators. Because of my close affiliation with commercial printing houses, I was invited to inspect the newest "secret" party press in Boston—a complete, modern shop set up to handle job printing by the offset method. The party asked me to look over the plant and offer any suggestions for efficient operation. The advantage of offset is that it can handle reprints without setting type, or if necessary can eliminate the linotype altogether, and print unlimited copies from typewritten masters.

I did a thorough job for the party. Then I went a step farther.

"Let me have a few samples of your work to show around," I suggested. "Perhaps I can throw some work your way." I was given a full set of all the types of work produced on the press. It was most considerate of the party to let me have them. They went directly to the FBI, where they doubtless are still on file—a set of "fingerprints" with distinctive characteristics through which any work turned out in the future by the same press can easily be traced. In addition, I obtained a complete inventory of the plant's equipment, including the model numbers for every important piece of apparatus.

As a good party member it was wise for me to help provide the necessary smoke screen for press operations. Accordingly, one day, when a good—and non-Communist—friend, Sam Baker, a salesman for the Lithomat Company, approached me with a problem, I was glad to help him.

"Herb," he said, "I have heard of a job to be done in a hurry. It's offset, runs about three hundred pages. But it is such a short run that the printer who has it now doesn't want to bother with it. The job would be done before they could get their presses rolling at normal speed. Any suggestions?"

"Sure. I know the solution," I said, thinking of the party offset press I had inspected. "I know a good printer just getting started. I'm sure he'd be glad to take it, and give you a good price, too." I gave Sam the name and address of the shop.

Some time later I called again at the printing shop on another mission. "Say," the printer spoke up after we had finished our business, "that was a nice job your friend Sam Baker had in his pocket. A United States government job."

"A government job!"

I tried to show some enthusiasm, but I must have paled. Perhaps I had made a terrible blunder. Sam Baker had told me nothing about the government, and naturally he did not know he was dealing with a Communist press. My first thought was the possibility of espionage. But the party had made a mistake, too.

"Yep," said the printer, "too bad we had to turn it down."

"Turn it down!" I exclaimed. "Why did you do that?"

"Security. We would have had to get clearance before we could have the job. We're in no position to be investigated by a bunch of FBI snoopers. I didn't think they would find a thing wrong with us, but headquarters said they didn't want to run the risk just now."

"Oh," I sympathized, with some relief. "That's too bad. What did you tell Sam?"

"Just that we weren't set up well enough yet to handle that many plates for quick delivery."

While party presses are available for quantity printing, many of the most highly secret documents were produced on the little headquarters mimeograph machine which I had rebuilt and frequently operated. In the fall of 1945, the party carefully screened 1,500 Communists in the Boston area to attend a super-secret training school in Marxism. I was selected as one of the sixteen candidates. Outlines for the course were prepared from a master copy provided by the party's national headquarters. Extreme caution was decreed to prevent the study outline from falling into the hands of any comrade outside the school. A limited number of copies was run off on the mimeograph, enough for each of the sixteen students and the instructors who would handle the training course.

It was a valuable document. It showed how Marxism was to be taught in Boston, and elsewhere too, no doubt, as a living and fighting force, applicable to our own times and our own country. It was a simple matter to get it into the hands of the Bureau. After each stencil was typed, I slipped out the thin fiber paper lining the backing sheet, stuffed them all into my pockets, and mailed them to the FBI. The government had the full course outline before any of the students saw it.

The secret teacher-training course was scheduled for eight sessions, one night a week, to be held in October and November of 1945 at the West End Communist Club off Scollay Square in downtown Boston. The appointed evening for the first session was cold and dismal. I worked late in my office on the square, then stepped out for a bite of supper at Joe and Nemo's Restaurant, famous—or notorious (depending on the point of view)—eating place of the burlesque stars. From there, cognizant of party instructions to avoid any chance of detection, I wound my way up the dark, narrow streets of Beacon Hill, then proceeded to the upper part of Hancock Street, and moved downhill again toward the square. The hill was almost deserted, in contrast to the evening crowds moving through adjacent Scollay and Bowdoin Squares. Walking down the rough brick surface of Hancock Street, I slowed my pace and surveyed the scene. It was deserted, except for passers-by at the foot of the street. A single street lamp on the corner cast deep shadows into the doorways of the old Beacon Hill buildings. No one loitered at the intersection with the square. I expected to find some kind of FBI lookout—a parked car, a truckman repairing a flat tire, a "drunken bum," some evidence of a plant—but I was unable to detect a single one.

Crossing the street toward the corner two-story brick building, I slipped in the doorway of Number 3 Hancock Street, ostensibly the headquarters of a bricklayers union, actually the blind for the West End Communist Club and the secret training school. I stood in a dim hallway from which led a broad flight of wooden stairs. At first there was no sound. Then I heard muffled voices from the floor above. I went up the stairs, turned down a narrow corridor into which the only light spilled through the glass partition of one of the offices. Opening the door I found a small room lighted by a single ceiling lamp. There was a table laden with overcoats, hats, and scarves. To the left was another table and three chairs. There were four or five rows of folding chairs facing the table.

At the table, Fanny Hartman sat in whispered conversation with a woman whose back was to me but whose hair, even under the dim light, was markedly red. I permitted my glance to move quickly over the faces of the students without lingering or showing any sign of recognition. There were only a few in the group who were known to me by sight or by name. I tossed my coat on top of the others, took a seat at the rear of the class, and rocked my chair back against the hot radiator. No word of greeting was spoken to me. One member of the class turned sideways and raised a finger in salutation. I smiled back and turned my attention to the instructors' table, squinting past the yellow ball of light hanging from the ceiling. Then I nearly fell out of my tilted chair.

The young woman with the red hair was Dr. Hulda McGarvey. I had previously encountered Hulda in connection with the Sam Adams School for Social Studies, and regarded her as one of many misguided liberals enticed into teaching posts in the Communist-front training school. But I was shocked to see her here in the inner circle of the Communist party. A graduate of Smith College and Columbia University, a former instructor at Mount Holyoke College, and an assistant professor of psychology at Smith, she was a highly regarded academician, unknown for any intimate Communist party connections.

Fanny Hartman glanced about the room, and, assured that her full class was assembled, passed out the course outlines. Then, as the woman boss of the district party, she went to work.

"Comrades," her soft voice was like the stropping of a razor in the still room. "You all realize that this is not simply a routine course in Marxism-Leninism. You are all experienced enough, I hope, to know most of the facts of Marxist-Leninist teachings. If not, you wouldn't be here. This is a course to instruct you how to teach others, how to train your own comrades. You will have the responsibility of training our cadres so that they in turn can go out and win the workers to the socialist struggle against the fascist imperialists of the world, and in particular, the United States.

"This is a long-range program, part of an organized campaign throughout the party to rid every unit of the last vestiges of Browderism, to deepen the understanding of Marxist-Leninist theory." She leaned forward in her chair for emphasis. "In particular, you

174

will study the application of Marx and Lenin to the conditions of the United States today. Your responsibilities will include organizing city and branch schools, and you will carry out a systematic checkup of Marxist study in every cell. You will lead some of the educational classes yourselves, and you will instruct others to lead similar classes."

The class members shuffled about in their chairs and settled down for a long session. I began making notes. Fanny delved into the importance of the tactics of proper teaching. A good instructor, she explained, can teach and influence any person along Communist lines no matter what his position in life.

"Take the *Communist Manifesto,* which all of you have read. Now this great work can be given to anybody to read and study— whether he is a member of the bourgeoisie, the petty bourgeoisie, or the proletariat. But the method of presenting it must be different in each case. We know that in the strategy and tactics of the class struggle, everything depends upon the conditions, the time, and the place. In the educational work of the party, everything depends upon the individual, his position in society, and especially his attitude toward that position. What does that mean?

"Of course," she went right on, not waiting for an answer from the class, "it means that for one person we must say that the *Communist Manifesto* is a great historical document, a masterpiece a hundred years old written by a great student of human nature and human history. Anyone, even the most reactionary capitalist or the most conservative bourgeois, might be convinced to read and study the *Manifesto* on this cultural, historical level.

"For the non-Communist workingman it does not have to be sugar-coated. In teaching the *Manifesto* to the working class, we say that it contains the answers to all of the evils under which these people work—wage cuts, high prices, depressions, and loss of jobs. It is the key, but only the key, to open the door to further Marxist understanding. Workers must be urged to use that key as an entrance to further study.

"Later, if we do a good job, it will become to them what it is to us, a guide to action—action, and not a mere historical document. It is especially a guide to action in so far as the need for revolution to overthrow capitalist imperialism is concerned. But we do not teach this to new members or to prospective members at the outset. We must lead them gradually, step by step, to lay the foundation first. That, of course, is the main purpose of our public courses in the Sam Adams School and others like it."

Fanny turned the class over to Hulda McGarvey, who started us off with the party definition of the three classes of society. First, she said, there is the bourgeoisie, the sixty top capitalist-class families who own and control the nation's means of production. These people inevitably are the enemies of the working class, and, with some notable exceptions in the case of disgruntled and idealistic members, cannot be won to the Communist side. It is this class which must be attacked without mercy, which in the end must be crushed and liquidated, together with their state machine for the exploitation of the working class.

The proletarians, the masses of the working people, are the natural allies of the party. They own no means of production, but earn their living through their labor. They are at all times at the mercy of the landlords, the bankers, and the bourgeois bosses. It is from the proletariat that most recruits must be enrolled into the Communist party.

The petty bourgeoisie represents a special class, Hulda said, and special conditions must be observed for handling it. This is the great middle class, especially in the United States, the "professional" people. Of course, the instructor explained, we know that the middle class is vanishing. It is being crushed between the inexorable contradictions of capitalist masters and capitalist slaves. But it is still large enough to constitute a separate class.

Actually, Hulda droned on, the petty bourgeois—small busi-

176

nessman, shopkeeper, "independent" operator—is a dupe and a fool. He is no more a capitalist than the ordinary workingman. He has no control over his destiny. But he imagines that he has. He is the tool of the capitalist who can and does crush and extinguish him at will.

Therefore, the petty bourgeois is in reality a member of the proletariat, the only difference being that he does not know it. We can sometimes win these people over if we present the facts properly. Certain members of the petty bourgeoisie can become extremely valuable allies. But since the average person in this class imagines himself to be a capitalist, he is dangerous to us because of his stupidity. In a crisis, he becomes an ally of the capitalists, and they must be crushed and destroyed together.

Hulda closed with a discussion of the application of socialist and Communist literature to the various classes. She stressed the necessity of gauging the proper "level" of a raw recruit, and said that it was impossible to start off immediately by teaching the urgency of revolution. To do so would scare the prospect away. He must be started at the right place, then brought along step by step, without losing control on the way.

There was a very brief question-and-answer period, but few questions were asked, all of them routine. We were dismissed, donned our coats, and disappeared singly or in small groups. Once again in the street, I surveyed the scene, and found no one in the vicinity of the building as I plodded up Beacon Hill.

Within a few days I found another cryptographic message on my desk requesting a personal contact with the Bureau the following morning. To meet the appointment I left the house early for work, and stopped at a diner near the city limits where I frequently filled my vacuum bottle with morning coffee.

The place was almost empty. The morning's run 'of hungry truckmen had come and gone. As I stepped to the counter I was greeted in a loud voice by a man behind me, seated in a corner booth where I expected to find him.

"Well," I effused, "fancy seeing you here." I walked over and shook hands, and we raised a blather of, "How are you? Fine, fine. How've you been?"

"Join me for a cup of coffee?" suggested the FBI agent who was indulging in a breakfast pastry. I accepted and sat down. We continued to chatter idly while my coffee was brought.

"How's the family?" I asked, knowing full well that he had none.

"Say,"—he reached into his inner coat pocket—"I have those pictures we took at the picnic." He produced a sheaf of snapshots and passed them across the table to me. On the top was a smiling young woman, a child on each side of her.

"Good shot," I said. There was no one near the booth now. I turned my back to the window as if to get a better light. The counterman was serving another customer at the far end of the diner. I peeled off the top picture.

Next was a close-up of me in semiprofile, wearing hat and topcoat, with the doorway of No. 3 Hancock Street plainly visible in the background. "Not bad," I said. There followed in succession pictures of Dr. Hulda McGarvey, Fanny Hartman, my old friends Joy and Margot Clark, and each one of the students of the secret Hancock Street school, all snapped as they left the building. The faces had the pale-lipped, ghostly translucence of infrared "black-light" photography. "I'll be darned," I said, recalling my careful scrutiny of the street corner during which I had tried in vain to pick out a possible hidden camera post. "I didn't even know you took these."

"No?" he smiled. We spoke freely and with no effort to subdue our voices. "Candid pictures are the best. By the way, some of that crowd that came with you I didn't know too well. Would you mind putting down their names for my album?" I turned the pictures over. Several of them, including some I didn't know, were already marked, "Identified." The rest I filled in as best I could, either with their party pseudonyms or their real names,

178

and in the end nearly everyone in the course was pinned down for the FBI files.

The special class continued, one night a week, two hours or more each session, constantly increasing in anticapitalist and revolutionary intensity. More than twenty-five textbooks were used, including *Political Economy,* by Leontiev; *Value, Price and Profit,* by Marx; *Socialism, Utopian and Scientific,* by Engels; *Imperialism,* by Lenin; and *Milestones in the History of the Communist Party, U.S.A.,* by Bittelman, who was later indicted.

This was ostensibly nothing more than a study of the classics, as any of these people would have insisted on a witness stand. But it was plainly no mere cultural pursuit. The austere nature of the classroom; the grim aspects of the students assembling intently once each week at an appointed hour to scrutinize the history of socialist and Communist revolutionary movements; the absence of humor; the discipline of the class; the purposefulness of the instructors sitting at the table with the naked light slashing across their faces—all these were the marks of a true conspiracy.

It was understandably necessary for them to speak in circumlocutions, to use the Aesopian dodges of Communist lingo. After all, the Communist party was even then working under the shadow of the Smith Act, making the teaching and advocacy of violent revolution a crime in the United States. The law was passed without fanfare in 1940 and was directed, at that time, more at fascist organizations than at the Communists. Now the Communists recognized the law as being applicable to their own teachings, which they took great pains to cloak in the greatest secrecy. Yet I was amazed at the transparency of the disguise.

The instructors—Fanny Hartman, Dr. McGarvey, and Comrade Sam—put across some of their points by "innocent" historical example, citing and elaborating upon pertinent passages in the revolutionary "classics." Constantly they admonished us to bear in mind that "we understand these things. But not everyone

179

you will teach has such understanding. Certainly a new member is not expected to have full knowledge of the tactics and strategy of the party. He must be led by degrees to a better appreciation of the facts by gradually raising the level of his understanding. Raise the level! Raise the level!"

But we understood. Otherwise, as Fanny said, we would not have assembled there in the chill atmosphere, poor light, and personal discomfort hour after hour to go over it.

We as students knew that when the instructors spoke of the materialist order of constant and inevitable changes in society, they meant now, today, not 1789 in France or 1914 in Russia.

We knew that when they told us man's destiny is conditioned by events over which he has no control, they meant today's man, not some historic creature caught up in some past upheaval.

We knew that when they said violent revolution is one of the abrupt changes decreed by the laws of nature, they were not speaking of history, but metaphorically they were endeavoring to shape future events.

We knew that when they said violent revolution was necessary for the overthrow of a capitalist czardom, they meant that it would be equally necessary for the ultimate overthrow of "capitalist imperialism" in the United States.

There was no room for misinterpretation of this line. No alternative political or social theses were taught. It was straight down the line toward Marxist revolution. We were under no illusions as to what was meant when we were told that the ballot box and orderly procedure do not suffice, that man is antipathetic to reforms by legal process, and that armed force alone will suffice.

We knew all this well from our years of Marxist indoctrination. I knew it. And still, when Fanny Hartman took off the gloves and slugged it out in plain language, it came as such a shock to me that I almost dropped my pencil and forgot to take my notes.

"Once we have taught that all of this is perfectly natural,"

Fanny said, "that it is all to be expected, then we are ready to state our position. And what is the definition of 'revolution?' Do we mean something like the Industrial Revolution? No. We mean violent revolution to be carried out by armed bands of workers, led by the Communist party, the vanguard of the working class. Only through such a revolution can socialism be established. Only with the Communist party as the leader can the revolution be successful."

A stillness fell when she stopped speaking. Not a foot shuffled. This was outright sedition, the first such blunt assertion of it I had ever heard in party councils. I felt a paroxysm of excitement as I transcribed her words for detailed quotation in my report to the Bureau. In the report I superimposed one of my rare interpretations onto the bare facts. "There are no holds barred now," I said. "This takes us back to the naked Bolshevik line with no trimmings."

One night a dark stranger occupied a place at the instructors' table. He was given no introduction to the class. His appearance was very brief, and he had only a few words to say to the class. But it soon became evident that his soft voice carried the weight of the national Politburo. He spoke of the reconstitution of the party, the reestablishment of rigid Marxism in every segment of party organization, the renewal of the struggle against bourgeois influences.

"Comrades," he added, "as a result of the war we have seen a great intensification of the contradictions between the two world systems—socialism and capitalism. In this country we shall see a sharper growth of fascism and the building of the class struggle which will eventually bring the establishment of socialism. The party does not consider the raising of the question of revolution as an immediate slogan for action. We must first reorganize the party in its vanguard role and function as the leader of the American proletariat.

"Under Browder's revisionism we have become soft. This calls for a special evaluation, and for an increase of our internal as well

181

as our external vigilance. Externally, we must defeat Red baiting. Internally we must take special measures to protect our party organization and membership. We must deal ruthlessly with agents of the enemy. You," he said, his eyes passing around the room and missing none of us, "will have special responsibilities in this task."

My "special responsibilities" soon became plain. After one of the class sessions toward the end of the course, Fanny Hartman stopped me at the door and drew me aside.

"There will be a special meeting of a new group at the office Saturday afternoon," she told me, out of earshot of the others. "Two o'clock. Be sure to be there."

On the following Saturday I passed the morning at the M. & P. Theaters office cleaning up some back work. Then, after lunch, I proceeded to district headquarters, rode the elevator to the sixth floor, walked down a flight on the fire stairs, and entered the Communist party headquarters.

The meeting was held in Fanny Hartman's inner sanctum. But I was surprised to discover that Fanny was not there. Present in the room was Justine O'Connor, Otis Hood, a gnomelike little man, and another big, hulking brute, neither of whom I had ever seen before. At a later date we were joined by the lanky and brilliant Daniel Boone Schirmer. But at this first meeting there were no introductions, not even by first names. The big man occupied Fanny Hartman's place, and seemed to take over her job as well. He talked more freely than Fanny and in a loud, positive voice. He gave orders bluntly. Many of his statements he put in the form of questions to which the answers were self-evident.

The group of six Communists came to be known among us privately as the Jack Stachel Group for New England. More formally, it was the District Educational Commission of the Communist party, operating directly under Jack Stachel as the national educational director. But we seldom saw him in person.

Everyone knew—and stood in awe of—the name of Jack Stachel. In the peculiar half-light of information shed upon the leading functionaries of the party, his authority was carried more by inference than by direct communication. It was my impression that not many comrades were permitted to meet him face to face. Stachel, then about forty-five, also known as Jankel, Jacob Zunser, and Moses Brown, had been a professional revolutionary all of his adult life. He had shortly before been made the national educational director of the Communist party and in 1949 was indicted as one of the top twelve Communist leaders.

The big man who ran the group at the outset was Emmanuel or "Manny" Blum, a New York–trained Communist sent by national headquarters to New England to replace Fanny Hartman as district organizer. There were policy differences between Fanny and the National Committee, the precise nature of which was never made plain. It was an unfortunate day for the party in New England when the domineering and bludgeoning Manny Blum displaced the sharp and rapierlike Fanny Hartman. But displace her he did, and the organization and indoctrination of the Jack Stachel Group was the first stage in the maneuver to shoulder Fanny out of power in the district.

The members of the group had no direct contact with each other, except on occasions when we were assembled for periodic reports. We were assigned to work in various Congressional districts into which the party was subdivided for political activities. I drew the Eighth Congressional District of Massachusetts as my territory. We were to operate in all of the branches and cells of our areas as educational and literature directors, visiting, talking, teaching, circulating—and inquiring. Manny Blum indicated the line of our inquiry.

"We do not worry about people like Budenz. Is he not already discredited by his own treason? Of what consequence is Budenz? We are probably enrolling more Budenzes into the party even now. Let us look at this sensibly."

183

Manny gave a laugh. We were a select group, in the privacy of his office now, and he could speak with even more than his customary frankness.

"Someone comes into the party in 1946. He works for us, say, ten years, fifteen years, hard labor. Then he quits the party. So? It is 1946 when he joins. It may be 1961 before he deserts us. We shall always have a certain number of deserters, traitors. But are we going to worry today because we will have a traitor in 1961? We will politely discredit him as a turn-coat; no one will trust him."

Manny smiled at the consternation written on our faces. Then his smile vanished and his swarthy face clouded.

"The time to stop a traitor is before he can become a traitor. In Russia they deal with such things realistically. Here? In this country we have a capitalist government which spawns traitors, offers them the sanctuary, the honor, and the reward for their treason."

"But," someone said, "shouldn't Budenz and others like him have their reward, too?"

"Not every traitor," Manny interjected, "accomplishes his plans. After all, it is most difficult. Naturally, to protect our party and our members, we should not make it easy for them, eh? Under such circumstances is it unlikely that they should—commit suicide? Or are there not other conditions that may cause them to reconsider? But we must recognize that some people will be weakened by bourgeois influences. It is up to us—to you—to find out who these people are. To discover them. To weed them out. To eliminate them. Destroy them."

In plain language, Manny was giving us a mission to spy on party members. The assignment gave me more than a moment's pause. First of all life was becoming enormously complex for me. On one page, I was the conservative businessman, suburban churchgoer, liberal Republican, civic enterpriser. On the next I was a deep-dyed member of the Communist party of New England, sitting in on its multifarious conspiracy. Between the lines,

184

I was a Federal Bureau of Investigation confidential agent, striving to perform a service. Within these categories, there were already more subdivisions than I could keep track of.

Now the party itself was grooming me for still another role, that of a member of a sort of junior review commission, with the task of strengthening the very movement I was trying to fight, by ferreting out its weaklings and potential traitors. I was burrowing so deep that I feared I might yet be trapped in the catacombs.

There were shocks and surprises at almost every turn, in business, in my family life, and within the party. There were so many snares and traps tossed in my path that it was almost impossible to avoid tripping up somewhere along the way. My father, for many years a railroad man in Boston, stormed red-faced into my office one day after his morning run from Portsmouth to Boston on the Boston & Maine. He was seething with anger. In his hand he waved a leaflet.

"I have been picking these up all over the North Station," he fumed. "Who do these people think they are, anyway? Who do they represent?" He glanced at the leaflet and tossed it disdainfully on my desk. "Railway Employees Branch of the Communist Party of New England!" Dad snorted.

I contrived to examine the leaflet with deep concern. It was a piece of routine agitational literature concerning the hours, wages, and working conditions of railway employees. It was issued in the name of the party branch whose title Dad had read. I knew the answer to his question. The railway employees "branch" was a figment of my own imagination, a designation invented by me with the approval of my party superiors, created for a special campaign among railroad workers. I wrote the propaganda leaflet myself, and helped with the arrangements for its distribution among Boston & Maine employees at the North Station.

I agreed with Dad that it was not so good.

But I could find no humor in some of my more recent discoveries. Here, in the so-called Stachel Group, I was dealing with the party professionals. Hood, Justine O'Connor, Schirmer, and Blum were all paid officials of the party, deriving at least part of their livelihood from their position. The gnomish man, who turned out to be Max Weitzman, and I were the only "volunteer" party workers in the new District Educational Commission. The cynicism and duplicity of the salaried officials was a revelation to me, even in my role as a Marxist.

Rank-and-file members were exhorted constantly to fight "fascism" in the United States, and it was our job as educational commissioners to keep up the fight. But in private, our conversation had a different color. Take for example the archenemy of the Communists, the House Un-American Activities Committee, which was shortened by party members, not alone for the sake of brevity, to the "Un-American" Committee.

"The House Commitee? Bah!" Manny Blum would say. "How much more are we helped than we are harmed? What can they do? They call us before the committee. So we put on a suitable performance. Everything depends upon the conditions, the time, and the place. Going before the House Committee is a chance for winning as many friends as we can to the party, and creating as many enemies of the American Congress as possible."

Boone Schirmer voiced agreement. "Lenin says, 'We do not seek to cover up the contradictions in capitalism, but seek to expose and unravel them.' We don't try to cover up the fascist trend or minimize the class struggle. The faster the development of fascism, the greater the increase in the class struggle. The bigger the growth of bureaucracy, the nearer the day of socialism."

Within the Stachel Group, a group dominated by professional party workers, there was then no genuine concern that the United States was, as we told the rank-and-filers, "heading straight for the fascist state." It was to the interest of the party that the country become more fascist, not less. And yet, outside of its secret councils, the Communist party posed with its own membership as the champion of antifascism.

186

The same double standard applied to the direction of the party's firing line, down among the lowly grubbers. "Work them into the most precarious positions, and hope that trouble will brew," we were told. "Once a grubber gets cracked over the head with a police club, we don't have to argue with him about the existence or nonexistence of police brutality."

It would not serve any purpose that I could see for me to become an expert snooper for the party. I had no stomach for it. If some member of the party could be persuaded to turn his coat, all to the good. In all of my party work there came a time when I had to draw a line. I was not anxious to root out any "enemy agents," among which the FBI had first place. Furthermore, I didn't like the implication behind the phrase "destroy them." This was an ambiguous term to which one might apply any number of meanings. Then there was the delightful proposition that "in Russia they deal with such things realistically." The prime example of the reward of a deviationist, which every casual student of history must know, was that of Leon Trotsky, who was assassinated by Stalin's agents in Mexico on August 21, 1940.

Instances came within the range of my experience which proved for me that disciplinary measures taken to silence a "traitor" could be of a very permanent nature. I attended one conference at which the impending liquidation of a member was discussed (it did not take place, I am glad to report); on another occasion a responsible party functionary bragged that a Communist suspected by the party of being a government agent had "successfully committed suicide"; and finally, I was told on reliable authority that a comrade, thought to be weak and unreliable, was literally driven to suicide by his Communist "friends."

The course I followed as a party counterspy in the Stachel Group was to lie low, take no initiative, and cover up as much as possible by concentrating on my less harmful functions as an educational and literary director. I visited the branches and cells in my area, lugging a brown zipper bag bulging with party pamphlets, helping to teach and organize Marxist classes and party activities on the community level. But I volunteered no reports on any findings or suspicions of party weaklings.

However, my back was put to the wall.

"What do you know about Comrade Whitey?" Boone Schirmer asked me without warning, one night at party headquarters. I thought I knew what he was aiming at, but I wanted to duck it if possible.

"Whitey?" I shrugged. "Not much. Married, no children, has his own house, good workman, good labor union leader in the AFL. . . ."

"But how good a Communist is he?"

I was not prepared to give Schirmer an answer, even if I had wanted to. "Of course I don't see much of him, because I am almost never in his branch, except for cell meetings."

"Look into it," Schirmer snapped, and turned on his heel.

Whitey was the chairman of the Melrose branch of the party, an underground Communist with a long record of party activity. Quite unaccustomed to the idea that I was supposed to investigate a branch chairman, I set out to do so with little enthusiasm for the job. I called at his home, became more and more friendly, met his wife, and even helped him strip wallpaper during a house renovation. Eva and I invited them to visit us. Because inquisitiveness was now not only excusable to my district superiors but also desirable, I was able to go much further with Whitey than I had ever dared to go for the Bureau.

Whitey accepted my offers of friendship, and strangely enough, I liked him personally. I didn't want to blackball him, nor did I want to perform the disservice of sending him deeper into the Communist party. My report did not condemn him, nor did it express any enthusiasm for his party abilities. Actually Whitey and his wife were both devoted, sincere, and idealistic party members who gave much time to their cause with no expectation of reward. I turned in to the Stachel Education Commission all the

188

details I could muster, but the report was indecisive. When it was completed, I cut off my connections with him, and returned to the party's underground. As a result of the report, Whitey was not advanced to a post which had been under consideration for him. It was the last complete investigation I was called upon to make. Evidently the party leaders concluded that I was not a competent undercover agent. They directed me to other work.

CHAPTER 12

"ANTHONY M. ROCHE will be our man."

Spoken in the shrouded secrecy of a Communist cell meeting in Malden, Massachusetts, in late 1945, this decision was the oral evidence to me that the Communist party had abandoned all sense of political principle and wrapped itself instead in a cloak of political pretense.

In 1945, communism in the United States returned, after a brief change of course, to its traditional policy of disruptive politics. During the war years, under Earl Browder, the party line was tied, however tenuously, to a hope that first socialism and ultimately a Communist state might be attained by constitutional methods through the ballot box. But when Browder was ushered out the back door, the party embraced once more its historic doctrine that, to quote the *History of the C.P.S.U.(B.)*, "the liberation of the working class from the yoke of capitalism cannot be effected by slow changes, by reforms, but only by a qualitative change of the capitalist system, by revolution."

So the party quit its brief temporary alliance with the Constitution and the ballot box and gave up all pretext of achieving its aims by collaboration with the American political system. But this was not to signify that the party would turn its back on politics, because the true Marxist knows his tools and how to use them. The restoration of revolutionary Marxism also carried with it the doctrine: "We must not cover up the contradictions of the capitalist system, but disclose and unravel them."

The nation's political machinery still remained as a tool that could be used for another purpose, not with any expectation of gaining office or winning reforms, but rather as a vast propaganda sounding board through which the party could "sharpen the contradictions" in the class struggle. If the Communists could no longer make use of constitutional politics as a direct roadway to their objectives, at least they could tear up the pavement to help force a Marxist detour. From campaign platforms throughout the nation they could harangue, disrupt, and harass. They could sow dissension and distrust, inspire divisions, create distinctions between classes, and set one against the other in bitterness and frustration. There would be no effort to present enduring political solutions, nor even to make sound political sense. If one theory held that unity and purpose in a nation could be sought through the electorate, then it followed for the Communists that the electorate could be exploited to generate disunity and confusion. Every election campaign from the local school board to the Presidency became fair game for Communist intrusion and infiltration—with or without the knowledge or assent of the candidates.

Anthony M. Roche was a Democratic candidate for Congress from the Eighth Congressional District of Massachusetts in the 1946 off-year election. The Roche campaign was an example of what can happen on the local level to an anti-Communist candidate, in an anti-Communist community, when a handful of ardent Communists seek to use him as a propaganda outlet. He had no opportunity to give his assent when the Communist party branch of Malden, Massachusetts, moved in on his campaign. He did not even know it. He had no idea that he had been carefully hand-picked ahead of time to serve as a grindstone for the "sharpening of contradictions." Roche had no Communist sympathies— far from it. He was a liberal spokesman of organized labor and a determined anti-Communist, too astute and independent to be made into a party dupe. Yet despite his astuteness and his hostility to Communists, he was tricked into their employment by the same methods that can be and are brought to bear on candidates for office in any political subdivision of the United States. Roche happened to be a Democrat. But in view of the objectives of the Communist party in the political arena before and after the Browder era, a Republican candidate would be equally vulnerable to Communist chicanery. Political principles don't matter. The Communist party can make use of them all.

I was one of the five Malden Communists who worked from the beginning on the Anthony Roche campaign in 1946. With other comrades in the district, I plotted behind doors, which carefully barred Roche and his advisers, to take over his campaign in spite of his own anti-Communist position. Beyond certain fundamentals, we were not concerned with what Roche stood for. He was picked not only in spite of but even because of his anticommunism. We didn't care whether he won, and in fact we never expected him to win. All we wanted was one foot on his campaign platform.

It was at a special meeting in the unkempt, bug-infested, walkup apartment of Alice Gordon that I was first tipped off that the Communist party had decided on a national level to make a special effort in the 1946 Congressional elections. I sat on an incredibly lumpy sofa covered with material grown slick and harsh through time and wear. Two poorly shaded bridge lamps illuminated the room and threw a wretched glare into my eyes.

"It is necessary," Alice said, "for the party to bring full clarity to the membership concerning the important elections ahead. This is the first postwar Congressional election. We are going to participate to the fullest extent."

I lighted my pipe, shifted from one lump in the sofa to another, and tried to express interest. "Does that mean we are going to run our own candidates in every possible district?" I asked.

"No, it does not," Alice replied. "In a very few places we will put up our own candidates. In some localities we will give open support to other party nominees.—DeLacy in Washington, Bobrowicz in Milwaukee, Marcantonio in New York. But in most instances it will not be necessary or even desirable to give open support to the candidates, particularly those of the Democratic party. If we did that, we would indicate support of Truman, whom of course we do not back. The campaign will enable us to achieve a greater activation of the entire party, all party members, and all party organizations. But it cannot be a policy of reliance on the Democratic party."

My interest was becoming genuinely aroused. This began to take on the appearance of the usual briefing session before assignment of a party task pursuing a new line. A brief familiarization course was usually held in these cases, and I could not but wonder what role I would be called upon to play in the elections.

"If we can't back the existing campaign platforms, and we are not putting our own candidates into the field, what are we going to do?" I asked, perhaps a little brazenly.

"The major objectives," Alice declared in typical Aesopian doubletalk, "will be the promotion of the class consciousness of the workers, and most important, the utilization of the experience of the election to accelerate the creation of a new people's party. We Communists are for a third party because the Democratic party cannot be transformed into a people's party."

As the evening wore on, I came, through my understanding of Alice's jargon, to the full realization that the party's main effort would be to infiltrate selected campaigns with or without the knowledge of the candidate, and certainly without public fanfare. Once captured, they would be utilized by us at every opportunity to stir up dissension, strengthen the "proletarian" idea among as many people as possible, and sharpen the class struggle for the day of crisis.

At the end of the meeting, Alice gave me the order: "You will be needed in the work of the Eighth Congressional District. You will report to Comrade Nat next Tuesday evening." The party

193

leaders never asked if one had a previous engagement. If something interfered, it was assumed that the necessary changes would be made to fit the party plans.

I had already acquired some background in political activity by the time the party steered me into the Malden election campaign. During the Browder era I had surveyed the Massachusetts Citizens Political Action Committee for the party leadership and had become, following party instructions, a member of a key committee in that organization. Despite my pessimistic report, the party did decide to capture the PAC as a Communist front, and I was assigned to help in that effort. By the time the first planning sessions got under way for the 1946 Congressional elections, a number of comrades were firmly established amidst the many non-Communists in the Political Action Committee.

Later in 1945, I had assisted in the unsuccessful campaign of my "old friend" Otis Hood, prominent district Communist, for the Boston School Committee. Hood ran for the post on an open Communist party ticket. Alice Gordon and I headed the advertising and publicity drive for his campaign. With only $1,500 in the budget, I aimed a heavy charge of direct-mail advertising calculated to hit the maximum number of voters. Working long hours over the kitchen table in the Gordon apartment, we devised slogans and wrote copy for letters, leaflets, and news releases, none of which, of course, carried my name. All of them stressed the "family man" angle of Hood's candidacy. In the end, garnering more than 25,000 votes, Hood ran a slow seventh on a list of ten candidates, of which only the top two were selected. But in the Communist party district headquarters it was considered a remarkable showing, and I shared in the distribution of laurels.

So I was already earmarked as a political activist when, in late 1945, I was summoned to the meeting with Nat Mills in Malden to take up the following year's Congressional campaign. The members of the branch planning committee for the drive, besides me, were Mills, Frank Collier, Gus Johnson, and another underground Communist known only to me as "Comrade R." The first question before us was whether to place our own open party candidate in the field, or devote ourselves instead to infiltrating the campaign of an acceptable non-Communist. There could be no question of our giving open support to any other major party candidate because none would accept our backing. We discussed the matter freely, although we knew that the decision did not rest in our hands. Ultimately, it would be settled in typical party fashion on a higher level, by the district headquarters. Liaison was maintained with the district leadership, and the orders came back in due time. We were to make a concerted effort to capture the campaign of one of the main party candidates, and use it to the fullest extent to carry on a vigorous propaganda campaign.

Comrade R was the kingpin. Young, sandy-haired, bespectacled, he was reported to be a printer by trade and a part of the organization of the secret press for the New England district. He led a respectable front life. His initial task was to assist our planning group in finding a suitable candidate by conducting a survey of the field, for which he utilized the services of a corps of "bushbeaters." These were secret Communist party members who were in a position to gain access to candidates, ask questions, propose offers of support, and draw out political views without arousing suspicion. Comrade R's workers represented themselves as spokesmen of an "independent labor committee" which had at its disposal an attractive "package" of 350 political-machine workers prepared to back the proper candidate in the election. The machine, of course, was made up of Communists in the area. In return for the support of this machine, they asked nothing. All they wanted, they said with disarming altruism, was to see a progressive candidate in office who would back the demands and the needs of the laboring man and his family.

The party's planning committee of Malden held a series of meetings to hear Comrade R's reports from the field. A number of candidates were ready and even anxious to accept the support of the proffered machine. Several of them were plainly unacceptable from the Communist party viewpoint. Others already had behind them well-established political organizations which were too strong for us to buck.

But there was one, Anthony M. Roche, who in spite of numerous drawbacks might fill the bill.

"He's running for Congress," I argued before the planning committee, "and so he will take in the entire district. We can reach more people through him than we could through one of the municipal candidates. Furthermore, he's a Democrat, and we can probably persuade him to tackle more issues in at least the right direction. He's practically a cinch to win the primary, so we won't have to worry about losing him in the middle of the race. We can start in on him right now."

"All right," Comrade R came back. "But he's an independent cuss. Told us he wouldn't make any deals with anyone, no matter who they represent. He doesn't want any strings attached to him and I don't believe he's going to have any. But that's not all. He's an anti-Communist, said so himself."

"All the better," I declared. "The more anti-Communist he is the more so-called 'respectable' people we can reach through him. And so far as the strings are concerned, we don't want to tie him up. All we want to do is support him. There are no deals involved. He'll certainly accept our help if it's free."

"Yes, but don't forget he's pro-Truman," was the rejoinder.

"Yes," someone else came in, "but he's a strong labor man and the best one in the field. We can't expect to have everything." It was among the ranks of labor that the party most strenuously sought to "disclose and unravel the contradictions" of capitalist society.

The planning committee's reception to the Roche idea was cool, but there seemed to be no alternative. We decided to go ahead with the campaign, with district approval. Anthony Roche didn't know it, but he had some new friends, of whom he might have said, like many before him, "God save me from my friends; I can take care of my enemies."

But if we had some misgivings, Roche had more. At first he was aloof. He did not want, for example, the support of one segment of organized labor to the exclusion of the other. So we formed a hypothetical Independent Voters for Roche group with the idea of embracing all labor. Chief among those who backed him publicly, with the tacit approval of the party's planning committee, were Nat Mills, a member of the CIO United Electrical Workers, Local 201; Paul R. Emerson, an AFL carpenter; Nathan Smith, an independent union member; and Franklin P. Collier, who was listed merely as a member of the Melrose Committee for Fair Employment Practices Legislation. We took pains to specify that organizations were listed for identification only, so as not to imply that these men were serving as spokesmen for their groups.

Had it occurred to Roche to investigate his new friends he would have discovered that Frank Collier was the manager of the Progressive Bookshop in Boston. If he was familiar enough with the Communist party he would have known that the bookshop was almost exclusively a Communist propaganda outlet. But if he was like the average Bostonian he would not have known that any such store existed, or he would have been unaware of its character. Had he inquired far enough he might have found a few who would "guess" that Nat Mills might be a member of the Communist party. But it is certain that he would not have obtained any proof, certainly not from any other member of the party. And so it was with all of the "independent supporters" who slowly closed in on the Roche headquarters with a carefully plotted flanking attack on his campaign.

Our first opportunity to ingratiate ourselves with him through service came in the primary campaign. We mailed out hundreds of letters to party members and friends throughout the district, who, in turn, launched a vigorous "Vote for Roche" effort. He

197

won the Democratic nomination by a margin of almost two to one over his opponent.

More secure in Roche's confidence by reason of the primary victory, we threw the Communist propaganda campaign into high gear. My role was to work my way in as Roche's publicity agent, to help him prepare his campaign literature and news releases. Though he wasn't to know it, I was also to formulate whatever policies I could for him and publicly advocate them in his name, behind his back if necessary. But I was held behind the scenes until the moment was ripe for me to enter. We planned each step by which I was to gain access to his headquarters. I first typed up a two-page memorandum of campaign suggestions. Foremost among them was a recommendation that Roche enlist in his entourage a man with training in advertising, public relations, or newspaper work to carry the burden of the campaign publicity. This memorandum, unsigned, was delivered to the party agents, who in turn passed it on to Roche so that it appeared to come from them.

We gave him a chance to study it, but no time to act. That was my cue. But before I went I drew a curt order from Fanny Hartman.

"Do you still have a party card?" she asked.

"Yes, the latest one."

"Don't run any chance of his seeing it. Destroy it. Tear it up in small pieces, or, better still, burn it."

I sent it to the FBI for safekeeping.

My name and qualifications for the job were mentioned to Roche, and I was taken to his headquarters by Paul Emerson and Nat Mills.

"I'd like to introduce you to Herb Philbrick," Paul said. "He's interested in your campaign."

"So you're in the advertising business," Roche queried, turning his brown eyes on me. Of medium stature, he had a pleasant, rugged face and an appearance suggestive of tweeds, a pipe, and a schooner of beer—a laboring man in the drawing room. I nodded. "That's swell. You're just the kind of man we've been looking for. Sit down."

I drew a chair up to his battered desk. "I admire your campaign platform," I began. "It represents the kind of candidate I think we ought to have from this district." I glanced at Frank Collier, sitting at the desk beside me, his expressionless eyes fixed upon me. Nat Mills leaned casually against the door behind me. Frank and Nat were expecting me to do my party duty. It was unfair to Anthony Roche and I wanted no part of it. But despite my instant liking for Roche, there was no stalling or turning back now. Hal Leary had admonished me, "We have no interest in any information about Anthony Roche. But the Bureau is plenty interested in what the Communist party is doing in the Roche campaign."

Roche was asking me what portions of his platform I liked best. "Well," I said, "I think you are sincerely interested in the little fellow." I picked up one of his campaign fliers. "Take this line, 'More Equitable Tax Laws.' I presume by that you mean that the heavy taxes should be reduced for the man with a small income, and passed on instead to big business. I'm all for it, and I think the voters are, too. War profits should be taken to pay the costs of war, from the big industrial cliques, the private monopolies, and the international bankers. These huge taxes can't be taken in five- and ten-dollar lots from the pay envelope of the workingman."

"That's what I do mean, in a way," Roche interjected, but I tried to brush aside his hedge.

"The only thing is that you ought to say so, spell it out. People want to know exactly what you mean. Take your stand on fair employment practices. It isn't enough to say you support FEPC. You have to come out in favor of strong laws to prevent discrimination on the basis of race, color, or religion. And you ought to urge strong antilynch laws. A strong stand can help you."

199

Roche seemed a little hesitant, so I tossed in a palliative. "I'm a businessman myself and naturally I don't want to see business strangled. Actually, I'm a registered Republican, a liberal Republican, but I'll have to turn to the Democratic party in this district."

"Well," Roche said, "you're the advertising man and you know how to do these things. I'll be very grateful for anything you can do to help in writing this stuff up. I just don't have the time to do everything."

That was what we were waiting to hear, and my party comrades were jubilant. From then on I had carte blanche to Roche's campaign headquarters.

To the Communist party, the biggest political consideration of the period from 1946 to 1948 was the economic crisis in the United States which the party was certain would come, and was determined to foster. It would be signaled by inflation and culminated by a sweeping depression as the nation tried to struggle back to a peacetime economy. The party anticipated that the depression would strike during the last quarter of 1948. It would be more devastating than the 1929 crash, and would thus serve the party's advantage. It might well bring the great opportunity for socialist revolt, and the Communists were confident that it would be the prelude to their seizure of power.

The period immediately following the war was, therefore, a period for build-up, for the gathering of forces, the closing of ranks, and the gaining of friends and allies. The 1946 election was a primary Communist "transmission belt," through which the effort was to be made to convince the broadest possible segment of the population that an economy-shattering crisis was on the horizon. The party set out to play on fears that the catastrophe would strike at the individual pocketbook. The frightening aspects of inflation, unemployment, public relief, lack of housing, and scarce jobs were amplified for the ears of returning service men and members of organized labor. The party believed, rightly or wrongly, that from the ranks of the returned service men, easily moved to deep resentments after a bitter fight to preserve their security and establish a firm future, they might enlist a large number of allies.

But in the long view none of the party's amplification was constructive. Its espousal of causes in behalf of the veteran and the workingman had as its primary objective the splitting of the nation into two camps, the "fascist reactionary" enemy on the one hand, and a militant force aligned toward socialism and sponsored by communism an the other. There was no room for moderation; no middle ground was tolerated. The program was to translate political issues of major or minor significance into terms of irreconcilable class struggle.

In a party study guide published during this period with my assistance, it was written: "Through organizing the people for this struggle to meet immediate problems, the Communist party points out the next step that needs to be taken in order to reach a final solution—socialism." This, of course, was for the consumption of disciplined Communists in party classes. But the fringe elements, the malcontents and fellow travelers, were submitted to gentler preliminary treatment by less direct methods, such as the propaganda we disseminated through the campaign of Anthony M. Roche.

In so far as specific issues were concerned, the primary one in the election was price controls, and the Communist party seized upon it with its usual duplicity. The difference between the public party line, as expressed in the *Daily Worker,* and the teachings inside secret cells was surprising even to one long accustomed to such contradictory views. Publicly, the party gave lip service to controls, urging them as necessary to the saving of the nation's economy and in the interests of justice. This appeal drew a huge popular response. But it did not represent the party's true objective.

Party members, including me, were sometimes prone to accept

public propaganda at its face value, and the leadership was frequently called together for seminars to freshen our Marxist-Leninist science on specific issues. In the midst of the Roche campaign, a branch executive meeting was called in Malden. Max Weitzman was the "expert" assigned from state headquarters as the educational speaker of the evening.

"Let us not forget," said Max in his discussion, "that it doesn't make much difference whether price controls as they are now proposed are on or off. Capitalism is caught in a trap of contradictions which the economy cannot shake loose."

Out of his explanation I understood that the party could count the issue of price controls a victory one way or the other. If a strong program of controls went through, the government bureaucracy necessary to enforce them would be accordingly reinforced. And Communists are pro-bureaucratic, in that they recognize bureaucracy as one of the "creeping diseases of capitalism." The party teaches that, as capitalism grows, bureau is piled on bureau in an effort to control the growth. Eventually, Stalin and Lenin believe, the government becomes top-heavy, and the whole thing crashes.

It was not out of a spirit of salvation and justice, therefore, that the inner circles of the Communist party supported a vigorous control program. They used price controls as another weapon in the party's ceaseless drive to throw all economic and social problems into the hands of an expanding government bureaucracy, confident that the resulting confusion and ineptitude could be exploited to hasten the day of crisis.

On the other hand, if the control program should fail, and Congress should follow the dictates of the extreme right wing of popular sentiment by killing the controls altogether, then the party felt that it would be served equally well. The termination of controls over the economy, the party blueprint said, would encourage inflation through runaway prices, and bring on the big depression even more quickly. The National Association of

Manufacturers, the party whispered in private, was in this respect a strong ally of the Communist movement. The most rabid reactionaries are invariably the Communists' best friends.

Anthony Roche was a moderate with respect to OPA price-control measures. He recognized the need for them, but he wanted them to be rigidly limited in both time and effect. He urged temporary controls that would be relaxed as soon as the situation would permit. Here he clashed with open party policy, which was clamoring for a more permanent and far-reaching control program.

We endeavored to strengthen Roche's platform plank on this issue. It was an ideal wedge of dissension to drive between production and the consumer dollar. It was the kind of thing that struck home. But Roche stood by his principles, and for a time would not be moved to follow our direction.

Then one day an angry picket line, composed of placard-waving housewives, many of them pushing baby carriages, materialized in Malden Square and began parading, shouting the stinging slogans that were blazoned on their placards. They cried for stronger price and rent laws to drive prices down. They stuck barbs into "gouging landlords," and ranted against the "swollen profits" of big business. They directed their line of march so that it passed directly in front of Roche's headquarters. The candidate recognized public sentiment when he saw it.

"People really are stirred up about this thing, aren't they?" he reflected.

Advisers at his elbow—hidden Communists—were prompt to take him up. "Too bad they aren't carrying placards, 'Roche for Congress,' too," someone remarked.

"If we let them know that Roche stands in no uncertain terms for price controls, perhaps they will," another said.

A stronger statement on OPA went into Roche's anti-inflation plank, and the party propagandists in his headquarters went to work to drive in the wedge.

What Roche didn't know was that the picket-line scheme was concocted behind his back in the party planning committee. Women members of the party were directed to round up non-Communist housewives in Malden and whip them into the buyers' strike. In the secret committee, we worked the campaign up into slogans and printed them on placards. We contrived the timing of the demonstration, arranged the route so it would concentrate on Roche's headquarters and the immediate surroundings, and primed the party workers in Roche's headquarters to be ready to make the most of the incident.

A half-dozen Communists who had by this time infiltrated Roche's headquarters leaped on the price-control issue by telephone, mail, and personal contacts. The campaign evolved a definite pattern. The party infiltrators exploited every question that held the slightest advantage. Most of the issues of the Roche campaign played directly into the hands of the Communists or of organizations largely controlled by Communists. His own campaign manager was successfully by-passed on many details. We swung the support of the Citizens Political Action Committee behind him, and lest he become suspicious of too many close ties, we ordered two of his closest campaign workers, Frank Collier and Paul Emerson, to resign from their official positions with the PAC. Through Roche's campaign we found new outlets for PAC literature, which in many instances was pure Communist propaganda. I personally delivered vast quantities of this literature to Roche's headquarters, all of it picked up, incidentally, at the Communist party's propaganda outlet, the Progressive Bookshop, even though it bore the imprint of the PAC.

Among the favorite devices for reaching people behind Roche's back were the campaign "house parties," small meetings usually held in private residences. Naturally it was impossible for Roche to attend all of them, and many were rigged with the specific intention that the candidate could not be there, because of a simultaneous engagement in another part of the district. Only one or two comrades would attend these sessions, but they were invariably transformed from ordinary political rallies into Marxist study classes which carried the issues far beyond those limits which Roche himself defined in his platform.

For example, a speaker would declaim, "The National Association of Manufacturers has spent two million dollars in its so-called public-relations program, which is in reality a campaign to crush price controls and to get more money out of your pockets and into the hands of the monopolists." Roche was no friend of the NAM, but his views were more temperate than the house-party speaker, who would add, "You working-class men and women will receive less and less money in relation to the value of the services you render. You will not be able to buy back what you produce by your labor. This is one of the contradictions which inevitably produce crises and depressions in our capitalist society."

And having planted this pure Marxist seed, lifted bodily from Lenin's teachings, the speaker would again align his remarks with Anthony Roche. "On whose side are you going to fight? On the side of Roche—the side of labor—or on the side of reactionary, fascist, warmongering big business?" By just so much the Communist propagandist succeeded in widening the class gap.

Sometimes Roche was scarcely mentioned at all. The entire meeting would be devoted to a discussion of the "issues" of the campaign. It always began in moderation, then the speaker would gradually draw the audience as far toward the Marxist line as he dared. At most of these meetings the discussion would fan sufficient flames of resentment to bring to light one or two prospective members of the Communist party. The "riders" which we hitched onto Roche's campaign planks touched every possible cause of civil discontent, to lure as many candidates as possible toward the party—racial discrimination, lynching, poll taxes, atomic control, Big Three unity, "peace," or any other inflammatory subject. There was always a place, a Communist-front organization, to which to refer the disgruntled, the embittered, the frustrated, and the confused. At one meeting I watched dozens of persons enroll in the National Negro Congress, which continued as a Communist front long after the Roche campaign was ended.

A few of those who responded to the campaign propaganda eventually were drawn into the ranks of the Communist party itself, and that was one of the most important sideline aspects of the election. We used the Roche campaign as a hook to bring in new members, to sell subscriptions to the *Daily Worker,* and to serve as a training ground in the fundamentals of party theory and practice. One new member wanted to go right out and proclaim publicly that the Communist party was backing Roche.

"But the Communist party is not backing Roche," he was admonished, and the neophyte was hard put to understand the distinction.

When Roche was no longer of any use to us, we abandoned him as unceremoniously as we had taken him up. Even before election day we began to pack up and drift away. By election night, almost every Communist was gone from his headquarters, and none was around to console him when the returns brought him a thumping defeat. We did not even bother to cover the polling places for him. We had no abiding interest in Anthony Roche as a prospective Congressman. We knew we could never control him. It was plain that the Roche campaign suffered more than it gained by the infiltration of the Communist party. He polled only 42,000 votes. The next time, he wisely avoided support from "progressives," and, without Communist party interference, drew more than 70,000 votes, and was only narrowly defeated.

A week after the election, a meeting of party branch executives was held in Malden. I ran into several of the Roche campaign workers. "By the way," I asked one of them, "how did Roche make out?"

"I don't know," he shrugged, and that was all.

Otis Hood came out from the district headquarters to give us a post-mortem on the election work. "The victory of the Republican party in the Congressional elections was a severe blow to the American people," he said, with evident glee in his perennial, round-faced smile. "It means that the control of the government will be more firmly than ever in the hands of big business." Then, with that incongruous facility for turning defeat into apparent victory, he added, "This confirms the view of the National Board of the Communist party. America is in for tough days ahead. The nation's relations to the rest of the world will be subject to an intensification of the get-tough bullying program of atom-dollar diplomacy. Now we'll see increased militarization and a speeding up of preparations for war."

"The Communist party," he explained, "played a significant role in the election campaign. Wherever its influence was brought to bear it was in the direction of crystallizing the unity and the independent action of the labor and progressive forces. It played a major role in clarifying the issues in the fields of domestic and foreign policy. It helped expose the forces of reaction. By putting forth its own views and, in a number of cases, its own candidates, it brought the party's policy and its program of 'socialism' to new hundreds of thousands of voters."

Thus the election was a victory for communism, despite the fact that scarcely a single major objective had been won through the ballot box. But that didn't matter. The gap between the classes had been widened, and the day of crisis brought closer, the crisis for which the Communist party was girding itself.

The preparations took on a new note of urgency in the party directives that came into district headquarters after the election. For more than a year, since the autumn of 1945, the Education Commission under Jack Stachel, of which I was a member in the New England district, had hammered away at "basic training" in Marxism for party members in every branch, cell, and neighborhood. Marxist theory had been pumped under high pressure into the party's blood stream as an antidote to the Browder anemia.

207

The main effort during this period was to purge the deviationists and weaklings, and to realign the party with its historic Marxist-Leninist doctrines. As early as August, 1946, the party was able to take note of its success in rooting up Browderism, and to declare, "We have demolished the whole rotten structure."

In every segment of the party the "level of understanding" had been raised, and party members who survived the great purge now clearly understood that their organization was no mere reform association, but a revolutionary party of the people. The ideological training and Marxist indoctrination must continue, we were told, especially for the benefit of new members. But the new educational directives, which, from my vantage point as an education director, I was among the first to see, ordered a new ingredient added to the training fare.

Now, we were told in effect, it was time to come down from the ideological to a more practical level, and to translate the theories we learned in the historic Communist texts into terms of contemporary realism. We must bring down to earth the lofty language of Marx and Lenin, and make it more understandable to the ordinary workingman, especially the non party-member. And there was more and more insistence on the role that labor was to play in the party's preparations.

Manny Blum opened this new phase of our educational work with a series of meetings, most of which were held at the Little Building, either in district headquarters or in a separate third-floor conference room. A few of these sessions, attended by party members whose identity required special protection, were held in a cubicle behind a partition in the rear of the Progressive Bookshop. I heard Manny deliver many harangues on the imminent collapse of the American economy and the necessity for complete preparation to meet the coming crisis. Now, he told us with particular emphasis, was the time to spread out, from the hardened, thoroughly indoctrinated core of the Communist party into circles where the party's sphere of influence could be broadened. And again it was to labor that he pointed, following the admonitions of Marx and Engels, Lenin, and Stalin that communism must find its greatest strength in the working class.

One of my assignments was to assist in the preparation of an extensive study outline for distribution throughout the district. I worked on this job with Comrade Frances, one of the party's "plain Janes," a heavy-set, studious, and serious girl whose party name, I discovered, was Frances Smith, but whose real name I knew to be something different. The study outline was drawn up under the title, "Prosperity and Depression in Capitalist Society." It sought to analyze American capitalism as viewed by Marx, and to set forth in the simple language of quantitative propaganda the theory of underconsumption, to prove to the man of limited education "that periodic economic crises are inevitable under capitalism." We used pictures, cartoons, figures, charts, graphs, and diagrams to dramatize the pamphlet. We showed that "the worker is always on the short end of the economic stick, and that salvation is possible only under socialism." It was not openly a revolutionary tract, but it did hammer and chip away at the foundations of free enterprise with unremitting cries of "crisis . . . crisis . . . crisis." It clearly pointed the way to "socialism," which party teachers said in secret sessions could only come about by violent revolution carried out by bands of armed workers. And Fabian socialism, the party traditionally held, is but the first step to communism.

At party headquarters, while this intensified educational campaign was getting under way, I noted an odd change in the atmosphere. Time after time, when I went to the Little Building on party missions, I found the district headquarters more crowded than in former days. But there was no sound of voices. An eerie quiet prevailed. Whereas formerly those on party business discussed their affairs openly and in normal conversational tones, now they were always whispering, drawn together into tight little groups of three or four in the corners of the rooms, exchanging confidences.

In this atmosphere resembling a displaced funeral parlor, Daniel Boone Schirmer took over as my immediate party superior, and it was with him, as chairman of the District Educational Commission, that I began to work most closely. Boone, as he was called, further contributed to the sensation that a conspiracy was hatching. He was tall and lanky, with a look of hollow frailty that his toughness belied, and he proudly claimed direct descent from Daniel Boone. He had drawn cheeks, high-boned features, deep-set eyes, and straight black hair; he looked like a woodman living off the lean of the land. We understood that he was financially secure, but his resources, if any, were kept hidden. His eyes were his most striking feature. They seemed darker in their recesses than they really were. They burned with a steady gleam, undimmed even in his quiet moments. Boone's power and zeal were such that he seemed to be in action even when he sat perfectly still. He rarely smiled, and I never heard him laugh outright. His moods ranged narrowly from passive resentment to nostril-flaring rage. Boone's single passion was the Communist party, and his intensity frequently overruled his good sense, so that he was led into grave tactical errors. He was, to me, the most dangerous of all party types, an antagonist who had an unwavering obedience and subservience to his masters, but it was built on something other than fear. Boone knew no fear.

One evening when the party headquarters was empty save for Schirmer and me, he pulled from his pocket a rumpled, hand-written outline.

"I need fifty copies of this form," he said. "Get it on a stencil and run it off. I'll help you."

I inserted a mimeograph stencil in a typewriter and went to work. The form had no title. It appeared to be a questionnaire dealing with individual party members, and started out with:

210

"Name . . . Address . . . Branch or cell . . . Length of time in the party . . . Education . . . Special training . . . Union member . . . What union." But as my eye traveled down the sheet I became aware that this was something more than a routine questionnaire. Its scope gradually widened. "Number of members in union . . . Number working in shop . . . Union officers . . . Influence in shop . . . Number of Communist party members." Then it became notably inquisitive. "Production facilities . . . Types of equipment in shop . . . Products manufactured . . . capacity. . . ."

Plainly this was more than a personnel survey. It was an industrial study of manufacturing-plant facilities and their products. As I cut the stencil and read it, I wondered why Schirmer should need only fifty copies—unless it was to involve only that many plants, important plants, perhaps. Boone stood over my shoulder as I worked, watching me closely. It was impossible for me to slip out the fibrous backing sheet for my FBI report. After the stencil was cut I went into the reception room, Schirmer at my heels, placed the stencil on the mimeograph, and ran off a few test copies. The machine was overinked, and the copies came out badly smeared. I started to toss the first sheets into the wastebasket, hoping to retrieve one of them later.

"Don't throw them away," Schirmer flared.

"But they aren't any good," I protested.

"Never mind that. I'll take them. Now run off fifty good copies." He watched me turn them out. "Good. Give me the stencil. I may need some more copies."

I wrapped the ink-soaked stencil in mimeograph paper and gave it to him. "I have some more work to do," he said by way of a dismissal. "Thanks for your help." We made arrangements to meet the next day for some other work. It was not necessary for Schirmer to tell me to keep quiet about the form job. I could see that something important to the party was under way.

As soon as I was out of the office I contacted Hal Leary, while

211

the curious form I had typed was still fresh in my mind. I informed him of the stepping up of party labor activity, and in particular the Schirmer questionnaire.

"When will they be used?" was the agent's query.

"I don't know for sure, but there is going to be a party builders conference in a few days, and I'll bet my last dollar it's connected with that."

"Are you going?"

"I don't know. It's going to be tight. Tighter than most. Invitation only. They're bringing in people from all over the district—Joe Figureido from Fall River, Oakie from Worcester, Sid from Springfield, Chase from New Hampshire. They all have ties with industry, big manufacturing plants."

"Try to get there if you possibly can," Hal said.

CHAPTER 13

IN THE DINGY Ritz Plaza Hall, up a broad flight of tread-worn wooden stairs on Huntington Avenue in Boston, the New England district Communists held an important "party builders" conference on February 2, 1947. By virtue of my position as a member of the Malden branch "Exec.," I did receive one of the coveted invitations to the unannounced, secret meeting. It was a workers conference, attended by about a hundred party members. But these were not the party thinkers, the threadbare Marxist ideologists with whom I had become accustomed to dealing in the party ranks. These were the red-necked, callous-handed labor leaders of shop and industrial branches and cells, the proletarian zealots with small theoretical understanding but big biceps and boiler-factory voices. Outside of the top district and branch leadership, those summoned to the conference were almost all representative of cells in heavy industry. They were selected for the influence they wielded with their fellow workers—Communist and non-Communist. In addition, there were a number of men who held key posts in the party's foreign-language groups, and the babble of many tongues was heard throughout the cheerless hall.

Manny Blum opened the session in the early morning with an address that bore heavily on the need for increasing the party's membership, and set the theme of the meeting. More important than numbers, Manny said, was the influence of the party in key industries. Over and over again throughout the long day the note was repeated—the "basic" industries, the "key" industrial plants, and the "decisive" workers. The published agenda of the conference echoed the same theme. "We greet this recruiting drive," the document said, "with enthusiasm, knowing that it will further direct our attention and activities towards becoming a party rooted among the decisive workers of New England." The program also stressed the importance of a special subreport on Communist work in the shops, to be given by Joe Figureido, branch organizer from the heavily industrialized Fall River–New Bedford area of Massachusetts. This was a conference called ostensibly to open a new drive for membership. But it was significant that in 1947, with new stresses rapidly developing in the world, and the Communist party already emphasizing its work among the ranks of labor, that now the key, basic industries should be so heavily underscored.

Joe Figureido's report turned out to be a disappointment, a routine address full of dogmatism that signified to me the absence of originality in the party's second-string leadership. As he droned on, I glanced around the room, to discover that I knew comparatively few of those assembled. I saw Boone Schirmer, Margot Clark, Max Weitzman, and a few others of long acquaintance. One of my favorite characters was present, Elba Chase Nelson of the New Hampshire state organization, the little Russian "Yankee" who always delighted audiences by her mixture of regional expression and Marxist doctrine which came out in her corn-cracking voice something like: "We cannot fiddle-faddle any longer with fascist imperialism." But most of those in the hall were strangers to me, and it was plain that a new element was assuming greater importance in the eyes of the party leaders.

Fanny Hartman's report was next. For background, she sketched in the threat of an American-Soviet war, even though the official party line held that war was not inevitable. American imperialists, she said, were plotting a war against the Soviet Union, and in proof she offered the statements of irresponsible private citizens who loosely advocated drastic atom-bomb measures to forestall

Russian aggression. These same plotters, she declared, owned and controlled the means of war production, and thus held in their hands the entire war potential of the United States. The major weapons in their possession were the big key industries, and it was around these decisive plants and factories that the nation's war apparatus revolved.

Although it was nearly submerged in a strong counterpoint, the theme of the conference now began to round out, and I sat up to take notice. The Communist party, even in its secret and semi-secret meetings, always manages to protect itself by skirting around the absolute point it is trying to drive home. But it circles the central issue enough, chipping away at the edges, to leave no doubt in the mind of a trained Communist that the point is there, and just what it is.

"What are these basic industries?" Fanny declared, falling into the Marxist habit of framing a question to hold a ready-made answer. One of them, she said, was the big General Electric Company plant at Lynn, Massachusetts, where the government was then engaged—and this was news to me—in the manufacture of jet engines for aircraft. Others were the railroad yards; communications, including radio, telegraph, telephone, and even the newspapers; the steel industry; shipyards; textiles; chemicals; and all of the heavy industries which were involved in the increasing tempo of the defense establishment. Fanny and the other speakers told the conference that it was urgently necessary for the Communist party to increase its strength in these industries in order to counteract the headlong rush toward an imperialist war. They did not say just how the party members were to accomplish this mission. That was left up in the air, at least for the time being, for each to determine for himself.

Otis Hood took the platform next and resumed where Fanny Hartman left off. He used a new term, one I had never before heard in all of my party activities—"colonizers." A party colonizer, he declared, was a devoted member who could be assigned party tasks in an important plant; or, if not already strategically placed, he would willingly give up his job in a nonessential industry or profession and move into one of the decisive basic industries. Here his primary task would be to surround himself with a solid phalanx of Communist party members, and through them to exercise his influence in the spreading of Marxism and the sharpening of economic and social struggles among Communist and non-Communist workers alike.

"The colonizer," I recall Hood saying, "will be elevated to a position of highest honor in the ranks of the Communist party."

During the long day's program, the details of this new industrial colonization program were worked out, to the subordination of the normal methods of building party membership, although this was supposed to have been a party builders conference. My old friend Nat Mills was designated as one of the colonizers at the General Electric plant in Lynn, together with Don Tormey, who was already prominent there as a labor organizer, Don Bollen, and Bob Goodwin. Nat later gave up his home in Malden and moved to Lynn to be closer to his job. Dave Bennett was assigned to the steel industry in Massachusetts. Gus Johnson, a carpenter by trade, shifted his work to the yards and shops of the Boston & Maine Railroad. The United Office and Professional Workers Union of the CIO had a delegate present, who was informed that its decisive area was in financial business, and that its critical point of concentration was in the big life-insurance companies, notably the John Hancock Life Insurance Company of Boston.

Puzzled over the relationship between this emphasis on vital industries and the questionnaire I had typed and duplicated for Boone Schirmer a few nights earlier, I spotted Boone during one of the brief recesses. He was in conversation with a delegate I did not know, and fingering a sheaf of papers in his hand. I passed them as close as I could without daring to stop and talk to them. Neither one noticed me.

"I want all three of these back," I heard Boone say. "Don't mail them. Get them to me personally." I walked out of earshot.

The heaviest colonization program carried out in the New England district under Boone's direction was in the General Electric plant, which coincidentally was one of the biggest defense plants in the region. I promptly reported the colonization plan to Hal Leary at the FBI, together with all the names I could muster, and the additional information that smaller, industry-wide conferences were to be called on the basis of plans set up at the party builders meeting.

After the February meeting, I sat in on several informal discussions at district headquarters with Manny Blum and Boone Schirmer. There I learned just how far the party expected to go in its membership drive. Manny held that the party did not require—and more than that, did not want—a majority at any level to carry out its mission. This sounded to me like a contradiction, until Manny explained it.

"The Communist party must be and must remain the vanguard, the leaders of the working class," he said. "They must represent the most advanced section of the workers, and not seek to embrace the entire working class. To do so would merely be to dissipate our energies. Marxism shows us how to *direct* the struggle of the workers toward socialism. Comrade Stalin points out correctly that only a party that has thoroughly mastered Marxist-Leninist science can go forward with confidence toward the goal. But we cannot fill the ranks of the party with undisciplined numbers who make no determined effort to master Marx. To do so would weaken the party and deprive it of the leadership that is necessary."

I wanted to be certain that I understood. "Therefore," I summarized, "the Communist party will always remain a minority?" I had in mind the reaction of most Americans who disparage the efforts of the Communist movement because of their small representation.

"Exactly," Manny replied, bristling with the confidence of one whose Marxist science is firmly grounded. "When did you ever hear of an effective group that had more leaders than followers? Even in the people's democracies, in the Soviet Union, the Communist party at the crucial point of the struggle was a small minority."

The industry-wide discussions, I learned subsequently, were held as they were outlined at the conference. They were small secret meetings, most of them held away from party headquarters. Their purpose was to go into further detail on the colonization program, taking each particular industry in the district plant by plant and shop by shop to study progress. Only the key leaders of the plan attended these meetings. As a white-collar worker I attended none of them. But I gathered from the district conference, and from reports of the industry meetings which filtered down to me, that it was plain now that party building in this critical period before the anticipated depression of 1948 signified the spreading of influence of the party and of Marxism among all ranks of labor, and especially among those who could be counted on to follow a militant leadership. Further, it was particularly evident that this effort was to be concentrated in essential industries—essential not only to the economy but to the military defense of the United States.

By the spring of 1947, my work shifted back to the political treadmill, and a period of frustration and comparative inactivity followed. The Communist party moved along with the old Political Action Committee into the coalition Progressive Citizens of America, the third-party movement. Dr. Harlow Shapley of Harvard was elected honorary chairman of the organization that was eventually to become the Progressive party. Angus Cameron, at that time editor in chief of Little, Brown & Company, was the chairman, Ruth Emery the secretary, and Marjorie Lansing the executive director.

I did not have a position on the executive committee of this group as I had in the PAC, but I was asked to serve on the publicity committee, and this was sufficient to the purposes of the Communist party to get me in with adequate cover. I attended a series of meetings in a cramped little two-room office suite at 6 Beacon Street, on one of the upper floors of the building, opening onto an air shaft. It was in the same building as the offices of the Republican party. The founding convention of the Progressive Citizens of America in Massachusetts was held in Boston, March 7, 1947, and for weeks thereafter our main effort in the publicity committee was organizational, the monotonous conduct of drives to enroll new members pending the launching of a third-party campaign for the 1948 elections.

Hal Leary repeated in paraphrase the same admonition he had given me in connection with the Anthony Roche campaign. "We are not interested in the Progressive Citizens of America as long as it remains a normal political movement. But we are interested in what the Communist party is doing and is planning to do in it." In an effort to run this down for the Bureau I attended scores of afternoon teas, rallies, receptions, and soirees, many of them intimate little gatherings held in middle- and upper-class homes in fashionable suburban areas and town apartments. They were usually called to "honor" a distinguished guest in connection with the PCA organization, and they always managed to tap those who attended for sums ranging from five to a hundred dollars and more. These affairs catered to the liberals in Boston professional life—writers, doctors, lawyers, and businessmen and their wives. There were very few among them, or among the forty to fifty regular workers at PCA headquarters, whom I recognized as members of the Communist party. The few I did encounter were small cogs in the machine, and I had little interest in them.

I was uneasy for two reasons. I was moving away from my central interest in all of these activities—counterspy work for the FBI in the Communist party. And I was afraid that inactivity was making me careless and undermining my usefulness. After one of these lengthy and dull meetings I became so disturbed that I called Hal Leary and made an appointment to meet him.

"Good," he said over the phone when I talked to him from a pay station. "I have something to talk to you about, also." We arranged the contact for the following Monday at a small restaurant in Porter Square, Cambridge.

I made my way there by subway and emerged in a cold spring rain. It was a little before six by the bank clock on the corner. I was to meet Hal at six o'clock sharp. The restaurant, almost empty, reverberated to the blare of a juke box in the corner. I bought a light meal at the serving counter and carried my tray to a white marble-topped table at the side of the room facing the door, where I could watch for Hal's arrival. The first man who entered after me had his rain-spattered coat collar turned up around his throat. As he walked down the center of the room without looking at me, I recognized him as a Communist party grubber I had seen around the PCA office. I bent down to my food as he passed me, giving myself a moment to consider my situation. I was indeed getting careless. Was I being "tailed" again, and without even suspecting it? It seemed unlikely, and this man's appearance was more probably a coincidence. But I could not risk being seen talking to Hal Leary now.

The door opened again and Hal entered. He was in the company of another man who was a stranger to me, and they were engaged in jovial and animated conversation. I waited until Hal looked in my direction for a cue. Then I picked up my glass of water, deliberately quaffed a drink while returning his gaze impassively, and set the glass down—the prearranged signal that the contact must be broken. Hal and his companion continued their conversation, went to the order counter, and then took another table apart from me. All four of us, the FBI agent and his friend, the spy and the Communist, ate with complete indifference to the presence of the others. I watched the comrade across the room. He was reading a book, apparently oblivious to the dramatic little tableau in the almost empty restaurant. I wondered if he really had followed me. If so, it would not do for me to dash out now, after throwing the government agents off our rendezvous. I decided it would be better to conclude matters on an explanatory note. If he was a "shadow" I might be able to satisfy him of my innocence. If not, my approaching him could do no harm.

I fished out my pipe and tobacco pouch and idled over to his table. "Hello, there," I greeted him. He started from his book and his face betrayed open surprise. I was convinced he had not even known I was in the restaurant. "Can you help me out with some matches for this stoker?" I asked.

"Why, sure," he said, producing a folder of paper matches. "I didn't see you here." He wasn't putting on an act. "What are you doing?"

"Oh," I said, making a ceremony of lighting my pipe, "I had a late business deal in this neighborhood and I thought I'd grab a quick bite."

"Join me?"

"Thanks, but I'm just finishing my coffee. Have to run along." I handed back the matches.

"Keep them," he said, "I have more."

I made some inconsequential comment about the rain, walked back to my table, and finished my coffee. Then I arose without looking in Hal's direction again, nodded a farewell to the comrade, and left the restaurant. Hal and his companion stayed behind, making no effort to follow me. I walked to a bus-terminal waiting room, making sure this time that I was not being followed. I purchased a newspaper and sat for ten minutes or so, as if waiting for a bus. Then, when I calculated that Hal had had time to finish his meal and leave the restaurant, I went to a telephone booth and dialed a number.

"Sorry about the mixup," I said, when his voice crackled over the radio-telephone circuit. "Thought my friend might become curious."

"O.K.," Hal replied, "we caught the idea."

"Where are you now?"

"On Memorial Drive heading west. And you?" I told him. "See any cabs around there?"

"Sure, plenty of them."

"Hop one and meet us at Smith's in about ten minutes."

This time I spotted Hal and his friend in a side booth at Smith's, and he signaled that we were all right. I joined them for a belated second cup of coffee and dessert.

"I want you to meet Don Richards," Hal said right off, without ceremony. "He's going to be your contact man from now on."

"Oh?" I said, shaking hands. Richards had reddish blond hair and a boyish face. His "hello" was in a thin tenor voice. He was of medium build and had a fair complexion. His greeting was friendly but reserved. Hal volunteered nothing more on the switch. I wanted to ask him what was up, but I knew it wouldn't get me anywhere. The change was accepted and the subject was dropped after Hal said, "That's the only thing on my mind. Wanted you two to get acquainted. What's on yours?"

I directed my attention now to Agent Don Richards, since he was the one directly concerned. "I'm a little confused," I confessed. "The party has tossed me into this Progressive Citizens movement, and I'm in it so deep that there isn't time for me to keep on with party cell activities. It's defeating me. Instead of getting closer to the comrades, I think I'm getting farther away from them."

"That ought to be a pleasure," Hal interrupted with a smile.

"It is, in a way. They are a different sort of people and it's nice enough to work with them and get out of the morass of Marxism a little bit. But the trouble is I'm afraid it isn't much use to you."

222

"What sort of work are you doing with this bunch?" Richards asked.

"Publicity, for the most part. And then, too, I go to a lot of pink tea parties for prominent people who call themselves liberals. Mostly they raise money. Good Lord, they took in twenty-five hundred dollars at two meetings in a row the other night. Small affairs, too, both of them. But where does it get me? You said yourself you didn't care about investigating this outfit."

"Well," Hal said, "let's see now. Are there any Communists, any other Commies besides you in there?"

"Sure, here and there. But they aren't important, and I don't tangle much with them. That's why I thought we had better talk about it. Take this meeting the other night. A lot of important people—wealthy ones, too, but I didn't run into a soul that I knew in the party. Not one."

"Who was there?" Richards persisted. I observed that he had a brisk, businesslike manner, precise and to the point.

I rattled off a list of names drawn from my best recollection of the affair.

"No Communists there," Richards mused. "Hmm."

"None that I know of, and I think I can spot 'em across the street by this time."

"Tell you what," Richards said. "I think you'd better stick with it. After all, you are in there on Communist party orders, and there must be others, too. I think it will turn out all right."

I continued my work in the Progressive Citizens of America, grinding out publicity material extolling the new Henry Wallace line of peace and abundance which he was already outlining from speaking platforms throughout the country. It seemed advisable not to attempt to disguise my third-party activities from my everyday associates, but openly to avow them. Otherwise I might trip myself up. After all, the Progressive Citizens was not yet recognized as a Communist front. Around the M. & P. Theaters offices, therefore, I was known as a Wallace supporter, and I even kept PCA literature supporting his movement in plain view on my desk. However, I took care not to become too vocal, and by all means to avoid being drawn into any political discussions with pro- or anti-Wallace members of the office staff.

One morning in late summer, when we were starting work on a publicity campaign for Wallace's appearance in Boston toward the end of September, a special messenger brought into the office an envelope with the letterhead of the PCA. It turned out to be a memorandum on a routine matter, typewritten, but scrawled across the bottom of it was a penciled notation in a hand which I recognized.

"Call F. H." was all it said. Fanny Hartman. It was the first direct communication I had received from the Communist party leadership in some time. The morning was busy, and before I was able to comply with the message, which meant that I would have to leave my office and phone from a pay station, I in turn received a telephone call. Over the wire came the Harvard-accented voice of one of the top leaders of the PCA asking me to meet him for lunch at Marliave's to discuss some of the arrangements for the Wallace appearance. This man, whom I shall call Harry, was to my view an insufferable, overeducated bore; a rich dilettante who dabbled in writing of sorts and in business enterprises which he did not need for his support. He lived in comfortable good taste. He was a fairly common mixture, a snob who professed to be a liberal. His speech was a ludicrous literary exercise. I had watched him in my PCA work until I had become convinced that he was too effete to be a Communist, or at least a good one. Even if he was not a Communist, I disliked him.

But Harry did hold down an important job in the third-party movement, and out of a sense of duty I agreed to meet him. After all, I thought, my job is to stick at it, and one thing might lead to another. It always has. At the appointed hour, therefore, I turned down the blind lane of Bosworth Street beyond the Parker House, and met Harry at Marliave's.

224

We chatted idly while the waiter brought our meal, and when he moved away Harry leaned across and in the seclusion of our booth he almost whispered, "Have you heard from Fanny?"

For a fraction of a second the question failed to register. I lowered my fork and scrutinized his sensitive face for a clew. He must, I thought, be talking about someone else. Surely not Fanny Hartman. I reflected on the girl on the PCA staff whose name was Frances, but who was sometimes called Fanny. And yet this name was mentioned within two hours of the note to me from Fanny Hartman, asking me to call her. It was inconceivable to me that Harry would be on first-name speaking terms with the hierarchy of the Communist party, or that he should even know who they were. Harry leveled his gaze at me.

"Who?" I asked. I was trying to set it straight in my mind just how much this man knew.

"Fanny," he repeated, and it was spoken in the same conspiratorial whisper. But he didn't give me the full name. With a glance at my plate I decided to play it straight and let him do the tactical maneuvering.

"No," I said, "I haven't seen her at all recently. She's still in the office, isn't she?"

Harry seemed a little confused himself, now, as if he feared he might be on thin ice. He changed the subject abruptly. Then he suddenly excused himself with a glance at his watch, muttering that he had to make a telephone call. A few minutes later he returned, his uneasiness gone and his composure entirely regained. He toyed with a fork with long, delicate fingers.

"Fanny tells me she left word for you to call," he said, and now I knew for sure what he was talking about. In his absence, I concluded, he had telephoned Fanny to make certain that there had not been some mistake. While he worked on his meal for a moment I tried to accept the disclosure that this strange, wealthy, ineffectual but fairly well-respected Bostonian, who moved in the highest civic, social, and business circles in the city, was a Com-

225

munist. He was apparently a bona-fide member of the party, and even his close acquaintances could not have known it. He was far enough up in the party scale to be used, evidently, as a courier. For he was saying, "There's a new group to be formed in Pro-4, and Fanny says—"

I felt myself start violently. "What did you say?"

"I said," his cultivated voice came back softly, "a new group is to be formed in Pro-4, and Fanny says that there will be another change in your assignment."

"Another one?" I forced a smile. The cryptic designation "Pro-4" catapulted my mind back three years to the 1944 state convention. That was the curious symbol that Fanny Hartman had scribbled on my credentials to get me into the convention hall. Pro-4. It was the second time in my party life that I had encountered the strange term. It was still a complete mystery to me.

"What is the group?" I asked. "Where will it meet?" I was still trying to adjust myself to the realization that this man apparently had close Communist ties. And at the same time, I realized with horror, he was swinging powerful influence in the new political movement of the Progressive Citizens of America. I thought I knew all of the comrades in the PCA, the little grubbers. But here was something else again—a wealthy college man who had no discernible cause for any complaint against society. Perhaps his was a brand of adolescent idealism on which the Communists had capitalized.

"You'll find out all about it," Harry was saying. "We will probably meet in Cambridge, perhaps in Boston. I think you'll like the general—tone—of the membership. It's useful work, too. And important. Vitally important."

"What about my present group in Melrose?"

"You will drop it. Drop out."

"Any explanation?"

"None is necessary." I told him that I had a meeting scheduled that very evening with my cell, at which I was to be the discussion

226

leader. He suggested that I go ahead with it. "After that," the courier continued as if delineating an order, "you will become a floater. You will receive further instructions. In the meantime, don't go near the headquarters. Break off all contacts with Melrose and any other groups. Don't say anything, just drop out. You will no longer affiliate with members on an official or even a social basis."

A "floater," I knew, was a party member, separated for security reasons from all normal party cells and organizations. He is a party free-lance agent who is contacted only by a few leaders, by courier, mail drop, or covert telephone calls. He holds no regular jobs with the party that bring him in touch with other members in large groups. The floater is but one step removed from the "sleeper," who is ordered to drop completely out of Communist life, sever all his relations with the party including the leadership, until he is called upon for a particular mission, perhaps years hence. In the meantime he leads a normal life, with all traces of his Communist ties banished, both in and out of the party. It may even intentionally be made known in party circles that he has been dropped out for disciplinary purposes or as an undesirable. Both floaters and sleepers have been used in Communist espionage and underground circles for many years, in all countries, as a means of concealment. I could not help wondering, in view of these drastic orders and the sudden reappearance of Pro-4, just what was in the wind.

Back in the office after lunch, I struggled the rest of the day between the work I had to do and the shock of discovery that Harry was, after all, a member of the Communist party, evidently in high standing. I was so stunned that I was unable to concentrate. The office closed and I stayed on alone to clean up my desk. A little after six o'clock, when the switchboard was untended and it was safe to talk, I called Don Richards.

"I apparently haven't been so out of touch with things as I thought," I admitted.

"No?"

"In fact I've been working right next to one of the boys for weeks and never knew it. I'll file on him. Did you ever hear of Pro-4?"

He didn't answer my question. "What do you know about it?" he asked instead.

"I've been invited to join a new group."

"Good. Don't be too anxious. Did they set a time?"

"Not yet. I've got to close out my other affairs first. They will let me know. I don't even know where."

"Fine. Send me all the details on your friend."

"Don't worry," I declared. "I won't forget him."

I followed the orders given to me by Harry and appeared that evening for the last time at the Melrose cell meeting. Then, except for a few PCA activities, I dropped my party connections, and waited. It was a long wait, and a welcome relief from the Communist merry-go-round.

Several weeks went by before I received a telephone call from Harry.

"We're having a small gathering tomorrow night," he said cheerfully. "Can you meet me at Revere and Charles Street at eight?" I assented. "By the way, will you pick up some material at the bookshop? They know about it. Get it ahead of time. It would be—better—easier, perhaps, not to come directly from the shop." I understood that he was again stressing a tight security policy.

I picked up the educational material that afternoon at the Progressive Bookshop, using an alias, Arthur Trobridge. Then I dropped a message to Don Richards, informing him that the meeting was to be held somewhere in the vicinity of Revere and Charles, but adding that I had not been given the street address.

In the autumn darkness of the next evening I waited on the corner of Revere and Charles until Harry drove up. He parked his car, and together we walked up the Revere Street hill a few feet

228

from the corner and turned into an apartment at Number 6. Lugging my heavy satchel of party literature, I puffed up two flights of steep, narrow, wooden stairs, at the top of which Harry knocked at a door. It was opened by a large, round-cheeked, and effusive brunet girl with a hearty hostess manner. She was introduced to me only as Norma. We passed through the cheerful foyer of the apartment toward a doorway leading to the living room.

In the door I paused for a breath and surveyed the room. The apartment was different from most of the party meeting places to which I was accustomed. The furnishings, while not lavish, were of excellent quality and quiet taste. At one end of the room was a fireplace set with white birch logs, apparently for decorative purposes rather than for fuel. Cleanliness showed the hand of a good housewife. There was a bright carpet on the floor, and the light-wood furniture was conservatively modern. A broad sofa stood in front of a solid bank of beige curtains which apparently screened a long window row. There were flowers in the vases, and the sound of bright, unrestrained conversation filled the room.

On the sofa and in comfortable chairs ringing the room there were six or eight persons, most of them women. Some of them conversed in pairs, others regarded me cordially and without obvious curiosity. There was an atmosphere of pleasant sociability. Norma took me by the arm.

"Come in and join us," she trilled.

Never had I seen a more innocent-looking gathering—the members of Pro-4, a cell of the Professional Group, Communist party, U.S.A.

CHAPTER 14

"Come in," Norma said again.

But I was frozen in the doorway, rooted to the spot. There on the sofa, slouched in a shadow and not at first apparent, watching me with a slow smile on his massive face, was a man, an old friend, the last man in the world I ever expected to find at a meeting of a Communist party cell.

The big man in the rumpled suit regarded me with a level gaze. The satchel suddenly felt like a lead weight in my right hand. My left arm stiffened to resist Norma's gentle tug. Incredulity swept over me. I felt a tingling along the nape of my neck as though my hair was rising.

Here was a respected, prominent Boston businessman, the vice-president and second in command of the largest firm of its kind in New England; a man with an area-wide and even nation-wide reputation for his business specialty. I had met him several times in business clubs at whose luncheons he usually occupied a place at the head table. A vast man, shaggy, unkempt, affable, slow-moving, factual. His wife was active in church and civic affairs. His children were college students. The top position he held in his firm gave him wide esteem along State Street. The job he did was looked upon as a tremendous asset to New England's commercial and industrial life. He was a contributor of frequent lead articles to trade journals in his field. A trifle eccentric, given to wearing sloppy and threadbare clothes and energetically supporting "progressive" movements, he was excused by conservative Bostonians

230

because of his warm personality, his hearty affability, and his intrinsic gentleness. He was an ardent supporter of Henry Wallace and the Progressive Citizens of America, where I had worked with him on membership and organizational campaigns. Some of his friends thought his political activities a bit odd, but they said of him, "He means well—and such a good guy."

And now, here he sat in a secret meeting of Communists.

I started to perspire. The conversation in the room died, and in the silence I felt eyes turned upon me. The surprise, the acute embarrassment, the panic of my discovery that this man was an intimate of Communists, gave way to fear—fear that I had stumbled upon a carefully guarded secret of the Communist party, and that for some reason I stood now on the verge of betrayal as an FBI undercover agent. The sweat beaded my forehead and trickled down my back. I tore my gaze from the level eyes of the big crumpled man on the sofa, glanced quickly around the room again, and forced a smile.

"Come in," said Norma, nudging my elbow. I struggled for a coherent thought to banish the shocked expression I was sure covered my face. I dropped the satchel of pamphlets and books heavily just inside the door and reached for my handkerchief. I wiped the sweat from my face and around my collar and recovered my breath.

"Golly," I gasped to Norma in an effort to explain my obvious discomfort, "I'll bet those fiendish stairs will help keep your figure. How do you manage to haul your groceries up here?" The polite laughter directed at the plump hostess by my side dispelled the tension. "Phew!" I added with feeling. But the ordeal was not yet over. The problem of greeting remained. I was still standing in the frame of the doorway as if transfixed by a spotlight. When in trouble, smile, I said to myself, and I did, despite my horror. Then I thought of the incongruity of the situation, the joke on myself, knowing this man for years, without the slightest intimation that he might be a Communist. The smile that started as an effort turned into the real thing and I was actually laughing at myself as I moved across the room toward him.

"Well," I said, as I grasped the hand that he extended as he remained seated, "I'm certainly glad to see you here, Comrade. I must admit I'm surprised."

"I suspected you knew each other," Norma said. I had control of myself once more. "Now meet these other people. Teddy, Jackie, Faith, Butch, Peg, Helen—this is Herb." There was only one among them whom I knew well. Comrade Teddy, a pert, pretty career girl, was an executive assistant to one of the leading non-Communist figures in PCA. In this position she was a veritable pipeline of information from the top level of the PCA to the Communist party. She had access to PCA plans, platforms, and decisions even before the membership. She knew thoroughly the organization's sources of income and political contacts. Now she greeted me with a superior little smile.

Others in the room I knew vaguely from work I had done previously in other Communist front groups. When the introductions were over I found a chair in the far corner of the room and dropped into it.

A Communist is all things to all people. Some regard him as an intellectual, essentially harmless but intense, spouting Marxism in abstruse terms. Another thinks of a Communist as a tough-fisted labor leader swinging a club on the picket line; others as a sinister professor, a suave diplomat, a swarthy saboteur, a bomb-throwing assassin. But every non-Communist, no matter what his station in life, is usually quite sure of one thing: that there are no hardened, disciplined Communists in his immediate circle of friends and acquaintances. No one he knows well and likes could possibly be among those who attend secret meetings and listen to discussions of revolution, violence, and the rise of the proletariat. Each man has a few friends he regards as "radical," perhaps. But none of them, he is sure, would go so far as to conspire. None preaches civil strife, or believes in it. Those who do that sort of

232

thing live in a world apart. They are shadowy figures in the darkness of unreality, fictional characters who occasionally break into the headlines as atom spies or Communist couriers, but they are not real. The average American cannot conceive of a Communist revolutionary living next door to him or occupying the desk just across the aisle.

So I had always thought. In spite of all my experiences over the years as a working Communist, I had convinced myself that the ardent members of the party, although I knew them and worked with them, belonged in a different world. Few of them could have been my good friends under any circumstances. I looked upon them as actors to be watched on a stage, who lingered only as illusions when I left the theater. I recognized their threat, their insidiousness, and their perfidy, but I never accepted them as an integral part of my own life.

Until now, when I was forced to a sudden awakening.

The discussion leader for the evening was launching into his discourse. "We are sorry you were unable to be here when we started our detailed study of *The State and Revolution*," he said, holding up a book. I became aware that he was speaking to me. "You know this work of Lenin's, don't you?"

"Oh, yes," my voice responded. "I've studied it before. I know it well."

The doctrine of *The State and Revolution*, with its political and philosophical analysis of the powers of a government and its discussion of the requirements of a successful revolution, was unusually strong medicine even for myself, a hardened pupil of many Communist classes. But here in this atmosphere of muted gentility, among a group of well-groomed and carefully mannered professional people, with one of Boston's business leaders seated across from me listening impassively, it was unbelievable.

"We have seen in our previous discussion," the leader droned on, "that the origins of the state are in capitalism itself; that the state is the product of the irreconcilable character of class antago-

233

nisms; and that this power, arising from society, becomes more and more separated from it. The state then becomes an instrument for the exploitation of the working class."

I looked at my friend on the sofa, certain that the ludicrousness of the situation would bring the smile back to his face.

"The social democrats," I was hearing, "the Browderites and the socialists have distorted the words of Engels to mean that the capitalist state can go through a process of withering away, can be changed for the better without a revolution. But the correct steps which must be taken are, contrary to the vulgarizers of Engels, very clearly indicated."

The big man across the room apparently accepted with perfect equanimity the fact that I—assistant advertising director of the largest entertainment organization in New England, a family man, father of four daughters, Sunday-school teacher, youth leader— should also be here in a nest of Communists, listening to a discussion of the state and how to overthrow it. I wondered if it had been a surprise to him, or if he actually regarded it as normal.

"First the proletariat must destroy the capitalist state. The capitalist state will not wither away of its own accord, and cannot be transformed. It must be destroyed. Second, the special repressive force of the capitalists must be replaced by another special repressive force, the proletarian state. Third, the proletarian state will wither away, but only after the consolidation of the dictatorship and only after the destruction of all remnants of capitalism."

There was a question period after the discussion. Our hostess, Norma, who, I discovered, was a newcomer to the group herself, holding the first meeting at her own apartment, was disturbed that democracy would also disappear after the revolution. Democracy under capitalism, it was explained, was merely another form of the bourgeois state, and it too must be destroyed.

But if there was any question of the group's not understanding the lesson, it was dispelled in the summary given by the discussion

234

leader: "The replacement of the bourgeois state by the proletarian state is impossible without a violent revolution. The abolition of the proletarian state, in turn, is only possible through withering away, when it is no longer necessary as a controlling force."

After the meeting was over, feeling weak from the shock of the evening, I excused myself as quickly as possible. Driving home in a mood of black despair, I could not put out of my mind the thought that in a world of such rude jolts there was constant peril that I might be discovered. Every member of the party, and certainly every member of this elite group into which I had now been introduced, was under constant suspicion and under the careful scrutiny of party security agents. The slightest defection, the smallest slip, might bring unpleasant consequences.

I must work out some special defenses. The first thing was to strengthen my Marxism, to practice more and more the mental attitude of the Marxist revolutionary. I must be more careful to place myself in the proper frame of mind before each meeting. I must never walk through a doorway, turn a corner on the street, meet a friend, talk with a stranger, or answer a telephone without having my guard alert and ready.

But the most difficult task facing me was also the most essential. There was one vulnerable spot which had to be eliminated. It meant cutting down one of the guideposts of my life and accepting the tragic fact. Where communism is concerned, there is no one who can be trusted. Anyone can be a Communist. Anyone can suddenly appear in a meeting as a Communist party member—close friend, brother, employee or even employer, leading citizen, trusted public servant. Now I could understand the instructions of the party leaders when I first joined: "Your membership will be secret. . . . Don't separate yourself from the masses. . . . Maintain your normal ties and lead a perfectly normal life." Anyone can do that, I reflected. No one is safe. No one can be trusted. There is no way to distinguish a Communist from a non-Communist.

235

When I trudged upstairs late that night, I had reached the lowest ebb of my life. My faith in my fellow man, one of the rocks on which my life was founded, was seriously undermined. Of all the ills of communism, none seemed more evil than this debasement of moral standards, this subversion of the traditionally American sense of fair play. I knew that I had collided with one of the complex questions of our day, and it would take time to find the answer, if there was any.

In my bedroom, Eva told me I looked ill. She was obviously alarmed. I was not physically sick, but I was indeed sick at heart.

"I've had enough of this business, Eva," I told her. "I just can't figure it out. It baffles me." But before I dropped off to sleep another thought took precedence in my tortured mind. There is only one way to find and expose the underground Communist. You have to get right in there with him, down in the muck. There is no other way.

Early the next morning I called Don Richards. "How did it go?" he asked.

"Perfect," I replied. "It was very interesting. We had a successful little session. It's hot. Really hot." Don made no direct comment when we met to talk it over, but he was plainly encouraged. "You're making progress," was as far as he would go. "Something may come of it yet." Don's natural reticence made his expressions of enthusiasm sound very mild.

The pro-group meetings went on and on. For the next year and a half my Communist party activities were centered almost entirely around the clever conspiracy of Pro-4. Shock was added to shock as I uncovered gradually the composition of the group, the surprising personalities who went twice a month to homes and apartments in Boston and Cambridge for cell meetings. I learned how the pro-group was organized, approximately how many members there were in its closely knit units, how it functioned with respect to the rest of the party, and where and to what extent it

236

wielded its powerful influence in behalf of Karl Marx, Lenin, and especially Joseph Stalin.

At first the young people I met appeared to be rather agreeable members of the white-collar class, a notch above the secretarial or clerkship level. I hoped that their involvement might have been the result of misguidance. Harry was one exception to this, and my prominent business friend was another.

Norma, our hostess at that initial meeting although on a higher level than an office girl, was less skilled than the others; she was the homey type and obviously frightened by some of the things she heard in cell meetings. She seemed to be a young woman who was infatuated with the scientific aspects of socialism, and she thought it was smart to know about them. In truth she would have been better off reading love stories instead for her relaxation, with a box of chocolates on the arm of her chair. Norma's husband, whose party name was Mike, was a certified public accountant, and I understood that he was a member of another pro-cell.

Then there was a girl whom I shall call Susan, a Bohemian type who thought she wanted to be a writer. Although she was a diligent worker in various front organizations and even on the pay roll of two or three, she seemed the least devoted to the dictates of Joseph Stalin of anyone in the group. It became obvious to me that she was unhappy in the party and was staying in because she was afraid of blackmail and knew no easy way out. Indeed, there *is* no easy out. Watching the pathetic figure of Susan, trapped in the party, reminded me of the dissertation of the heavy-handed Manny Blum on the matter of potential "party traitors" and the "conditions that may cause them to reconsider." One of those conditions—blackmail.

Susan had courage, however, and showed a spark of independent spirit at the time of the Tito-Stalin split during the summer of 1948. She seemed to derive sly enjoyment reminding her fellow comrades of their previous worshipful attitude toward the "great Yugoslav patriot." She was a sad and sensitive person, and she lived alone in a small two-room apartment with a Murphy bed, in Cambridge. Sometimes I had the distinct impression that she was clinging desperately to her sanity.

Another member of Pro-4, Butch, was a young artist, also with rather Bohemian ways, who lived on Beacon Hill. He was not very bright politically but was attentive, quick, and talented in other ways; despite his political naïveté, the party put his artistic talents to good use.

Peg Gilbert—Mrs. Margaret Gilbert—served us as a wonderful shield for our pro-group activities; she was held in such high esteem by her neighbors that we could meet at her house with relatively little fear of arousing suspicion. She was a plain young woman with straw-colored hair, the mother of two children, and the wife of a labor-union organizer. She herself was a professional, paid worker in a number of front organizations and a charming hostess at numerous Communist social affairs. Why exactly Peggy Gilbert was associated with this group is a mystery to me. Certainly no one in her neighborhood would ever believe that "nice Mrs. Gilbert down the street with those lovely children" might be party to a conspiracy.

A stylish, attractive young woman in the group—Helen, by name—was our courier. She was extremely quiet and wore her expensive clothes like a professional model. Never did she indicate by so much as a word exactly what her job with the group was, but her frequent trips to New York and to Europe—with no visible means of support—led the rest of us to the correct conclusion that she was not only a courier but an international courier. Subsequently I was to learn more about the contacts between the Russian and American Communist parties, although always in general outline and seldom in detail. Altogether there are four major Soviet espionage networks in America, each operating independently of the others. The two thousand pro-group members in America serve as the major source of information for one of these espionage systems—and the glamorous, silent Helen was their contact in my own Pro-4.

All of this I learned by painfully slow degrees, over the weeks and months of our meetings. It was entirely possible to sit next to a person a dozen times at meeting after meeting and learn only his party name, nothing more.

Our meetings were held at the homes of these and other members of the pro-group, and initially I wondered if it might be possible that they were not really Communists after all, but merely dupes who had been lassoed into what they regarded as intellectual discussions about Karl Marx and the history of revolutionary movements.

But as the meetings continued, and they remained in attendance, this hope was lost. We paid dues at our meetings to the Communist party. We contributed a special pro-group "sustaining fee" to the party treasury. We talked about Communist party affairs, directives, and personalities, and openly discussed the party line. Our meetings followed the normal routine of all party cells— first a discussion of cell business and activities, followed by a dues collection and sale of literature, and topped off with an "educational" discussion based on the Marxist classics.

This was the pattern, and it was manifestly impossible as time went on that anyone could be there without a full realization that he was deep in the Communist movement. All of the members, like me, had been ordered to destroy their cards, and all functioned in secrecy, unknown as Communists to their friends, and unknown even to the rank-and-file members of the party, who were entirely unaware that the pro-group existed.

Between the fall of 1947 and the spring of 1948, as the cell to which I belonged grew and its membership was gradually rotated, other faces came into the picture.

Harry Winner, the quick-witted and affable Malden rubber-company executive and Samuel Adams School instructor, was one of them. Although I'd met Winner before at various functions

239

and on one occasion we had spoken from the same platform, I did not know him well until he began attending our meetings. As a party type, he was the direct opposite of such ominous conspirators as Daniel Boone Schirmer or Jack Stachel. His was a warm, jovial nature; he thoroughly enjoyed his human relationships in and out of the party and was perfectly at ease in any group. When the city of Malden celebrated its centennial anniversary a few years ago, Harry Winner, one of the most popular men in town, was selected chairman for the occasion.

Curiously enough, one of those closest to Winner was Dirk J. Struik; and they made an interesting study in contrasts. Dirk was cold and calculating—perhaps the prototype of the pure scientist. He was not only a great mathematician but an expert in Marxist theory as well; he combined these two fields in his flat assumption that Stalinism was founded in science. I have heard him lecture many times at the Samuel Adams School; he could hold a class of Communists and non-Communists alike absolutely spellbound, reeling off names, dates, facts, and figures in accurate detail without even glancing at his notes.

The more I saw of Pro-4, the more varied and fascinating its membership became. Two young men whom I had known from my earlier days in the Young Communist League reappeared, this time as Boston attorneys and respected members of the bar. There was a successful author and a prominent Jewish leader. A labor-union leader of great ability and with many valuable contacts among Boston newspapermen joined Pro-4.

Culture simply oozed out of our pro-group; graduate and honorary degrees were a dime a dozen. One of the most popular members of the group was a woman of great talent who could boast a family listed in *Who's Who,* a European education, and a degree from a fashionable Eastern college. She had written a dozen successful books and was a leader in all sorts of women's clubs and professional groups.

The question of money raising in our pro-group was one which

240

at first amazed me. At one of the early meetings, I saw sums of $15 to $25 passed along casually to our treasurer; it was not long before I realized that Pro-4 had ample resources on which to draw. The members were nicked for dues, "sustaining fees," and innumerable "drives, funds, and causes." In one such drive alone, our eighty members produced more than $3,500 in cash. One of our older and wealthier enthusiasts, Mrs. Sara Gordon, the wife of an affluent jeweler, used to hold receptions in honor of such party stalwarts as Paul Robeson and Elizabeth Gurley Flynn in her swank hotel apartment with its magnificent sweeping view of the Charles River. At such affairs, money raising, in good taste of course, was an important item.

These people were all well-known, established residents of the Boston area, some of them suspected among the citizenry at large of having leftist tendencies, but none regarded openly as a member of the Communist party. Many of them were among the most respected and most expert in their particular fields of endeavor; a few were wealthy.

The cell to which I belonged numbered ten to a dozen members before security measures required that it be broken down into smaller units. I learned that there were other cells also in the group, including a teachers' cell in the public schools; a small cell of government workers; two cells composed of writers, authors, newspapermen, and radio workers; two of businessmen; a cell for lawyers; another for doctors; cells for college professors, including one at MIT and one at Harvard; a cell for phony ministers—a few of whom were ordained; and a cell for social workers. In all, it was estimated, the pro-group membership in the Boston area numbered about eighty persons; in addition, there were a few pro-group floaters who were never permanently attached to any one cell.

Altogether there were some fifteen cells in existence in the fall of 1947 when I first joined the pro-group. Each cell numbered from three to a dozen or fifteen members, ours being one of the largest. The membership was reorganized from time to time as members moved away or new ones were brought in, or as their job status or party missions were changed.

The pro-group operated with almost complete independence from the district leadership. Major party directives were passed to the group directly from the Communist party national headquarters in New York. Each cell had the prerogative of overruling district headquarters on such matters as membership. Quite often, a name submitted by the district leadership was turned down for lack of qualifications by the pro-group. Each cell designated a single representative to serve for it on the Pro-Council, which was the top governing body of the pro-group. The elections were held on a remarkably democratic footing, because these people were all thoroughly devoted Communists, and there was little or no fear of defection among them. Cell members rarely commingled except on the Pro-Council level.

This elaborate organization had a definite purpose, one of crucial importance to the Communist party. The members of the pro-group represented the intelligentsia, the party intelligentsia as distinguished from that of the bourgeoisie. They were the vanguard of the vanguard. Their mission as a group, through individual influence in their communities, businesses, professions, civic organizations, and local governments, was to direct the thinking on all issues toward the tenets of Marxism-Leninism and toward conclusions that would aid the Communist party. The particular value of the pro-group members, who diligently came together every two weeks for their own realignment, rested not alone on their influence and the high regard in which they were held in their communities, but also on the absence of any apparent ties with communism.

Their hands appeared clean. They functioned through the elaborate party network of front organizations, and almost every pro-group member was energetic in his front activities. Some were active in scores of organizations of all kinds. The arrange-

242

ment was somewhat the same as that in the Anthony Roche campaign for Congress, although on a much larger scale. But whereas in the case of Roche a special underground committee had to be established to infiltrate the campaign, the pro-group stood as a permanent force, mobilized and highly mobile, prepared to move swiftly and efficiently wherever an issue arose or an organization afforded an opportunity for the spread of Stalinism. The pro-group was large enough to cover every important field of endeavor, and there were among its members experts in every segment of the cultural, commercial, and professional life of the community. Yet it was small enough to escape detection.

No task was too large or too small for the pro-group to tackle, and no outlet was overlooked. The activities within my own cell ranged from the foisting of a Communist peace crusade on a church meeting to the rewriting of a major speech for a presidential candidate. We directed strategy in a labor-organizing drive; we served as a major money-raising arm for the party; we secured and passed on to higher echelons confidential information about important industrial firms. We did not frequently require orders from the cell or from pro-headquarters. We knew what to do without being told. Occasionally, however, direct orders were given in our biweekly meetings.

Shortly after I became a member of Pro-4, such an order was given to me. It involved my own Wakefield Baptist Church and placed me in an embarrassing situation, but one from which I could not escape. It was a typical professional-group order—nothing written, but simply a mutual understanding within the group. It was known that I was active in the Mr. and Mrs. Club at the church, which I had helped to establish and of which Eva and I were the first presidents.

The subject of the club came up in connection with the intensive "peace crusade" then being conducted by international communism. It was a part of the campaign to allay fears of war, inspire disarmament, and lull the world to sleep in the face of

Communist aggrandizement. The Mr. and Mrs. Club, with its church background and its youthful atmosphere, seemed an ideal place to foster the campaign. Accordingly, it was suggested that I make arrangements for a speaker to address the club on the subject of "peace." The speaker was a member of the professional group, a secret Communist, and a respected Bostonian. The event was held, and the speech followed the party line to the letter. It was a complete apologia for Russia and for the Soviet Union's obstructive tactics in the United Nations. The speaker urged us not to blame Russia for taking a position of defense against the "imperialist nations" which surrounded her. He declared that the Soviet Union had done its best to prevent World War II, and that only when these efforts were ignored by the free world did Stalin enter a nonaggression pact with Nazi Germany, forced upon him for his own protection.

It was a good speech from the Communist point of view, although it fell on deaf ears among most members of the club, few of whom were so naïve as to fall for it. Needless to say, I sat through a very uncomfortable evening.

That was an example of a small task, trivial in itself, but when multiplied by many similar jobs taken on by each cell member, and then again by the three score and more professional group members active in every phase of Boston community life, and still another time by the two thousand pro-group members throughout the country, it was a contribution of significance.

As in every section and activity of the party, there is a fundamental Marxist precept on which the pro-group is based. In a booklet we studied, *Culture in a Changing World,* by V. J. Jerome, Karl Marx is quoted as saying, "Before the proletariat fights out its battles on the barricades, it announces the coming of its rule with a series of intellectual victories." The first problem is to win men's minds. When that is accomplished, the rest is easy.

Many of the pro-group's offensives to win men's minds were more dramatic. Henry A. Wallace was brought to Boston for a

244

major political rally at the Boston Garden during his 1948 presidential campaign. A part of his address was broadcast on the radio. A copy of this speech came into the office of the Progressive party on Beacon Hill the day before the event, and ultimately found its way into the hands of my businessman friend from the pro-cell. He regarded the speech as woefully inadequate, fuzzy, and confused. My friend called me at my office and asked me to hurry over. I sat down with him for more than two hours, and worked over Wallace's phraseology. My friend rewrote the speech during the night, and by noon the following day it was mimeographed. Whether Wallace had time to read it before the broadcast I never knew. But in any event, comrades in the pro-group were delighted with the speech as it was given.

During my two years in the pro-group, I handled a multitude of similar assignments, although naturally I withheld myself from as much activity as I could, volunteering only enough to keep me in good standing. On one occasion I was given one of our frequent blind orders to go to an apartment on Walnut Street. The reason for the mission was not described. On arrival I found myself in the lavish apartment of Elizabeth Moos, at that time mother-in-law of William Remington (later tried for perjury in regard to his denial of membership in the party). She was expecting me. We sat down and discussed arrangements for a Boston reception for the Very Reverend Hewlett Johnson, the famous "Red Dean of Canterbury" and a foremost apostle of the Communist "peace crusade."

The pro-group worked most intensively on the Progressive party's campaign for Henry A. Wallace, which was one of its major activities during the period of my membership. "We have assigned some of our most important people to this task," I was told in a pro-cell meeting. We were under strict orders in our Progressive party work to maintain absolute secrecy as to Communist party participation in the affairs of the organization. On Sunday, February 8, 1948, the state convention of the Progressive

Citizens of America was held in Boston to draw up a resolution, later to be transformed into the platform of the Progressive party. There was a liberal sprinkling of pro-group members throughout the convention and its leadership. A good many floaters were on hand, who had no connection with any cells. A glance at the platform is the best evidence of Communist influence.

It called for complete rejection of the Marshall Plan for strengthening Western Europe; the withdrawal of all military personnel, equipment, and aid from Greece and Turkey (on whose borders Communist pressure was constantly applied); the rejection of universal military training and drastic reduction of military expenditures to an "absolute minimum"; support of "democratic" China; repeal of President Truman's loyalty order and "revocation" of the power of the FBI. On the domestic scene, the Communists wrote into the platform measure after measure which would make the people even more dependent on their government for everything in their lives—jobs, health, security, housing, education, *et al.*

No one really expected a Wallace victory. But as in the Anthony Roche campaign, Communist ideas were planted and class strife promoted. The entire program for the convention was discussed in detail at pro-cell meetings. Then it was handed over to a public committee of three persons for formal drafting. Finally it was returned to a party floater, the wife of an eminent scholar, and a woman against whom there is no legal evidence of the Communist party membership which she actually held. She made the final revisions and passed the program on to Wallace's campaign committee.

The Bureau queried me, "Where do these orders come from? Who gives them?" In my cell, they usually came from Martha Fletcher, the cell leader. They came to Martha from "Jan," who received them by courier from New York. The district headquarters were not only by-passed on numerous occasions, but in

246

fact orders were usually sent from the pro-group to local functionaries.

One cell member, a top public-relations man, was assigned to the field of labor to assist Communist unions in drawing up material which would best appeal to workers in organizational campaigns. Such a task included interviews with workers and union officials and careful studies of company counterpropaganda and business affairs. Sometimes several cell members took part in these studies, and the information was routed through my cell to other professional-group members who then went to work on preparation of the actual propaganda material.

Another skilled career man said to be in the pro-group worked in the heart of Boston's financial district and had ready access to facts and figures. He received periodic requests from the Communist party for information as to the financial strength of Boston corporations, the composition of their directorates, their rates of earnings and profits, and similar material for use in compiling anticapitalist propaganda. This same man was in a position to influence thinking in high places. He made strenuous efforts to plant the fear in the business community that the defense effort was the only thing holding together the nation's economy, and that without it the whole structure would collapse. He could and did steer this statement into the public press through non-Communist business officials who gave him their ears.

One of the pro-group members managed to get himself a post on the governor's study commission for the drafting of a fair-employment-practices law. After the drafting was completed and the law was passed, it was arranged through a Communist labor union to put pressure on the governor's office to have the same man named as a permanent commissioner to help administer the law. It was defeated when the details of the plot were laid before Governor Maurice J. Tobin by a particularly alert newspaperman.

247

While the members of the professional group were subjected to the usual discipline so far as loyalty was concerned, they were permitted greater freedom on the intellectual level than those in the lower ranks of the party. It was entirely possible to "deviate" in exploratory fashion, at least in small ways. On matters of broad general policy, no swerving from the party line was tolerated. For example, when Marshal Tito turned against the Cominform and was branded as a renegade by the international party, pro-group members who previously had lauded him as a hero had to jump through the Stalin hoop with the same nimbleness as the others.

But, as Stalin declared, "everything depends on the time, the place, and the conditions." Society is constantly changing, and the Communist party must have enough flexibility to meet these changes. Not every order comes from Moscow, nor even from the national headquarters. The pro-group section of the party, throughout the country, led by the best minds the party could muster, held it within their power to call the tune on local matters.

In Boston there is an organization known as the Twentieth Century Association, considered a respectable non-Communist group with a fifty-five year history in the community. It is an organization literally supported and backed by Boston's best families.

On March 25, 1947, at Number 3 Joy Street in Boston, Philip Jaffe and Julian Friedman gave a report on China and on "China's People Today." (Jaffe, at one time editor and owner of the magazine *Amerasia*, was arrested by the FBI in 1945 for "unauthorized possession of defense data" but was later acquitted.) Louis Lyons, formerly of the Boston *Globe* and at present curator of the Nieman Foundation of Journalism at Harvard University, was the chairman for the evening. What Lyons and those present did not know was that "arrangements" for the meeting had been made through the subtle influence of two pro-group members, one

248

of them also a member of the Association. Dirk Jan Struik, professor of mathematics at Massachusetts Institute of Technology, also assisted in the project, and the speakers were obtained by way of Maude Russell's Committee for a Democratic Far Eastern Policy, an organization listed by the United States Attorney General as subversive.

The front is the stock outlet for pro-group operations. The fronts which we used were of four general types, with many degrees of shading between them. Failure to distinguish between these groups and to understand the Communist party's methods and aims is one of the greatest weaknesses of the anti-Communist forces, and a source of many injustices. Blanket condemnations such as those of the House Un-American Activities Committee, which black-list entire organizations because of the presence of a few Communists, frequently harm innocent persons. Guilt by association merely strengthens the hand of agitators in their attacks upon the infringements of civil liberties.

First, there is the Communist front that has been planned as such from its inception. The Civil Rights Congress is an example. This type of front is conceived and directed by Communists and operates behind a screen of apparently respectable pro-group members. Non-Communist organizations and individuals are drawn into the front in response to its name and its statement of purpose. Even though it is heavily disguised, its basic aims will normally coincide with the Communist party line. No matter who the innocent sponsors may be, a careful examination of its platform for comparison with party declarations will usually unmask it as a Communist front. It may be drawn around specific issues with which many liberal-minded persons are inclined to agree. But Communists leading such groups usually permit one issue to run into another, until inevitably they tip their hand to the clever observer and reveal their espousal of the whole Communist platform.

The second type of front is the coalition, in which the party openly joins hands with other organizations, Communist or non-

Communist. The Progressive Citizens of America (PCA) is a typical example. The idea of a third party in the 1948 elections was carefully considered by the Communists ahead of time, but it was not exclusively their idea. There were many other liberal and independent voters who felt in all sincerity that they could not support either of the two major parties. They also felt that the PCA (and later the Progressive party) was a "noble experiment" in cooperation with the Communists. They soon discovered that such cooperation is an idle dream. The Communists took over the PCA lock, stock, and barrel, and later made a shambles out of the campaign and a fool of Mr. Wallace. It is a tragic fact that countless loyal Americans were caught in a trap when the House Committee on Un-American Activities listed the Progressive Citizens of America as subversive.

There is a third type of front which is based on an organization representative of humanitarian, non-Communist interests, but infiltrated by undercover Communists in a deliberate campaign to seize control and turn the group to their own purposes. Boston's Youth for Victory group was one example, and on the national level, the American Youth Congress was another. Often, after seizing and using the group, the comrades will find that they have no further purpose for the organization and will suddenly withdraw their support and their workers. The organization, by this time dyed a deep red and in public disrepute, then collapses.

In the fourth type of front, infiltration is also involved. But here the Communists use an organization as a refuge and a badge of respectability to conceal their underground activities. Countless associations and committees with spotless records harbor a few Communists without ever knowing it. I knew Communists in the Advertising Club of Boston, who would point to the organization with pride in public and scoff at it in party meetings. The strongest anti-Communist groups make the best blinds. Usually the Communist does not work actively inside this type of organization, but uses it as a credential to worm his way into other organizations. To the top pro-group operators, this fourth type of front is the most important of all.

At the time I joined the pro-group, one of the most active fronts in Boston was the Joint Anti-Fascist Refugee Committee. It was a favorite fund-raising project of the party, playing with elaborate virtuosity upon the sympathies of ordinary citizens for the victims of the defeated fascist armies. The list of sponsors of this group revealed a remarkable absence of known Communist party members, which would make it appear that Communists had been deliberately blackballed. Indeed, if a legitimate liberal organization had shown such discrimination, the Communist party would have been the first to complain. But the pro-group Communists pulled all the levers that controlled the Joint Anti-Fascist Refugee Committee. They appeared as initial sponsors, thus giving the front an air of respectability. They approached other well-known citizens of the Boston community and enlisted their support and the use of their names—and their money. They staged elaborate benefits for which the arrangements, including the sponsorship, were all worked out in Pro-4 meetings. One of these, I recall, was a benefit motion picture, *Man's Hope*. Another was a personal appearance and speech by O. John Rogge. In our pro-cell, we arranged for the hiring of an auditorium—in this case the New England Mutual Hall. We assigned comrades to work on sponsors. Their orders were to obtain the very best, most respectable people: among those who were successfully taken in for this type of fund-raising dodge were Judge Jennie Loitman Barron, Dr. Channing Frothingham, Rabbi Joshua Loth Liebman, and dozens of other noted Bostonians. Using this formula over and over again, garnishing it with speakers who were brought in through the efforts of pro-cell members, the Joint Anti-Fascist Refugee Committee was able to raise tremendous sums of money in Boston alone. Only after considerable public pressure did some of the Boston blue bloods disown the organization, and then, for good measure, some of the pro-group Communists publicly disowned it, too.

Secure as the pro-organization seemed to be, it was not invulnerable. In November, 1947, we were given a scare. To a meeting at Norma's one night came a militaristic young man, Pete the courier, our liaison agent with the district party headquarters. He bore an important message from the leadership. Pete looked the part of the courier; he had close-cropped hair which gave him a Prussian aspect, and the effect was enhanced by a belted trench coat. His visits were always brief. He never addressed anyone in the cell by name, even by first name. His suggestions were accepted by us as party directives. On this particular night he addressed us on the subject of security, and gave us a list of security precautions.

The primary concern, he said, was the protection of the pro-group as a whole, even to the sacrifice of an individual member. He reiterated the order that no member of the group should go to the district office for any reason. He told us not to telephone the state office, but if we had messages, to route them through the cell chairman who, I later learned, relayed them through Jan, the head of the all-powerful Pro-Council.

We were to exercise extreme caution in any contacts with each other outside of cell meetings. It was advisable, he suggested, not to meet in each other's homes privately, but to confine ourselves instead to public places such as restaurants. Pete cautioned us against the keeping of records or the listing of any names. He ordered us to spread out our cell meetings by shifting their location from one member's home to another, and advised us especially to avoid holding successive meetings on the same day of the week. A variable pattern is the first requirement of security. Accordingly we met one week on Wednesday night at one apartment, then on a Friday somewhere else, and even shifted the hour of the gatherings to avoid a rigid pattern.

Not long after Pete's security lecture, the party took a swift dive for cover. The cause of the flurry was a warning from O. John Rogge, former assistant attorney general. He said that his ex-boss,

Attorney General Tom Clark, was preparing to use a New York grand-jury investigation on subversive activities as a springboard for the launching of a new series of raids against the Communist party. Rogge said they would duplicate the notorious Palmer Raids of the 1920s, and that the government's "witch hunt" would be marked by midnight roundups of party leaders, seizure of records and documents, and a framed plot against the Communist party reminiscent of Hitler's carefully staged "Reichstag fire."

The top brass scrambled for cover. District leaders fled the Little Building headquarters and ran into hiding out of the city, taking the party's important records with them. The tipoff said that the raids would take place November 15; it was not until several days after that date that the party relaxed its vigilance and sheepishly emerged from the bushes. No one ever explained this raid which did not come off. The party crowed about its security system and took credit for upsetting the government's plans; but I, for one, was never convinced that any such raid was planned in the first place.

The "Palmer Raid" scare brought new tension into the party. We avoided the telephone. Notices of cell meetings became friendly invitations, such as, "Dear H. I am having a few people in Wednesday evening at eight. Hope to see you then. N." There was no address, and no full names were used.

Despite regulations to the contrary, it was necessary for me to work through district headquarters from time to time because of my specialty in the preparation of leaflets and propaganda material for the district Educational Commission. An exception to the rule was made in my case, but they were the most covert operations. If there was material for me to pick up, a rendezvous was arranged at a soda fountain. I purchased a copy of the Boston *Globe*, entered the drugstore, and took a stool next to the party courier, who had a copy of the *Globe* on the counter beside him. I placed my paper next to his, and after a brief interval he picked up my copy and departed. When I finished my coffee, I took the

253

remaining *Globe*, the folds of which later yielded the source material for a party pamphlet or flier together with instructions for turning it out.

When it was necessary for me to take the bundles of completed material to party headquarters, no contact was necessary. I carried my work to the Boylston Street subway and stuffed it into a parcel locker. Then I inserted the key in an envelope addressed to the headquarters, and dropped it in the mail. The headquarters workers took the key, entered the subway station by a tunnel running under Boylston Street, and retrieved the material without ever going aboveground.

With new vilification directed against the FBI for its supposed part in the Tom Clark "Reichstag plot," I found cell meetings to be more and more a strain on my nerves. I began to lose my appetite, and frequently went to meetings without dinner. I became acutely aware of my dual personality, and the necessity of preventing one from infringing on the other. Driving off to a meeting after a busy day at the office, I would pull the car over to the curb and settle back for a few minutes to shift my mentality into Marxist high gear. I scanned the textbook for the evening's educational meeting, absorbing the rude terminology and bludgeon phrases to tighten my discipline and prepare myself for shocks that I knew would come.

One such shock was the appearance at a meeting of my old friend, the beautiful and charming Martha Fletcher. I knew Martha as a fellow traveler from the old days of the AYD. To walk in and find her in a pro-cell meeting was in itself no great shock—I was prepared by this time to encounter anyone there.

But then came a cell meeting one snowy night at Martha's Grove Street apartment on Beacon Hill. I remember distinctly a small triangular room at the very rear of the apartment with an office desk in the middle and a white porcelain oil stove beside the desk. There was a china closet in one corner of the triangle, a sofa in another corner, and a wooden window seat in the third.

254

A table held a small aquarium with tropical fish, one of them a cannibal, Martha said, which had to be kept in a separate compartment of the tank or it would devour the others. Outside the apartment, elevated trains crossed the bridge from Cambridge and dived into the tunnel under Beacon Hill with a roar that forced us to suspend conversation momentarily.

Martha sat behind the desk, the center of attraction, poised, calm, and efficient, directing the meeting with the warmth of her personality and the vibrancy of her youth. It was my assignment that evening to lead the discussion, which centered on an article in a recent issue of the Cominform bulletin dealing with the intensification of party discipline and action, and especially with the employment of civil disobedience as a primary weapon. The article said that it was impossible for Communists to display an excess of zeal in the pursuit of Communist aims. I had marked out the important sections of the document for discussion and had prepared a list of supplementary questions to provoke comments from the membership. It was intended to be an inspirational discussion, but I observed in Martha a growing impatience. She glanced at me frequently, and her lovely features hardened.

Apparently my conduct of the discussion was too thin for Martha's blood. Her customary warmth vanished; her voice lost its softness. Her eyes glinted with irritation and impatience.

"This lacks specific objectives," she said harshly. "The time has come when we must be realistic. Civil disobedience is nothing new in American history. There are opportunities for it on all sides. We Communists must be vigilant to support incidents of civil disobedience wherever we find them, and to initiate them where necessary."

Martha's attack was a vicious rebuke to me. I made no effort to regain the floor. She called up the memories of Crispus Attucks and John Brown; she raged against Henry Wallace as a social reformer and an idle dreamer—another example of party

255

duplicity in politics. The Communists, and even Martha, were supporting the Wallace campaign in the open, while deriding him behind his back. Martha raged against the "liberals," the "privileged workers," and the "petty bourgeoisie" who stress class collaboration and object to revolutionary struggle. She told us that we must be prepared for civil disobedience which would turn to revolt if a severe economic crisis struck the country, or if the capitalist world embarked on an imperialist war which could be converted into a civil war.

The alarming demonstration of party fervor put on by this attractive young girl lapsed into an impromptu quotation from Stalin which carried her to even greater heights of ardor.

"Furthermore," she said (and I passed on her exact words to Don Richards), "we should arm the workers for it, and we should arm them now."

It was this firebrand—ostensibly a youth leader in the Unitarian Church in Massachusetts, an associate director of American Unitarian Youth, a fiery campaigner for the Progressive party, and a diligent worker in many other organizations, a brilliant, persuasive, and bewitching young woman—who became the chairman of our pro-cell.

To hear her speak with such vehemence unnerved me to the extent that, when I reached home that night, I could not sleep. I went to my hideaway, which in the Melrose house was concealed in an old coalbin in the cellar, and labored until early morning over a long report for Don Richards. "Does she know what she is talking about?" I asked in a rambling digression, and the words on the paper reflected my confused thoughts. Did Martha realize that revolutions, carried out by bands of armed workers, as she called them, meant bloodshed and destruction and a final denial of all Christian principles?

After the conclusion of our studies on the state and revolution, Professor Dirk Struik of MIT came to a meeting at Peg Gilbert's in Cambridge to give us a summation. In a two-hour talk, Dr. Struik analyzed the conditions for socialism and revolution in almost every nation in the world. Some areas, he said, were overripe. One of these was Indonesia, where civil strife was even then in progress. It was another shock to me, another imponderable, when I heard this tall, lanky Dutchman, a naturalized citizen of the United States, a brilliant mathematician and a keen Marxist student, urge all Communists everywhere to support their Indonesian comrades by every possible means in their civil uprising—a revolt directed against his own native land.

Martha Fletcher and Dirk Struik set the tone of the meetings in those early spring days of 1948. Events seemed to be moving swiftly toward a climax. Jittery over the Palmer Raid scare, the party at the same time was beginning to wonder whether the big economic depression would occur as soon as the Cominform and the national board had scheduled it. The threat of war and the elections were in the air, and the party was preparing for every eventuality.

One eventuality was the possible passage of the Mundt-Nixon bill, then up for consideration in Congress, which would have outlawed the Communist party. It brought Pete the courier back to our cell with drastic security orders. We were to be broken down organizationally into groups of no more than five members, Pete explained. There was to be a solid wall of security around each cell. We were never to mention in our cell the name of any member of another cell. Personal or business telephones were never to be used for calls to other cell members. Pay stations were permissible, but we were cautioned that the phone at the other end of the line might be tapped. All written notices of meetings were banned. Our meetings were arranged, with details of time and place, in advance from one session to the next.

The breakdown of the party hit the pro-group hard, and hampered my efforts to gather intelligence. We were split into smaller cells which henceforth never contained more than five members. The regular ranks of the party drew up a similar organizational

257

plan, but it was not put into effect until later. Our units were scattered throughout the Boston area, out of touch with each other except through a new administrative structure. The chairman of each cell in the pro-group served as a member of the Pro-Subcouncil, on which no more than five cells were represented. The Subcouncil, in turn, sent a single delegate to the Pro-Council, the governing body of the entire pro-group. It was this Council which maintained direct links, first to the national party headquarters in New York, and next to the district headquarters.

However well intentioned the Mundt-Nixon proposals may have been, they were greeted with the same hoots of derision in the party as usually accompanies an anti-Communist blast from Congress. Boone Schirmer said, "It's good. They make us appear even stronger than we really are." For those of us trying to do a careful job of fighting communism from inside the party, the mass hysteria that seized the nation was a heavy blow. Although security restrictions had been tight before, it had been possible to move around with comparative freedom and learn what was going on. But the new party breakdown that followed introduction of the control legislation vastly multiplied the difficulties of my intelligence work. Luckily, I had already drawn up a fairly complete picture of the pro-group and its membership for the Bureau. After the breakdown, it would have been almost impossible to get it. I was close to a number of ardent Communists in the larger cell, but I lost track of them after the group was split up, and I seldom knew thereafter what they were doing. It was for reasons such as these that the FBI, including Director J. Edgar Hoover, publicly opposed outlawing the Communist party. Many people felt it would merely drive them underground and make them all the more dangerous and elusive. Although this type of campaign against them might serve the political ambitions of some of the more vocal politicians, it would not hurt the party.

There was another even more personal aspect to the matter. The sound and fury in Congress was genuinely alarming to me, and even more so to Eva. I ran an ever greater risk of exposure as a Communist, which would result in ostracism from my business, social, and community life. My wife and children would suffer most of all. We were certain that someone would attack us on the basis of my AYD treasuryship, the Cambridge Youth Council chairmanship, or some other front activity of the past years. We could easily be the victims of a broad smear campaign which might wreck our lives. And I knew the Bureau's standing rule— "If anything happens, you're on your own."

We actually made plans to move Eva and the children to another part of the country under another name if the Mundt-Nixon bill should land me in jail or expose me. I discounted this possibility, but not Eva. It was a heavy strain on her from day to day.

But in the end, it was not necessary. Luck was with us, and although I did not know it, my time in the party was fast running out.

It was in the midst of these new security maneuvers that the Party was dealt a severe blow. On July 20, 1948, the Federal Grand Jury in New York slapped conspiracy indictments on the twelve top leaders of the Communist party, including Chairman William Z. Foster. Horror and outrage spread through the ranks, but it was not long before the party, rising to the challenge, purged its own jitters and restored its confidence. Rallies were held to denounce the Smith Act, under which the twelve were charged. Pamphlets, leaflets, newspaper and magazine articles compiled with the assistance of the best legal minds in the party set out to convince the American people of the innocence of the victims. There was arrogance in their tone. They defied the law, the courts, and the Justice Department. They swiftly and efficiently organized campaigns for funds for defense of the twelve. The entire energies of the party were directed toward the trial.

In the meantime, an emergency mobilization plan was organized in case the party had to go entirely underground. In Boston, the system was given two trials in the pro-group and regular party cells. The plan was designed so that all members could be rallied at a moment's notice in a predetermined location. It was also to correct deficiencies the party discovered during the Palmer Raid scare, when it found itself floundering without a substitute chain of command or adequate hideouts and communication networks.

The two practice mobilizations were held in July and August, 1948, and they demonstrated the efficiency of the new administrative setup throughout the party. Warnings were flashed, for example, from headquarters to the chairman of the Pro-Council, who notified the other members of the group. The notification, by courier or code telephone call, was in the form of an innocuous message, such as, "Aunt Martha is sick, can you come over?" Each Pro-Council delegate flashed the word to his subcouncil, and the five members of this group passed it along to their cells. By virtue of the new organization, each leader at every level was responsible for no more than five others, and the alert was thus filtered quickly down through the ranks. From that time on each cell in the party maintained a standard mobilization procedure with a predesignated rallying point, a recognized warning code, and a tight system of communications. It was the beginning of an underground organization which has been constantly polished and perfected since.

Shortly after the indictments, I received a telephone call one day at the office from Don Richards. "Can you duck out for a minute?" he asked.

"Sure." I grabbed my hat and told Eddie Alfano I had to go down to the bank.

"Can you cash a check for me?" he asked. "Save me a trip."

I told him I would and waited while he endorsed the check to me. Then I dashed out of the office. Fifteen minutes later, I was seated in Don's two-door jalopy, a wreck of a car whose exterior appearance belied its high-speed engine and its well-equipped interior. We parked on the Esplanade along the Charles River near the Hatch Memorial Shell.

"What's doing?" Richards asked.

"Nothing new. Routine. Mostly trial stuff, civil rights, that sort of thing. The comrades are screaming about The Twelve."

"What do you know about the indictments and about The Twelve?" Richards asked.

"Quite a bit. That's all we've talked about."

Richards looked straight ahead of him through the windshield, his eyes wandering into the distance. He was silent for a long minute.

"I have instructions to make an inquiry of you," Don said, and it was not his normal manner of approaching a subject.

"Anything I can do, you know. . . ."

"This might not be easy. The Justice Department wants to know if you might be willing—would volunteer—to appear as a government witness at the trial of The Twelve. They want you to tell your whole story."

CHAPTER **15**

A BLAST OF WIND across the Charles shook the car, and my breath came out in a long whistle. The road that had twisted down almost nine years took its last crazy turn, the most unexpected of all.

"Here's the story," Richards said quietly. "I'm not urging you one way or the other. I have to separate myself from my opinions and my interests in the case. I'll just give you the background and the government's view, but I hope you understand that the decision is yours. At least in part," he added as if in afterthought.

"In the trial, the Justice Department will need witnesses—live witnesses who will appear on the stand. We can't try a court case simply by going before a jury with records and telling them that 'Confidential Agent X' took part in certain activities in the party and reported them to us, or that so-and-so made certain revolutionary statements to him. That won't do. The witness must give his testimony directly and the defense must be permitted to cross-examine him. But this is an unusual case. To prosecute it, we have to wreck a good bit of what we have built up. If you go on the stand, obviously you will be ruined in the party forever and your usefulness to us will be ended—done—finished."

I waited, expecting Richards to say something more. "That's all there is," he concluded.

For a few minutes I thought about it in silence. I knew what a shock my appearance on the witness stand would be to the party. I also recognized that there could be serious danger to my family and to me if it should leak out in advance that I was to take the stand to spill the story of my years in the Communist party. At the same time, I reflected, it would relieve me of a task that was becoming more of a burden than I could carry. I had been neglecting my business and other matters of importance to my family. I had almost no home life. Instead of going to advertising meetings as I should and widening my circle of business acquaintances, I had been dashing off evenings and week ends to more and more Communist party affairs. My average was at least three meetings a week—cell meetings, conferences on special projects, luncheon sessions with various pro-group and party leaders.

"Well," I said, "if I could shuck off this load and still do a job for the government—it would be good, Don. No doubt about that. Frankly, Eva and I have been worried. We've been wondering how we ever were going to break away. We haven't been able to see any clear way out. This could be a happy solution. My four daughters are getting old enough now to read and to understand something of what is going on. I don't want them to grow up with any wrong ideas about their Dad. Then, too, Eva is concerned about all these investigations and smear campaigns. What would happen to me in Boston if I should be accused as a Communist? We worry about that more than anything else."

"Then your answer is yes?" Richards put in impatiently.

I thought for a few minutes. It was not an easy decision to make. "No," I said. "My answer is no."

Richards sat quietly a moment. "Are you sure you mean that?"

"Yes. There are other things to consider. I know exactly what effect this will have on the party, and as you say I'll be through. But the situation with these characters is going to get a lot worse before it gets any better. The party right now is like a keg of TNT. It'll take a lot of rough handling, but if anyone sticks a fuse in it, it'll go off. The party is going underground fast. It is becoming a tighter and harder core all the time, and the harder it becomes, the more difficult it will be for you to work anyone into it. It will become almost impossible for anyone outside the party to find out just what is going on. But I'm in there now. And I think I ought to stay."

"I understand what you mean," Richards said.

"I'm on the verge of learning a lot more that would be valuable to you. I'm well established in the pro-group. Every day I pick up a scrap of information here and a scrap there that helps round out the full picture. Every day I meet new people. On the functionary level I'm in close touch with Boone Schirmer, the hottest one of the gang. Then, too, I'm not sure whether I believe it is the best thing to put these people on trial at this time. Maybe it's good, I don't know. But I know that it won't stop the Communist party, even if they do succeed in putting a dozen or so in jail."

"You know, Herb," Don intervened, "you could be subpoenaed. They can make you testify."

"I'd go quietly, Officer, don't worry." Don gave one of his rare smiles.

"Seriously," I continued, "that would be a better way to handle it. After all, I'm only one person working in a very small sector, and my field of view is limited. I can't possibly see the whole picture. So how can I decide whether or not I should testify? The decision isn't up to me. I have no right to make it. So I'll do nothing. I won't volunteer. Personally, I think I should stay where I am. But if the Justice Department wants me on the stand, they can say so, with your subpoena. Naturally I'll go then. Don't you think that's the best way?"

"All right," said Don, slapping his hands together suddenly and putting on a brisk air. "You can count on me to take back your answer just as you gave it to me." Don made no direct comment on my decision, but he appeared to be happy about it. No intelligence agent likes to spend years building up a network of information only to have the whole thing wrecked before his eyes.

"Now," he added, reaching into his inside jacket pocket. "That was the only question I had to ask you. I want you to understand

264

that there is no certainty that you will be subpoenaed. It may be a long time, if ever. But in the meantime there is a lot of work to be done, building up the case. The Department's attorneys want to begin checking over your story."

Without my saying anything, Don read my apprehension. "Don't worry, it won't tip your hand. We'll keep it as tight a secret as we can, and you'll have every possible protection we can afford. I hate to give you short notice, but it would be good if you could take a little trip."

"When?"

"Tonight." He pulled an airline ticket out of his pocket and handed it to me. "Boston to New York," it read. "The late afternoon plane," Don said. "You'll be back before midnight."

"I'm supposed to go to a Mr. and Mrs. Club affair at the church tonight," I declared, "but I can get out of it."

"Your wife will understand, won't she? I would suggest that you don't tell her anything about this just yet."

"I agree. There's no sense causing extra worry, or raising any false hopes until we're sure I'll be called. Eva expects almost anything these days. I'll just tell her I have to work late. It won't be any different than most of my evenings."

"Right," Don said. "Now. You are traveling under the name of Hubert Brooks. That's the name on the ticket and the name on record with the government attorneys. You will be met at the plane in New York. But you be Hubert Brooks, and don't forget it. Wait to be approached. Make them identify themselves. There will be two agents and a Mr. Shapiro. They will not want to know your right name so you needn't give them any clew to your identity. Don't talk about your business or where you live or who you know outside of the party. Best of all, don't talk about anything except in answer to questions. But so far as the questions are concerned, you can answer them fully."

Don then gave me a name and a telephone number, and instructed me to commit them to memory. "If for any reason you

265

miss your contact at the airport, if no one meets you, wait ten minutes, no more. Then call the number I have given you. Ask for the man whose name I have given you, and simply tell him Hubert Brooks is calling. He will give you instructions. Don't write the name or number down on anything. If you don't have to use that method, then forget them."

We looked at each other. I had a strange feeling of exhilaration.

"Everything clear?" Don asked. I nodded.

"One thing more I want to emphasize. Don't talk to anyone on that plane, coming or going. Don't talk to anyone at the airport except those who will identify themselves. Don't ask any questions of strangers. And most of all," he said, with a reassuring pat on my shoulder, "don't worry."

I hurried to the office. On the way up in the elevator I suddenly realized I had forgotten to cash Eddie Alfano's check. I could easily trip myself up by a foolish little thing like that, I thought; I descended again, walked across to the United States Trust Company, and cashed the check.

Back in the office, Eddie asked me, "What took you so long?"

"Met a friend and had a bite of lunch with him. I didn't know you were in a hurry. Sorry."

"Oh, no, none at all. It doesn't matter," Eddie said.

I cleared the work off my desk, then telephoned Eva to make my excuses for the evening. She knew better than to ask me pointed questions over the telephone, and accepted the matter quietly. Then I hopped a cab to the airport.

In the early evening I landed at La Guardia Field. Just inside the apron gate a man approached and flashed a Federal Bureau of Investigation card.

"Hubert Brooks?" We shook hands, chatted a moment, and then threaded through the terminal to the parking lot. Beside a sleek black limousine stood another agent and a third man, who was introduced as Irving Shapiro, a Justice Department attorney. The two agents climbed into the front seat of the big car and

Mr. Shapiro joined me in the rear. The car purred out onto the parkways of Long Island, moving away from the city. Almost immediately I understood that we were not going to stop, that the interview was going to take place in the car.

During the long ride Mr. Shapiro fired questions at me in rapid succession. He scratched notes on a large pad of ruled yellow paper under the dim illumination of the ceiling light of the car.

"Are you a member of the Communist party?"

"Yes."

"When did you join?"

"Nineteen forty-four."

"What was AYD? Did you attend its founding convention? Where? When? When did you become New England treasurer? How? What was the Communist Political Association?" In this fashion, by staccato questions and answers, we ran through most of my party life in sketchy outline. Then Mr. Shapiro's questioning took a different line.

"What does proletariat mean? Bourgeoisie? What was Browderism? What is democratic centralism?" We engaged in no informal conversation of a friendly, personal nature through more than two hours of interviewing, as we rolled over the parkways of the Island. Mr. Shapiro scarcely looked at me the entire time. But at the end, as we neared the airport again, he said, "You seem to have all the technical stuff down pat."

"I ought to," I laughed. "I've had the best training the party could afford, and all of it free."

At 11:55 that night I was in Boston once more, aboard the last train for Melrose pulling out of North Station. The trainman gave me a reassuring greeting. "Working late again, eh?" At home Eva was still up, listening to the radio news. Everything had shifted back to normal. I said nothing to Eva about the sudden turn of events.

There were two more similar trips to New York on successive Saturday evenings. Don Richards gave me a little more advance notice on these. The tickets were delivered to my office in a blank envelope bearing my real name, but I still traveled as the noncommittal Hubert Brooks. Mr. Shapiro continued his note taking as we sped over dark miles of Long Island and Westchester County parkways. The planes shuttled me back and forth between Boston and New York.

Then it was over as suddenly as it began. Silence fell. I heard no more. I tried to forget about it, put it out of my mind entirely, but that proved difficult. Although I still felt that I would be more valuable to the government as an FBI contact than as a witness for the prosecution, I also realized that the trial was my only chance of getting out of the party and back to a happy, normal life. But when I heard nothing from New York, I returned to the old routine.

The Progressive party campaign of Henry Wallace for the Presidency was in high gear, but the comrades had other pressing business on their minds. The indictments and the approaching trial of The Twelve drew attention from the election. Having diligently infiltrated many of the top places in the New England Progressive movement, the Communists now began to pull out, leaving the Wallace party to stand on its own feet. As a matter of fact, the stock of Henry Wallace among the Communists dropped rapidly as the election drew nearer. He was privately taken to task for the errors of his "progressive capitalism," the notion, deadly to Marxist-Leninism, that a reformed capitalism can succeed. It was a similar idea to that which frightened the Communist party away from the late Wendell Willkie.

Although the district Communists continued to give token support to Wallace, the membership was concentrated instead on efforts looking toward the coming New York trial. Orders which came down through the pro-group were to ride hard on a civil-rights program to whip up public sympathy for The Twelve as victims of "political persecution." Our instructions were to leave a skeleton force in the Progressive party, and turn our heavy guns on the Civil Rights Congress, a well-established Class A Communist front, and on the liberal, non-Communist Civil Liberties Union.

"We have always kept a token representation in the Civil Liberties Union," we were told. "Now we must strengthen our ties with this organization and with all groups in which there is a chance of tapping a sympathetic response." Pro-group members were especially valuable in this infiltration drive because of the respectable front of noncommunism which all of them maintained. We were given secret orders. Mine were to join the ranks of the Civil Rights Congress. Others were given similar instructions concerning the American Civil Liberties Union. The move into the ACLU angered me. The organization was well known as a powerful liberal influence on the American scene. With underground Communists hard at work within the group there was acute danger of its complete subversion. The trail of the Communist party in the United States is strewn with the bones of such organizations which have been infiltrated, sucked dry, and then cast aside.

But I had no such objections to my assignment in the Civil Rights Congress, already widely reputed as a Communist front despite the presence in its ranks of many non-communist dupes. As directed I made my way to Hank Cooperstock, a New Yorker who had originally been sent to the Boston district to replace Don Bollen as the head of American Youth for Democracy, and who then took over the leadership of the Civil Rights Congress in the district. Cooperstock directed me to Jack Lee, a Negro who was head of the Young Progressive Citizens of America.

Working in Jack Lee's office at 27 School Street on the shoulder of Beacon Hill, we turned out reams of propaganda material, the object of which was to undermine the Smith Act and the public's faith in it. We portrayed the law as an instrument of suppression affecting every segment of American life and every individual from his cradle to his grave. From the national office of

269

the Civil Rights Congress at 205 East Forty-second Street in New York came a steady stream of ammunition for the propaganda barrage. We bombarded the public with leaflets, fliers, and speeches, in meetings and through mailing lists. By the old Communist device of creating the broadest possible base of appeal, we enlisted many non-Communists in the cause. We did it by surrounding the central issue of the trial with concentric social implications. We urged a "fight for the rights of the Negro people . . . for abolition of Jim Crow and religious and political persecution . . . for the rights of labor . . . for the defense of the Bill of Rights and the Constitution . . . for freedom of speech and public assembly." On the basis of the forthcoming trial, new membership blanks for the Civil Rights Congress were issued. "The unconstitutional indictments of the leaders of the Communist party," the blank said with arrogant assumption, "are a threat to the liberties of all Americans. The issue is democracy against fascism. I am proud to join with millions of my fellow Americans in this freedom crusade. I won't let it happen here."

A primary objective of the agitation through the Civil Rights Congress was the raising of $250,000 for a "freedom fund" to pay the expenses of the defense of The Twelve. New members were asked at the time of enrollment to make a pledge to the fund. A large Civil Rights Congress conference was held at the Hotel Bradford in Boston, on Saturday afternoon, December 4, 1948. By this time affairs in New York were moving slowly toward the actual beginning of the big trial. The defense legal staff began its obstructionist tactics early by throwing a challenge at the constitutionality of the method for selecting a panel from which to draw a jury. The arguments on this and other points dragged on for dreary weeks.

At the Hotel Bradford conference, Len Goldsmith, national director of the Civil Rights Congress, made the principal address, blasting the Smith Act as unconstitutional and an infringement of civil liberties, and categorically elevating the CRC to the top position among all groups in the nation seeking to preserve civil rights.

"We need," Goldsmith said, "two hundred and fifty thousand dollars for the defense of The Twelve, and we need it now. We do not have all year to raise this money. We must have it in our hands before January 17. I would remind you that the deportation case of Gerhart Eisler had already cost our defense fund thirty-two thousand dollars and will cost us more." Just how much more, Comrade Goldsmith probably didn't calculate. On May 6, 1949, Eisler stowed away on the Polish liner *Batory* and escaped behind the Iron Curtain, forfeiting $23,000 in bonds posted for him. In his appeal for defense-fund bonds, Goldsmith told us to take out mortgages, if necessary, on our homes and automobiles.

"Of course," he added, "our major fight will be to prevent the case from coming to trial." So it was that I joined hands with others, under Communist party orders, in an effort to wreck the very case which, in my role as a Federal operative and potential witness, I was helping the government to build.

I had to play my hand with cautious bluff in an atmosphere of increasing tension. When in our meetings the air was filled with invective against "spies, stool pigeons, FBI agents, and enemies of the working class," I felt with more and more uneasiness that it was directed against me, and it was with difficulty that I maintained my outward calm. After a meeting, I would find my shirt wet with perspiration and my nerves like taut wires. I began having attacks of nervous indigestion and on several occasions Eva insisted that I stay in bed a day or two to catch up on my sleep and calm down.

During the early winter of 1948, the government broke its silence and informed me that I would probably be subpoenaed for the trial. I was called to New York and Washington for a new series of conferences with the Federal attorneys.

Don Richards impressed upon me the necessity of establishing a "cover" for my activities. There was always the possibility that I would encounter someone en route who would become inquisitive about my mission. I had to have a ready explanation for it, and a timely occurrence gave me one that was plausible.

A group of government attorneys, one of whom was named Frank Gordon, had successfully prosecuted an antitrust case against the "big five" motion-picture companies, including Paramount Pictures. A consent decree was won by the government in the case, with the result that M. & P. Theaters was broken up. An offshoot company, American Theaters, was formed, and I joined it as assistant advertising director. But I let it be known that I wasn't happy about it, and I dropped a hint in the pro-group that I was in disfavor with the company because of my activities in the Progressive party and the hysteria over the Hollywood Red hunt. The news spread through the party that I, ostensibly a non-Communist, was threatened with loss of my job for political activity. This not only created sympathy for my cause, but also served as a tailor-made cover. If anyone should ask me why I was shuttling to New York and back, I could simply say that I was job-hunting.

Don checked with me frequently to see that all of my movements were carefully screened. He told me that if I went on the stand I would be an important link in the government's chain of evidence, and he wanted to run no risks with me. It became necessary for me to tell Eva that I might take the witness chair and to let her in on the plans. She was delighted and only too happy to cooperate. When I made Saturday trips to New York, she purposely invited guests for the evening, and then explained at the last minute that I was kept late in town with business affairs. It came to be accepted as a matter of course that I was too busy for social life. When my week-end flights to New York or Washington became all-day meetings, I deliberately gave the Communist party leadership in Boston a false scent, in case they should miss me. I would prepare material requested by the district headquarters on Friday night, then hold it for mailing by Eva Saturday afternoon so it would bear a late postmark indicating that I was still in town at that hour.

My regular—or rather my irregular—mode of living over the years helped me to cover my trail from any prying eyes. For a long time I had practiced subterfuges, to avoid detection as a member of the Communist party, to dodge professional Red hunters, and to escape any suspicion of FBI liaison. The pattern of life which had become second nature made it difficult for any investigators to keep track of me. Now I concentrated more than ever on variations of this pattern.

My telephone at home was unlisted, and few even realized that I had one, so there was little chance of surprise checkups at odd hours to see if I was at home. I rarely took the same train to or from the office on successive days. My lunch hours never followed a regular schedule. I usually decided purely on impulse where and when I would eat, if at all. It had always been normal for me to devote my week ends to free-lance advertising jobs, to church work, or to some other activity, so there was no irregularity in my working long hours on Saturdays and Sundays now.

Occasionally the shift in my attitudes had to be abrupt. After one all-day conference in New York, going over the details of the case against the Communist party leadership, I hopped a plane to Logan Airport in Boston and less than two hours later I was at dinner with a member of my pro-group cell at her apartment. The subject of our discussion at the table and afterward was the planning of methods to raise additional money for the defense of The Twelve.

I continued to file regular reports by secret communication methods to the FBI. The transmission of these reports was carefully guarded. Among the organizations on which I reported was the Boston School for Marxist Studies. During the winter months, the Educational Commission received a directive from national headquarters ordering the selection of a few comrades for a course

of advance training in Marxism to offset what they called "the increased tendency toward fascism throughout the United States."
Vanguard leaders, the directive said, must be ready for action.

The result was the establishment of the Boston School for
Marxist Studies. Only party members with carefully tested back-
grounds were to attend. Boone Schirmer sent the outline material
for the courses in the new school to me for preparation. I was to
write a series of four-page circulars for the four different classes
to be held. I worked on the material at my office and transmitted
it to party headquarters via the parcel lockers in the Boylston
Street subway.

But something went wrong. A few of the circulars were routed
for distribution through the Progressive Bookshop. Frank Collier
placed them on a lower shelf at the rear of the shop. Among his
frequent customers at this time was Cornelius Dalton, a reporter
for the Boston *Traveler*. Dalton snatched a copy of my mimeographed folder and hustled it away to his office. There he read it,
and learned that a series of Communist party study classes was to
be held in the Ritz Plaza Halls, at which students would pursue
the same kind of Marxist-Leninist studies which had brought
conspiracy charges against The Twelve. He broke the story in his
paper, and it caused an immediate public uproar which forced
the management of the Ritz Plaza Halls to cancel rental of its
quarters to the party. Plans for the Boston School for Marxist
Studies were hurriedly revised, and the courses were postponed
until new arrangements could be made.

As a result of Dalton's exposé, the school was now cloaked in a
secrecy that was almost absurd. I tried to get into the labor class,
which I knew would be the most interesting and revealing course
of study, but this was denied me. So skittish was the party over
the secrecy of the school that I had difficulty finding out where
my first class was to be held. I called the district headquarters, but
the girl told me she could not give me the address over the telephone. I was ordered instead to see Manny Blum, and to do so I

made my first visit to the district headquarters in over a year. For once I found the voluble Manny silent. He would not even speak the address aloud to me in the office. Instead he scribbled it on a piece of paper and handed it to me. It said, "33 Fayston Street," the home address of Otis Archer Hood.

In the raw damp of a February evening I picked my way over icy sidewalks up darkened Fayston Street to the duplex apartment building where Hood lived. The members of our class included young and old comrades, none of whom I knew. There were four college students, the wife of a successful Boston businessman, a young Greek photographer, and two Negroes. The meeting was held in a front room of the house, where Hood had arranged a large table spread with a supply of Marxist literature and surrounded by chairs.

The first session was routine, to establish the theme. We plunged into a study of *Value, Price and Profit,* with Hood as the instructor emphasizing the contradictions in capitalism which, he said, produce wars and recurring economic depressions. "The teachings of the Lenin-Stalin party," he told us, "provide the knowledge of the laws of capitalist development and social struggle, and furnish us with the assurance of ultimate victory. They teach us how to apply these laws in directing and leading the proletariat in the revolutionary struggle."

Later in the course, in March, a storm broke over the heads of the party because of a statement by a French Communist that his comrades would not participate with their nation in any war against the Soviet Union. It provoked long discussions in our classes. William Foster and Eugene Dennis issued a statement to the press in which they masterfully dodged the direct issue, and still gave the proper line to disciplined Communists, by saying, "United States Communists will oppose a Wall Street war."

In our secret meetings this view was clarified. Hood reminded us that the state is owned and controlled by capitalists and that war is a necessary part of capitalist oppression. The question then

275

was, "What is true patriotism?" The answer was that a true patriot was one who would fight on the side of the "working people," and not on the side of the capitalist, "who knows no patriotism and would sell out his country at any time for his own selfish interests." Therefore, Hood said, it was unthinkable that American Communists should ever fight against the Soviet Union, the land of the working classes. If United States imperialists, he added, should insist upon creating such a war, then Communists must do everything in their power to oppose the military operations of the country. In other words, any war the Communist party chose thus to label would be a "Wall Street war."

Indirectly, through the Boston School for Marxist Studies, I learned what some of the methods of opposition would be, below the ideological level. One of them was sabotage. The Communists, recognizing that in the aftermath of a revolution it would be necessary for them to restore a productive economy as quickly as possible, wisely planned to avoid wholesale destruction of valuable machinery through sabotage. They spelled out a policy of preserving irreplaceable machinery which was regarded, after all, as the rightful property of the workers. Instead, the plan was to incapacitate temporarily entire plants and their crucial machines by knocking out power supplies, wrecking transmission lines, conduits, cables, generators, transformers—any facility which would render productive machinery useless to the governing authorities, but leave it essentially intact to be restored immediately by the revolutionary forces. In concrete terms, they would not destroy rail locomotives and rolling stock, but would merely deny their use by ripping out the track. The saboteurs would strive for a complete paralysis (rather than destruction) of the critical points —bridges, dams, water-supply lines, communications, etc.

Otis Hood, in keeping with his usual demeanor, was very pleasant about the whole thing. "After we have won the revolution," he said, "destroyed the capitalist state, smashed the ruling power, and taken over the means of production, then we shall have a

276

world without war, without oppression, without hunger—a world of peace."

He spoke as if he believed it.

The trial of The Eleven—eleven now, with Chairman Foster excused for illness—opened in January, but it wasn't until March that Louis Budenz, the former head of the *Daily Worker,* and a re-formed ex-Communist, took the stand as the first government witness. I made two trips directly to the United States courthouse in New York to confer with attorneys close to the trial.

These jaunts were still carefully guarded, but the procedure was changed. When I reached New York, I called a number furnished me, and said, "This is Hubert Brooks." A voice on the other end of the line told me where to go and when. My identity was still a closely held secret, kept by the Bureau even from the top lawyers of the Justice Department. If anything should happen and I should not be called for the trial, the Bureau wanted to be sure that I could continue my membership in the Communist party.

I held a full day's conference with United States Attorney John F. X. McGohey. Mr. McGohey was scrupulous in his search for details. In his study he had amassed a tremendous knowledge of Marxism-Leninism, and developed a remarkable appreciation for its devious course.

It became more and more apparent that the government was building a large part of its case upon evidence that was in my possession, and that they would have to place me on the stand. But back in Boston, Daniel Boone Schirmer called me one day and asked me to meet him for lunch at the Waldorf Restaurant on Washington Street. Over our coffee, he began plying me with questions.

"How are you coming on the new job?" he asked.

"All right, I think. I have several other irons in the fire."

"Do you expect to be traveling much?"

"Some. A trip now and then."

277

"Where?"

"All over New England."

"Will you use your own car or a company car?"

"Probably my own."

"Will you have your week ends free?"

"Yes."

Then he glanced around him and leaned toward me to make a point. "We need some reliable people for some special work. We need couriers to operate both in and out of the metropolitan district. What about your neighbors? Are they suspicious of you?"

"No one has ever given any indication of it."

"Is there any room in your house for—temporary shelter?" I told him my little home was too crowded to take anyone in. "We need supply depots. Have you any storage space?"

"I'm building a garage now. I can easily tack a shed on the rear of it." Boone was enthusiastic about the idea. We drew a plan for it on a paper napkin—an innocent-looking shed stuck on the garage, with a loading platform inside at the level of an automobile trunk compartment. I actually started the construction according to the plan we roughed out. But the loading platform was never used for the intended purpose. It was converted instead to a stage for one-cent-admission plays put on by my children and their neighborhood chums.

Following my enigmatic luncheon conversation with Boone, I immediately flashed the FBI. I outlined what he had said, and I took the view that the courier proposition Boone had mentioned was most promising. "I still think I had better stay in this thing where I can see what is going on. See if the government can't get someone else to testify," I pleaded. Don Richards promised that he would do all he could.

But the government was all set. Richards brought back the information that I would be called to the stand, probably as soon as Budenz was finished. "Have a suitcase packed and ready to go," Richards told me. Together we set up a plan of action. A series of

278

code telephone calls was worked out between the Bureau and me, and also with Eva. We arranged to get Eva and the children out of the house as soon as word came that I was taking the stand, both to avoid any possible reprisals, and to duck newspaper reporters until my testimony, expected to take several days, was completed. Eva casually told her sister-in-law in nearby Lynnfield that I might be going out of town, and asked if she could bring two of the children to stay for a few days. She also notified her mother in Somerville that she might leave the other two youngsters with her for a day or two. She couldn't tell any of them why. In order to throw off anyone looking for us, we told the children that we might go to Rye Beach, New Hampshire, for a short visit with my parents. Delighted with the idea, they told all their playmates and spread the word around the neighborhood.

I typed out letters to a half-dozen of my closest associates and relations—to Sam Pinanski, my boss at both M. & P. and American Theaters, to the Reverend Ralph Bertholf, the minister at the First Baptist Church of Wakefield, to my parents, and to others in my family. These letters were to explain in detail my long affiliation with the Communist party and the FBI. They were sealed and prepared for mailing. Some were given to Edward Soucy, at that time special agent in charge of the Boston office of the FBI, and some to Eva. They were to be mailed when I took the witness stand.

Meanwhile, the party went to work on another activity. The CIO United Office and Professional Workers of America, subsequently expelled from the CIO as Communist tainted, started an organizing campaign among white-collar workers of the John Hancock Life Insurance Company—one of the key industries cited in our colonizing and party-building conference in 1947. The campaign to install the union as the bargaining agent of the employees was of paramount interest to the Communist party. Orders came to my pro-group cell for every member to get behind the campaign.

I was instructed by Carol Levy, a courier from party district

279

headquarters, to join the UOPWA and lend my efforts to the propaganda aspects of the drive. As a Communist, therefore, I was installed in the union's campaign headquarters at 173 Milk Street near the Boston water front. I ground out questionnaires and fliers and assembled statistical material with which to attack the company and needle the Hancock employees into sentiments of discontent with their pay and working conditions. We attached coupons to all the fliers, by which a Hancock worker could give us his name and address, and "authorize" the union to serve as his bargaining agent.

When the replies poured in from these fliers, my pro-group comrades got down to the grubbing level. They were used as drivers for union organizers, and themselves were assigned to pay personal calls on workers at their homes, to persuade them to cast their lot with the union. We were not to hold any mass meetings, but rather to conduct our recruiting as quietly and unobtrusively as possible. New members were told to keep their union affiliation secret, lest they lose their jobs. At first the new union was organized into cells, much the same as the Communist party, and cell meetings were held regularly.

But I didn't stay around to observe the successful conclusion of the John Hancock campaign. On Tuesday, April 5, 1949, I had lunch with Carol Levy to brush up on the propaganda program. Shortly after I returned to the office, my telephone rang.

"Hello." I recognized the nasal accent of Don Richards. "That printing job you ordered is ready. Can you pick it up about five o'clock?"

"I'll be there," I said. The moment was at hand. Don's message told me by prearranged code that he would meet me at my house at five and that I must be ready to go. I would probably go on the witness stand the next day. But I could not be sure. The way the trial was going, with endless objections and arguments by the defense staff, I might cool my heels for a week or more. Don instructed me beforehand to establish a good "cover" in case I did not come to work for several days. I feigned a bad cold, and complained to Eddie Alfano that I wasn't feeling well.

I planted the same impression with others, in conversation with Bob Foster, the comptroller, over the moving of a filing cabinet in our office, and with a man in the booking department over the dates of a movie screening for advertising purposes. I let Mary Connors, our switchboard operator, know that I was feeling mighty low. Then, blowing my nose diligently, I told Eddie I was going home, caught a train, and found Don Richards at the house, my suitcase in his car. Eva waved to me from the doorway as if I was going away on another of my frequent short business hops. The youngsters were all on hand to add to the domesticity of the scene.

Richards drove me straight to the airport. "You're still traveling incognito," he told me on the way. "Be careful. But once you get into the hands of Mr. McGohey, it will be all right to forget about security. You can tell them who you are. Fact is, you'll have to."

I boarded a plane for New York. At La Guardia Field I called the blind telephone number and was told to proceed to the information booth at Grand Central Terminal. There I met a Bureau agent whose name I did not know, but with whom I was by this time on friendly terms. He took me to an automobile parked on East Forty-first Street. Another agent sat behind the wheel. We drove through the evening traffic to Foley Square, and at the United States courthouse we ducked between iron gates into a ramp leading down into the building. Armed guards were posted at an entrance marked for official visitors. We entered a small elevator which whisked us upward in silence. When it stopped, one agent stayed with me in the car, while the other went ahead to see if the hallways were clear. I was hurried through corridors past a door which one of the agents held open, and which clicked on a spring lock when it closed after me. We went through a series of offices where the desks were all deserted. No

281

one observed me. Finally I entered a small inner room in which there were a few chairs, one blinded window, and a table stacked high with papers. The door opened, and Mr. Shapiro stepped in. We exchanged greetings.

"That's all your stuff," Shapiro said, indicating the material on the table.

"Quite a file. I didn't realize there was that much."

Mr. Shapiro smiled. "That's only a small part of the truckload of reports you turned in."

Mr. McGohey came into the room, together with Frank Gordon, the same Gordon who had won the antitrust case against Paramount. "This is a fine thing," I said, greeting him. "First you ease me out of a job, and now you're going to give me the third degree."

I expected Mr. McGohey and his staff to run through my testimony again, and I was keyed with excitement. But instead, the prosecutor placed me entirely at ease, sitting and chatting informally for over an hour. He barely touched on the trial, except to ask me a few questions about my identity, my real name, where I lived, my schooling, and my business experience—enough to round out the preliminary testimony I was to give. The two FBI agents who came with me remained throughout the conference, one of them in the room and the other just outside the door.

Afterward, the two took me in a car to a restaurant for a late dinner. I got to know the FBI men as Jim Johns and Jack Parsons. With both of them constantly at my side, we drove to a small hotel on a quiet street. I never did know the name of it. In the tiny lobby, the two agents stood aside, one by the door and the other by the elevator, while I stepped to the desk to register as Hubert Brooks, of the Ace Advertising Agency, Boston.

In a little single room on an upper floor, Jack instructed me, "I don't want you to open the door or use the telephone until we call for you tomorrow morning. Bolt the door and keep it bolted. Anything else is O.K.," he said with a grin. "Take it easy."

As I stood forlornly in the middle of the room, the two agents

282

walked out. I locked the door behind them and went to bed to pass a sleepless night.

The following day my bodyguards were on hand for an early breakfast. Then I was smuggled in the cellar ramp to the Federal Building and spirited again to a secluded room on an upper floor, where the vigil of waiting began. At about eleven o'clock Jack beckoned to me. Feeling light on my feet, my heart pounding in my throat, I was taken to a small elevator and dropped to the courtroom floor. For almost an hour I stood in the darkened elevator. Through the open door I could glimpse a corner of the courtroom and the bailiff's stand. My mouth was dry. At noon the call turned into a false alarm. The court recessed for lunch, and I was whisked back to my chamber above. Luncheon was brought to me. Shortly before two o'clock, I was taken to the courtroom floor once more.

This time I had not long to wait. There were some preliminary arguments in the courtroom. I glanced at my watch. It was almost 2:05. I thought of Eva. I felt confident that Don Richards would flash her the word at the moment I took the stand. We had arranged it that way, utilizing FBI communications, so that Eva could round up the children and leave the house. I wondered what the reaction would be in Boston. In the midst of my reverie, I heard the voice of Mr. McGohey.

"Mr. Bailiff, will you call Mr. Herbert A. Philbrick!"

CHAPTER 16

"THE FEDERAL BUREAU OF INVESTIGATION!"

My own pronouncement of those words echoed back to me in the vastness of the Foley Square courtroom. Under Prosecutor Frank Gordon's careful priming, I had exploded a bombshell in the faces of the eleven Communist party leaders facing trial for conspiracy against the United States. Within a few minutes after I took the stand, it was written in the record that I had been a member of the Communist party for four years and of its fringe groups and front organizations for five more, and that throughout that time I had been in constant communication with the Federal Bureau of Investigation. The top eleven, ranged behind the long defense table, glared at me as I gave the preface for my testimony of those nine years.

I sat back in the witness chair. The tension eased in my throat as a great weight rolled off my shoulders. It was more than a momentary relief. For nine years I had sealed my lips on those words—The Federal Bureau of Investigation—scarcely daring to utter them even in closest privacy with my wife or with special agents Hal Leary and Don Richards, the only three persons with whom I shared my secret. Now for the first time I was permitted to speak them in public. With five words I was able to shrug off the burden of those nine years, and to square myself with my family, my friends, and the world.

It was the end of the tightrope for me. But it was a cause of consternation among The Eleven. The rest was so much an anticlimax to me after the secret was out that I scarcely sensed the drama that gripped the courtroom when I started my testimony as the government's first surprise witness. The next morning, Walter Arm reported it in the *New York Herald Tribune*.

"His appearance," Mr. Arm wrote, "was a complete surprise to the defense. Defendants and their counsel stared at the soft-spoken agent, first incredulously and then in evident distaste. They whispered among themselves and shook their heads. A member of the defense committee tiptoed from the courtroom and hurried to a telephone."

The government's sense of timing had been perfect. Louis Budenz, disenchanted Communist who quit the party after long association, renouncing the convictions he had once held, had been the first witness. The defense was prepared for him, and attorneys for The Eleven maintained their arrogant attitude throughout his testimony. Then the Department of Justice placed me on the stand. I was the first FBI informant to testify, not a party malcontent either, but a FBI contact who had been opposed to communism and Communists from the beginning. It was the first time that the government ever had publicly acknowledged that it had undercover agents actually working inside the Communist party. There were similar witnesses to come, seven in all, but it was given to me to be the first. Until I took the stand at a little after two o'clock on April 6, 1949, I was a "member in good standing" of the Communist party in the United States. Until that moment the comrades, despite any suspicions, had no certain proof that intelligence operatives were behind their lines, watching their important moves. The astonishment at the defense table was well founded.

Mr. Arm reported that my first statements on FBI activities "drew an audible gasp from the left side of the spectators' benches—a section generally filled with relatives and friends of the defendants and with fellow travelers. Throughout his testimony, the defendants slumped in their chairs and watched him

285

silently. . . . The five defense lawyers, however, were far from silent . . . they were constantly on their feet with objections to the testimony as constituting 'prejudice' and 'unfair surprise.' Judge Harold R. Medina was kept busy overruling them."

The initial testimony established that I had been a member of the Communist party in New England for FBI intelligence purposes. Mr. Gordon then began to draw from me the account of what I had learned during those nine years. Louis Budenz had furnished basic material for the record, describing the organization of the Communist party in the United States and naming the eleven defendants as its top leaders, comprising what Budenz called the "politburo."

I was to carry on from there. The indictment against The Eleven contained ten counts, of which the first was all-inclusive. It charged that the Communist party leaders "unlawfully, wilfully and knowingly, did conspire with each other . . . to organize as the Communist Party of the United States of America a society, group and assembly of persons who teach and advocate the overthrow and destruction of the Government of the United States by force and violence, and knowingly and wilfully to advocate and teach the duty and necessity of overthrowing and destroying the Government of the United States by force and violence. . . ."

My testimony, as we worked it out in long pretrial conferences, had two main purposes. First, I was to contribute all that I could from my experience to the conspiracy aspect of the indictment, to show that the party operated in secret, met behind closed doors in private apartments, organized itself on an underground pattern, and spread its doctrines, not openly, but by planned subterfuge.

I was to trace the dissolution of the "reformist" Communist Political Association in 1945, and the reconstitution, under a carefully prepared and preconsidered plan, of the Communist

286

party—a party dedicated, according to the indictment, "to the Marxist-Leninist principles" of violent revolution.

Second, but of no less importance, I was to contribute my testimony to the weight of evidence regarding what the Communist party taught and advocated in the meetings which I attended. We were to introduce as exhibits numerous books and pamphlets used by me in secret training schools with Communist comrades— material which, over the years, I had bundled up and passed along to the Federal Bureau of Investigation. I was to discuss the teachings in those Communist textbooks, and tell how the most pertinent and most revolutionary ideas expressed in them were defined, expanded, and explained by party instructors.

To the tune of a running commentary of objections from the battery of defense lawyers, we began with the dissolution of the Communist Political Association and the reconstitution of the full-fledged, revolutionary Communist party. The defense even objected to the admission into evidence of my membership card in the Communist Political Association, the card that I had spared from the wastebasket in Alice Gordon's apartment, and sent in to the FBI. Defense objections, designed to throw everybody in the courtroom off the track and to confuse the judge, the witnesses, the prosecution, and the jury, were typified by the exchange over my CPA card.

THE COURT (Judge Medina): Is Mr. Philbrick's name on it?
THE WITNESS: Just the first name.
THE COURT: Just the first name?
THE WITNESS: I think.
MR. GORDON: Yes. That card just says "Herb."
MR. SACHER (for the defense): I thought your honor saw it.
THE COURT: Well, to tell you the honest truth I did see it and I didn't notice that part. I suppose you will take exception to that. I didn't notice that part. Is that all right?

MR. CROCKETT (another defense attorney): I do take exception to your honor's ruling—

THE COURT: You see, Mr. Sacher starts something. He made the remark that he thought I had looked at it and how funny it was that I hadn't noticed the name "Herb" there. You see, one thing starts another and then when one of your number starts it the others all get up and take the opposite view and do the old whipsaw game.

MR. CROCKETT: I object to the court's remark. . . .

And so it went.

But they were unable to obscure the fact that I had been a member of the old Communist Political Association; the fact that I received a personal invitation from Dave Bennett to attend the New England convention of the Association in July of 1945; or that the entire convention was rigged in advance by the party leadership. I testified to the details of the convention, including my observation that it was necessary for each speaker to write his name on a card and send it to the chair before he could gain the floor. I told the court that before any delegate could participate in the convention panel discussions he was required to organize his material in advance, and that this was a device for the district leadership to determine what speakers were going to say before they said it. The defense objected strenuously to both lines of testimony, but Judge Medina permitted them to stand.

I recalled the Duclos letter, Anne Burlak's abject acceptance of its decrees, and her demand for a return of the new party to the principles of Marxism-Leninism. My testimony included the vote at state level on the dissolution of the CPA, the reconstitution of the party both nationally and in the district, and the establishment of the New England organization. My next disclosure was the report by Justine O'Connor calling for a state educational commission to revive Marxist ardor among the membership, and my position on that commission.

After my testimony, linked with that of other witnesses, had helped to nail down the charge that The Eleven had deliberately reestablished the Communist party for revolutionary purposes, Mr. Gordon led me into the full details of the teachings within the secret sessions of the party. He introduced the complete outline for the teacher-training course at Number 3 Hancock Street. It was at this point in the trial, from the four-year-old report to the Bureau that I had written out with shaking fingers, that the government drew up for the jury the definition of "revolution" as the term was understood by Communists. Anticipating a defense argument that "revolution" meant peaceable reform, Mr. Gordon took me back to the Hancock Street School where, under the glare of a naked light bulb, Fanny Hartman posed the question, "What do we mean by revolution?" He asked me what the class teacher said, and I testified, "The teacher defined revolution as a violent revolution to be carried out by bands of armed workers against the existing state government."

The defense counterattacked swiftly with a simple motion to strike out my testimony, but Judge Medina repulsed it with an equally simple "denied."

At the end of my first day on the witness stand, I was taken in close custody again by my FBI bodyguards, bundled out of the building the same way I came in to avoid newspaper reporters, and kept under guard through the night. They gave me a résumé of events back in Boston. There was some confusion among my non-Communist friends. First reports from the courtroom had flashed the word that I was identified only as a member of the Communist party, and the news broke in Boston before the explanation came out that I had worked all the time with the FBI.

Eva, I learned, had been alerted by Bureau agents in Boston at 2:05 P.M. and had left the house at 2:20 to stay with her sister-in-law at Lynnfield. She made her getaway just ten minutes before a platoon of reporters and photographers surrounded the house. I was not concerned at the time about formal reprisals against my family by the Communist party, although in talking it over with Don Richards I had explored the possibility that some individual hothead in the party might become violent. It was to protect Eva and the children against any such eventuality, and further to avoid the close questioning of the press which might jeopardize my testimony as a government witness, that we decided to send my family into hiding.

The party, meanwhile, scurried around Boston, trying desperately to find out just who I was. Some of the pro-group members were so shocked to find they had been infiltrated by the FBI that they could not believe that their Comrade Herb and the witness Philbrick were the same man. Still others had worked closely with me in front groups for many years without ever knowing me as a Communist. When the district leadership recovered from the shock a few days later, they started a determined campaign of vilification in an effort to discredit me as a witness. But it was all vitriol, and had no foundation in fact. In leaflets and fliers distributed in Boston and New York, they called me "cheap informer," "spreader of fantastic tales," "present-day Judas," "stool pigeon," "labor spy," and "wormy character," among other things. But they did not refute my testimony. And ultimately, in order to save face, the party, rather than deny I had ever been a member, admitted it by announcing publicly that I was officially expelled. Thus they were forced to confirm the fact that I had been a member in good standing.

Thursday morning in the courtroom, the testimony went deeper into the teachings of the Communist party, particularly into those of the Hancock Street school where I had been trained as an instructor in Marxism. Now Mr. Gordon began bringing into evidence the documentary material in the form of the classic literature of the party, the books and pamphlets which were used throughout the party as instruction "manuals"—a word which was abhorrent to the defense, and which they repeatedly tried to expunge from the record.

The first one was Karl Marx's *Communist Manifesto*. It aroused a futile defense battle to keep out of evidence a document which they said "is over a hundred years old and is regarded as a classic of economic and political discussion." They claimed that its admission would simply place the ideas of Karl Marx on trial, but again Judge Medina overruled them.

Mr. Gordon brought out from me that we studied the *Communist Manifesto,* and other works in the party library, not as dead history but as material that was never out of date. With this established, he then read from the work: "In short, the Communists everywhere support every revolutionary movement against the existing social and political order of things. . . . The Communists disdain to conceal their views and aims. They openly declare that their ends can be attained only by the forcible overthrow of all existing social conditions. . . ."

The defense seized its prerogative to read from other portions of the *Manifesto* which Mr. Gordon had omitted. It was a maneuver obviously intended to bolster the defense contention that history was taught as history, and that the party's teachings were in the nature of peaceable, intellectual discussions. But much of their reading merely served to strengthen the government's case.

Although the firsthand, personal-experience testimony of the counterspies played the larger part in convicting the defendants, their own textbooks were vital factors. One of the most condemning books offered in evidence was my original classroom copy of *History of the Communist Party of the Soviet Union (Bolsheviks)*. Passages stressed in classes I attended were marked in the book, and Mr. Gordon excerpted them for the jury.

"Hence," he read, "in order not to err in policy, one must look forward, not backward.

"Further, if the passing of slow quantitative changes into rapid and abrupt qualitative changes is a law of development, then it is clear that revolutions made by oppressed classes are a quite natural and inevitable phenomenon.

"Hence the transition from capitalism to Socialism and the liberation of the working class from the yoke of capitalism cannot be affected by slow changes, by reforms, but only by a qualitative change of the capitalist system by revolution.

"Hence, in order not to err in policy, one must be a revolutionary, not a reformist."

Defense Counsel Harry Sacher persisted in his reading of other long portions of the book, including the critical Communist phrase that "everything depends upon the conditions, the time, and the place." Mr. Gordon immediately countered by asking me what I had been taught about the historical timing of revolutions.

Thus, with an assist from the defense, the jury learned that the Communist party visualized two circumstances as being "pregnant with revolution"—first, a serious economic depression, and second, a war which could be converted into a civil war directed at the overthrow of the existing order.

The catalogue of inflammatory literature and party teachings continued. From Stalin's *Foundations of Leninism,* properly introduced as the very book used by me in the Hancock Street school, the prosecution brought out Stalin's view that "Lenin is therefore right in saying the proletarian revolution is impossible without the violent destruction of the machinery of the bourgeois state and its replacement by new machinery." He condemned the party again by this passage from the same book: "Only the revolutionary party of the proletariat can serve as this general staff. The working class without a revolutionary party is an army without a general staff. The party is the general staff of the proletariat."

From the Hancock Street school and the Malden and Melrose cells of the party, Mr. Gordon traced my admission into the sanctum of the professional group, Pro-4. We touched on the study there of Lenin's *State and Revolution.* I was permitted to testify with the book in front of me to refresh my recollection, although

292

the defense battled constantly to have the book put aside. "Don't worry," Judge Medina said to me, "you have a right to look at the book if you want to."

We piled evidence on evidence. "Such a course of events," I read into the record, "compels the revolution to concentrate all of its forces of destruction against the state power and to regard the problem as one not of perfecting the machinery of the state but of breaking up and annihilating it."

The policy I had followed throughout my long years as a Bureau informant, of turning in to the Bureau every scrap of documentary material that came my way, no matter how trivial it seemed at the time, paid off handsomely in the trial, and enabled me to give far more detailed testimony than otherwise would have been possible.

I testified on what lessons we, as Communists, drew from the failure of the Paris Commune after the French Revolution, and generally about the way the party "used" history instead of studying it. I was able to draw for the jury the picture of the pro-group, its secret meetings in members' apartments, its breakdown into smaller groups of no more than five members, and its plans for speedy mobilization in case of emergency. The colonization program in key industries in the Boston area was sketched in as a highlight of the Communist party's program for increasing its potential strength to destroy.

Finally, on Friday morning, after I had had four sessions on the stand, the state finished my direct examination, climaxing it with the account of Martha Fletcher's tirade on civil disobedience and hammering home for the jury the fact that Martha and her comrades, when they spoke of fomenting civil strife, were unmistakably talking about civil disobedience in the United States.

"You may examine," Mr. Gordon said.

The defense was taken by surprise that the direct examination ended so abruptly, with the government satisfied to drive home a few cardinal points. There was a whispered conference at the

293

defense table, and then the cross-examination was started. It appeared to have three main objectives—to learn how the Federal Bureau of Investigation operates and to examine the Bureau's files, to find flaws in the testimony, and to discredit me as a "paid" informant of the government.

They began with a long fishing expedition into my employment status, endeavoring to characterize me as a lackey of big business. I was questioned closely on my relationship with the FBI, and the defense finally demanded to see reports that I had submitted to the Bureau. This endeavor to open secret government files was firmly denied by Judge Medina.

The judge, on the other hand, gave the defense every possible assistance in trying to establish whether I was paid large sums by the Bureau for my work. Defense Attorney Crockett brought out that my house in Wakefield cost $5,000; my car, purchased in 1947, cost $2,400; even that my motion-picture camera cost $20 and my projector, $90.

"Mr. Crockett," the judge asked, "is it your intention to follow through all the things that the witness may own and find out how much he paid for them and then draw certain inferences from that?"

"No," the defense counsel replied, "I do not propose to go through all of these things that he may own and how much they may cost. I did want to find out when he suddenly—or, strike 'suddenly'—when he took on this hobby of motion pictures."

"Well," the court replied, "I don't think you need to strike the 'suddenly.' I think I get the drift of what you are working up to, just as Mr. Gordon did, and it is perfectly proper. If this man has been receiving large sums of money from the FBI or from the government I think it is perfectly proper to bring that out, and I will allow you all the latitude you desire to do so."

But it did not work. I testified flatly that I never received funds from the Bureau beyond reimbursement for my expenses. On redirect examination, Mr. Gordon examined my finances in detail. He established that in 1942 I paid $300 in cash against a $3,500 mortgage for the big house in Wakefield. I fixed the house up and sold it in 1944 taking out a $1,000 profit, which I used as a down payment on the $5,000 house in Melrose. In 1947, I increased the mortgaged balance to $6,000 in order to purchase my automobile, and I am still paying it off. Furthermore, Mr. Gordon permitted me to explain that I took out a short-term note for $90 from the bank in order to purchase a projector for my hobby. (One result of this testimony was the receipt through a Boston newspaper of an anonymous donation "from a friend" of a five-dollar bill to help pay for my projector. The bill is still framed with its accompanying message on my office wall.)

The defense was unable to discredit my testimony, and in fact made little effort to refute what I had reported. When I finally stepped down from the stand on Tuesday, after four and one-half days and 582 pages of testimony in the transcript, the defense moved to throw all of it out of court together with the supporting exhibits. But the only grounds they could muster to support the motion were that "the information that forms the basis of the testimony and all the exhibits introduced by the government were fraudulently obtained by the witness at the behest and in cooperation with the FBI, an agency of the United States Government, which agency financed his activities." Such activity, Mr. Isserman contended for the defense, was "unconstitutional, undemocratic and incident to a police state." There was more along the same line, and to all of it Judge Medina replied, "Motion denied."

Subsequently he commented, "As I understand it, you and your colleagues take the view that if someone with knowledge of the FBI or the police is in places where they observe persons who are later charged with crime, that what they see and hear is protected by the Constitutional provisions and may not be proven."

295

In his summation of the prosecution's case at the end of the long trial, United States Attorney John F. X. McGohey made several points based upon testimony I had given.

"When they reconstituted the party [in 1945]" he said, "they went back to the old Communist party organized to establish socialism in the United States according to Marxist-Leninist teaching. That teaching is, as the evidence shows, that socialism can be established only by the violent overthrow and destruction of our constitutional form of government; through the smashing of the machinery of government and the setting up of the dictatorship of the proletariat by violent and forceful seizure of power, under the leadership of the Communist party.

"If this were a legitimate American political party seeking members to gain office by the ballot, one would think that one vote would be as good as another, one recruit as good as another. But we find that throughout the indictment period party recruiting drives were aimed at workers from the key industries.

"Why this desire to have party members in the rubber, transportation, communication, auto, electrical, coal and steel industries, and in plants where jet airplane engines were being manufactured? This policy lays bare the sinister purposes behind the defendants' activities.

"It was for the purpose of inculcating revolutionary theory in party members that the party operated classes and schools wherever in the United States Communists are to be found. Are history classes conducted in secret and unannounced, assembled in someone's apartment, or in a room entered through a dentist's office, or at a rural camp? Are history classes confined to selected members of the Communist party?

"Students at these schools were instructed not to use their regular names or their full names. Such conditions of secrecy are unnecessary to study history, but the defendants apparently believed such conditions necessary for their schools. These schools were held to train professional revolutionaries.

296

"No matter where the school was conducted, in any part of the United States, or who the teacher was, or whether the classes were for beginners or advanced students, certain texts in revolutionary theory and practice were regularly used. Those are the books which we have placed in evidence here; and here they are."

My work was done.

As soon as my testimony was completed, I flew that evening to Boston and joined my family. Leaving the children with relatives, Eva and I took a week's vacation on the road through New England where we could not be disturbed. Then we returned to the Melrose house, and I went back to my job with American Theaters Corporation.

My neighbors and my fellow workers welcomed me back. Everyone was highly amused at the turn of events. None of them said, "I knew it all the time."

There were a number of newspaper, magazine, and radio offers. While there was no compulsion involved, the Department of Justice had made it plain that they would prefer me not to elaborate on my public testimony, at least while the trial was still in progress. I turned down all offers.

My services to the Bureau, naturally, were ended. Local police furnished protection for my family for some time after the trial. But my testimony against the Communists was by that time a matter of record, and no reprisals could remove it. The protection proved unnecessary, and after a time we settled back into a normal routine and went our own way.

The comrades in the party shunned me. I encountered a few of them on the Boston streets. Most of them ducked me. Once I met Boone Schirmer, and he snarled at me and turned his back.

There remained a few old friends who had turned away from me because of distaste for my various activities whom I wanted to see again. Foremost among them was Gordon Case, my old schoolmate and companion from the first days of the Cambridge

Youth Council. Gordon had walked out on me at the Touraine Hotel meeting in 1941 when I had embraced the new Communist line on the war after Russia had been attacked by Germany. I had not seen him since. Now he wrote me a long letter, saying that he was happy to know the truth of my associations with the Communists, and to find that what he had feared had turned out to be unfounded.

I received many other letters, a few from malcontents and cranks, but most of them, in support of my work, from persons in all walks of life throughout the country.

The Eleven stand convicted, their conviction affirmed by the United States Supreme Court. But the Communist party and its conspirators are still at large. The control of the party and its violent revolutionary doctrine is a paramount question of national policy.

In recounting that conspiracy as I saw it, I have tried to show factually some of the things about the party that are not generally known, and to indicate some of the reasons why Communists act the way they do. In appraising the party, its philosophy, and its threat to America, I have tried to take the view of a peace-loving, Christian pro-American. It is my earnest hope that my personal history may make an affirmative contribution, however small, to better understanding. It is certainly not my desire to create greater misunderstanding, more hatred, or more fear.

What is a Communist?

In what may loosely be described as the whole party, there are many different kinds—the power-hungry leader, the sheeplike follower, the very poor, the social outcast, the misanthrope, the misguided intellectual. Perhaps the neophyte Communist can speak with unashamed truth when he declares—a bit wistfully—that he clings to a dream of a bright new world without war, without poverty, without hunger. Perhaps that was the dream of Karl Marx.

But the seeds of Marxism bear evil fruit; the methods used by the followers of Lenin and Stalin are depraved; and any new world the Communists create becomes a nightmare instead of a dream.

For the "professional" Communist is another breed. He is neither a sheep nor is he a dupe. He knows precisely and exactly what he is doing. He believes in science and materialism rather than in ideals and emotion. The latter are merely tools for him to use on others, and he uses these tools with great skill.

He is specially trained to be all things to all men. In order to achieve maximum success, he carefully cultivates the proper veneer to conceal his motives and intent. Thus the most highly skilled— and the most dangerous—Communist is often a man of charm, wit, social standing, good manners, executive ability, brilliance, and achievement. Certainly he will not carry a dagger in his teeth, wear a long black coat, or convey the slightest hint of conspiracy. Thus he plans not only to escape detection; but he hopes that gullible Americans, even when faced with cold facts, will insist "Why, he couldn't possibly be a Communist—he's too nice (or smart, or handsome) a guy." Therein lies the reason why so many inherently loyal citizens, evidently unwilling to think evil of any man, are misled into sympathy for Communists as well as their fellow travelers and supposedly worthy causes.

The Communist seems to be fascinated by his highly developed ability to carry out party objectives while behaving like a non-Communist in the midst of anti-Communists. He seems to derive a grim thrill out of taking the chance of being a Communist. His complete dedication seems to be equally matched with almost fanatic zeal. He will work long hours, pass days or even months away from his family, alienate his friends, even go to jail. Whereas the Communist seems to find some enjoyment from all of this, I found none.

The trained, hardened, disciplined, dedicated Communist therefore carries on his fight against capitalist society in a cool and calculated manner. Amateur Red hunters, ambitious politicians, demagogues, and rabble rousers are no match for him. The fight against the professional Communist leader will not be won by flag waving or name calling. Patriots and would-be patriots who go in for bombast and two-fisted punching find that their smashing blows against the Communists too often sail through a mist of angry controversy without landing on a solid object.

There is a desperate battle between communism and anti-communism, nonetheless. It is an underground war, calling for long, hard, tough infighting. No one knows that better than the FBI. On the legal level and before the bar of public opinion, it calls for strenuous and continuous intelligence and counterspy work by government agencies charged with those responsibilities. It takes experts to fight experts. If the inexperienced Red hunter cannot distinguish between a Communist and an innocent liberal, then he is also unable to distinguish a bona-fide Communist from a government counterspy. Every precaution must be observed, for example, to protect the expert intelligence agent in the ranks of the Communists. Such measures as the outlawing of the Communist party could conceivably destroy government intelligence work without seriously damaging the underground party, and thus in the end merely serve to strengthen the Communist hand. It is difficult enough now to work operatives into the party and keep them there. Under an outlaw policy, it would be well-nigh impossible.

What can the average citizen do as his part in the war against communism?

The most important single thing is to avoid behaving the way a Communist says the individual must behave in a capitalist society. If the Communist had his way, he would force all non-Communists to the extreme right, toward fascism and state control. The Communist seeks by every means to create a split in our society, to provoke class hatreds and intense conflict. All capitalist governments, the Communist is taught, inevitably become states of fascist oppression, thus creating the demand for a violent revolution as the only possible cure.

However, if we do not behave in that manner, we will con-

300

tribute to the downfall of communism. If we adhere to our traditional American dream of a society of freedom, of personal rather than state responsibility, of individual as well as collective intelligence, and of civil rights rather than rigid civil controls, then we will have disproved the Communist theory of the inevitability of capitalist deterioration.

Time after time I learned in my party experiences that the Communist movement is not genuinely antifascist, any more than it is genuinely in favor of civil liberties, better housing, peace, or any of the other causes its leaders so ardently espouse. If every basis for Communist discontent today were suddenly removed and their every demand granted, tomorrow the professional leaders of the Communist party would find or provoke new causes of discontent, and would draw up a fresh list of demands. Any suggestion that the country is moving toward fascism is always greeted in the Communist press and party pronouncements with rejoicing, however much it may be disguised by righteous indignation. The evils of society provide the Communists with their fuel. We must readily admit those faults that we have under our capitalist system of free enterprise, and work indefatigably to eliminate them. We must lead a positive political and social life, not a negative, bitter, or denunciatory life.

The Communist depends upon hatred, uncertainty, and fear. "Let the ruling classes tremble," wrote Karl Marx. The best answer for that is reaffirmation of the faith that ours is a nation and we are a people founded upon belief in God and the sanctity of each individual. Therein lies our strength. The Communist believes only in the strength and the will of the party. We believe that the strongest nation is the one which has the greatest possible individual freedom. But there can be no individual freedom without equivalent individual responsibility.

A Short Glossary of Communist Terms

I notice they have a curious way of expressing themselves. . . . It seems like some special jargon. Possibly the jury would like some explanation of some of these expressions to give more continuity to the evidence.
—Judge Harold R. Medina, during the trial of the eleven Communist leaders.

Activist: The two major types of Communist activists, labor and political, have similar functions. They are catalysts who enter, among other things, strike situations and political campaigns; stir up trouble, dissension, and bitterness; and then drop out of sight entirely.

Bourgeois: Those who own and control the means of production, *i.e.,* the important capitalists.

Cell: The basic unit of Communist organization, today limited to from three to five persons. A *branch,* the next highest unit, is composed of one representative from each cell. Above the branch level is the *district,* of which there are thirty-two in the United States. New York City and vicinity lies in District Two; Boston and most of New England in District One; and Washington, D.C., in District Four.

Coaster: A go-between, usually between couriers (see below), to complicate the communications system further. Often a coaster is an innocent person—an elevator operator, a bootblack, a newsboy—with whom a message is left by one comrade and picked up by another.

Colonizer: A party member who infiltrates a key industry, of importance to the United States defense effort, acting under party orders to take special destructive action in a time of crisis.

Couriers: Those who transmit top-secret messages and material between Communist groups and members. Small children are often used to divert suspicion.

Democratic centralism: The system by which important decisions are made by the party leaders and then passed down to the membership for rubber-stamping, thus avoiding true democratic procedure entirely.

Deviationist: A party member who errs either to right or to left; one who disagrees with the leadership. His actions are sometimes called "infantile disorders."

Fellow traveler: A person with Communist sympathies who is not actually a card-carrying member of the party. The term was supposed to have been invented by an American ex-party member, but it is actually used by Stalin in *History of the C.P.S.U.(B.).*

Floater: A comrade separated from membership in any cell or branch. He carries no card and attends no meetings; his only connection with the party is through secret couriers. He is called on for special tasks which require that his party affiliations be entirely unknown.

Grubber: The lowliest of Communist workers, who sells the *Daily Worker,* marches in picket lines, and circulates petitions. Newcomers to the party almost always do at least a minimum of grubbing.

"Khvostists": Coat-tailers, from the Russian word *khvost,* meaning "tail of an animal." Usually a term used in scorn to denote the abject follower or the opportunist.

"Kulak": A Russian term denoting the middle- and upper-class farmer, a landowner and a deadly enemy of the Communists.

Obstructionist: Closely allied to deviationist. Any Communist with a stubborn or independent streak.

Patriot: The party teaches that a "true patriot" is one who in a war fights on the side of the working class of the world—led by Russia—and against his own country's capitalist bosses and their medium of control, the government.

Petty bourgeois: The shopkeeper, store owner, or small businessman. According to the Communists, the petty bourgeois *think* they are capitalists, but actually are but tools of the system.

Proletarian vanguard (or the vanguard of the working class): The vanguard, in this case, is the hard core of the Communist party which is to lead the proletariat to victorious revolution.

Proletariat: The working class, those who toil with their backs and hands, often called the "masses."

Trotskyite: First, a follower of Leon Trotsky; second, a left-wing Communist who believes in immediate world revolution; third, loosely applied to all party traitors. There are also "Browderites" and "Kautsky-ites," followers of party heretics who deviated to the right.

White chauvinism: The private Communist expression for racial prejudice against the Negroes. The Communists have other uses, or misuses, of the word chauvinism; a man who tends to relegate women to a secondary role is a "male chauvinist."

The Communist and the Liberal

Unfortunately some people confuse Communists and liberals when, in truth, they are worlds apart. While it is difficult to distinguish the skilled underground comrade from even a conservative Republican, if he wants to hide his identity, nevertheless I can offer certain guideposts from my own experience which may be of some aid:

1. A Communist believes the individual must be sacrificed for the good of the masses; a liberal has high regard for the value and integrity of the individual.

2. A Communist interprets and misinterprets history for his own purposes; a liberal studies history honestly and learns from it.

3. A Communist uses the ills and defects of the capitalist system to foment anger and class strife; a liberal points out those ills, but tries to cure them.

4. A Communist believes that the government is the master of the people; a liberal believes that the government is the servant of the people.

5. A Communist will attack socialists and progressives even more violently than he attacks conservatives; a liberal tends to agree and to compromise with people holding the same general point of view.

6. A Communist, to attain his seemingly bright idealistic goals, uses any means at his disposal—lies, blackmail, bloodshed, murder; the liberal, although he may have some of the same ends in mind, uses honorable means.

7. A Communist uses the arts—literature, painting, music—in a strictly functional sense, to further the aims of world communism; a liberal appreciates the arts for their own sake.

8. A Communist is absolutely indefatigable in "serving" an organization he wishes to control. He will do anything, even stay at a meeting until 3 A.M., by which time, unfortunately, the non-Communist liberals will have gone home.

9. A Communist, although he pretends to be independent, always takes his orders from above; a liberal makes up his own mind.

10. A Communist, because he takes orders from above, is sometimes trapped by an overnight change of party policy; a liberal can change his mind but he does so slowly, painfully, and by his own volition.

11. A Communist participates in secret, underground activity. He feels that he has something to conceal. A liberal works toward his goals aboveground and in the open.

12. A Communist is committed to violence, although he seeks to hide it in every possible way; a liberal is just as dedicated to peaceful methods. One is revolutionary, the other evolutionary.

13. A Communist, like any other totalitarian, is vitally interested in youth movements through which he can capture the minds of young people; a liberal is interested in educating but not controlling the minds of the young.

14. A Communist is suspicious of everyone, not only his enemies but his fellow comrades. The party spies continually on its own members. A liberal has no reason to be suspicious, and for that very reason sometimes falls into Communist traps.

15. A Communist believes that a small, tightly knit group (the vanguard) should lead; a liberal does not distinguish so clearly between leaders and followers.

16. A Communist tends to use Marxist jargon (see Appendix I): a liberal struggles along with our native vocabulary.

APPENDIX III

On June 28, 1940, both Houses of Congress passed the Smith Act, aimed as much at Fascist underground organizations as at Communist. The specific sections of the law under which the eleven Communist leaders were indicted, tried, and convicted follows:

It shall be unlawful for any person—

(1) To knowingly or willfully advocate, abet, advise, or teach the duty, necessity, desirability, or propriety of overthrowing or destroying any government in the United States by force or violence or by the assassination of any officer of any such government;

(2) With the intent to cause the overthrow or destruction of any government in the United States to print, publish, edit, issue, circulate, sell, distribute, or publicly display any written or printed matter advocating, advising, or teaching the duty, necessity, desirability, or propriety of overthrowing or destroying any government in the United States by force or violence.

(3) To organize or help to organize any society, group, or assembly of persons who teach, advocate, or encourage the overthrow or destruction of any government in the United States by force or violence; or to be or become a member of, or affiliate with, any such society, group, or assembly of persons, knowing the purposes thereof.

The general indictment of the twelve Communist party leaders, under the Smith Act, charged:

. . . that from on or about April 1, 1945, and continuously thereafter up to and including the date of the filing of this indictment, the defendants unlawfully, willfully, and knowingly did conspire with each other and with divers other persons to the Grand Jurors unknown, to organize as the Communist Party of the United States a select group and assembly of persons who teach and advocate the overthrow and destruction of the government of the United States by force and violence and knowingly and willfully to advocate and teach the duty and necessity of overthrowing and destroying the government of the United States by force and violence which said acts are prohibited by the Smith Act.

INDEX